GPU Programming with C++ and CUDA

Uncover effective techniques for writing efficient
GPU-parallel C++ applications

Paulo Motta

‹packt›

GPU Programming with C++ and CUDA

Copyright © 2025 Packt Publishing

Portfolio Director: Kunal Chaudhari
Relationship Lead: Samriddhi Murarka
Project Manager: Ashwin Dinesh Kharwa
Content Engineer: Alexander Powell
Technical Editor: Rohit Singh
Copy Editor: Alexander Powell
Indexer: Tejal Soni
Proofreader: Alexander Powell
Production Designer: Prashant Ghare
Growth Lead: Vinishka Kalra

First published: August 2025
Production reference: 1280825

Published by Packt Publishing Ltd.
Grosvenor House
11 St Paul's Square
Birmingham
B3 1RB, UK.

ISBN 978-1-80512-454-2
www.packtpub.com

To my wife, Katia, and my daughter, Helena, for their love and support, and to our families, for their encouragement.

– Paulo Motta

Contributors

About the author

Paulo Motta is a computer scientist and software engineer with more than 20 years experience in software development. Paulo has worked in both academia and industry, including at Microsoft. He is a senior member of the IEEE and a member of the ACM.

He holds a PhD in Parallel Systems from PUC-Rio, where he developed a platform to abstract low-level hardware for parallel applications on top of the Cell Broadband Engine processor. His post-doctoral research at LNCC (Laboratório Nacional de Computação Científica, Brazil) involved redesigning a quantum walks simulator, leading to GPU-enabled middleware presented at IEEE Quantum Week. He also supervised GPU-focused research projects at LaSalle College that have been published at SBAC-PAD and SPLASH.

He enjoys teaching, writing, and sharing knowledge.

I want to thank everyone who has supported me in this journey, especially my wife, Katia, and my daughter, Helena, who both encouraged me. I am also deeply thankful to the mentors I've had over the years, and to the editorial team at Packt for their great support in bringing this book to life.

About the reviewer

Aditya Agrawal is a postgraduate student in Computer Science at IIT Madras. He is working on multithreading to extend OpenMP (a popular parallel programming library for shared-memory parallelism) with synchronization primitives. He has worked in a wide range of domains including data science and web development, and is currently exploring the domains of compilers and high-performance computing. His experience working on the CUDA programming language stems from a graduate course in GPU Programming, where he was introduced to the world of parallel-programming using the CUDA framework for NVIDIA GPUs. On completion of his postgraduates studies he aspires to work in the compiler field.

Dedicated to the memory of my mother, whose love and support have always been such a help over the years, as I found out who I was and what I wanted to do. Thank you mummy for always supporting me and I wish you to always stay happy and keep that sweet smiling face wherever you are.

Table of Contents

Chapter 6: Parallel Algorithms with CUDA   97

Chapter 7: Performance Strategies   125

Part 3: Moving Forward 167

Chapter 8: Overlaying Multiple Operations 169

Chapter 9: Exposing Your Code to Python 197

Preface

Welcome to an accelerated world! Technology that in the past focused specifically on graphical and image processing is now used to speed up computations in a wide variety of domains. Graphical Processing Units, or GPUs for short, can be programmed to enable applications to reach solutions many times faster than would be possible with a CPU (Central Processing Unit).

When programming GPUs we are dealing with a very different paradigm to that involved in parallel programming for CPUs. GPUs have a distinct hardware architecture, and usually run on a separate, specialized hardware card that does not allow direct access to the main system memory. This means we have to understand how to control the device and its internals to make better use of its potential.

Besides that, the type of problem that requires this kind of acceleration usually involves some relatively advanced mathematics, which can be intimidating at first.

All of this presents us with a dilemma when we are learning GPU programming: how can we address the key concepts and technical structures in a simple way?

In this book we focus on providing a solution-oriented approach for each GPU concept, illustrated with simple examples that do not require advanced math. Our aim is to allow you, the reader, to develop your knowledge about this new programming paradigm by hopefully facing only modest technical challenges during the learning process.

Two of the chapters are somewhat theoretical in flavor. *Chapter 1* sets the stage for parallel programs thinking, while *Chapter 5* provides explanations of some of the resources we use in our first practical examples. All the remaining chapters are practical in style, allowing you to learn how to solve code acceleration problems by implementing code solutions. Thus programming plays a central role in this book, with the theoretical concepts orbiting around it.

Computational performance is of course of major importance today, in the AI era, and hence it is of fundamental importance to understand how GPUs work, rather than just try to use them blindly. That way you can avoid potentially erroneous or disappointing results.

Who this book is for

This book is primarily for the developer who already has C++ knowledge and is interested in learning how to use GPUs to accelerate their applications. Advanced mathematics is not required.

Developers will learn how to accelerate real code by using GPUs, and will acquire insight into what needs to be taken into consideration when doing so. The solution-oriented approach presents information in a way that can readily be applied to different scenarios.

The book will also be helpful for any IT professional contemplating getting into GPU-accelerated software, since it provides the foundational knowledge needed to make informed decisions regarding its use.

What this book covers

Chapter 1, Introduction to Parallel Programming, provides a gentle first exposure to the parallel paradigm by using analogies with tasks that arise in our daily routines. We discuss the difference between having multiple programs executing at the same time and having multiple processor cores working on the same problem at the same time. We talk about the types of parallelism, present GPU hardware architecture, and discuss how it differs from CPUs. We complete the chapter by discussing the challenges and advantages of using GPUs.

Chapter 2, Setting Up Your Development Environment, provides guidance on how to set everything up for GPU programming. We present an alternative to using Docker to organize the environment, and employ pros and cons reasoning to help the reader decide on the best approach for them.

Chapter 3, Hello CUDA, provides the bare minimum terminology to introduce a first program that executes on our device, together with instructions on how to compile and run it. Then we see how, using a second program, to inspect particular hardware details regarding our device. We proceed by guiding the reader through the setup of a more efficient programming environment, by working through the installation and configuration of VS Code and necessary extensions.

Chapter 4, Hello Again, but in Parallel, broadens our scope to the execution of programs that really use parallelism. First we see the SIMD execution model and how some problems map really well to our explorations of parallelism. We then move to an example that does not require data transfers, and investigate how to measure program performance. Finally we see how to transfer data into and out of GPU memory.

Chapter 5, A Closer Look into the World of GPUs, pauses code development to present concepts that map and address GPU cores, and we also see how to launch GPU execution kernels. We learn about another level of parallelism allowed by CUDA streams, and about the necessity for asynchronous data transfers. Finally we discuss shared memory, an important type of fast memory that improves performance by helping reduce access to global memory.

Chapter 6, Parallel Algorithms with CUDA, returns to our code explorations, but we now have the benefit of a deeper understanding of how to control the GPU. First we discuss how to design parallel algorithms, and then meet the classic example of matrix multiplication. Finally, we learn the importance of thread synchronization to avoiding erroneous results.

Chapter 7, Performance Strategies, explores techniques to identify bottlenecks and overcome them. We learn how to use a visual profiler that allows us to check the performance details of our programs.

Chapter 8, Overlaying Multiple Operations, outlines another level of optimization possible when we use the GPU hardware to overlap data transfers and processing at the same time. Using techniques covered in previous chapters we can see the blocks of time necessary for data transfer and data processing. Then we explore the use of multiple GPUs on the same machine to provide a different approach to parallelism.

Chapter 9, Exposing Your Code to Python, explores how to pack our code as libraries that can be used from Python in two distinct ways. We also explore the importance of handling memory correctly to avoid unnecessary data copying.

Chapter 10, Exploring Existing GPU Models, discusses some of the existing libraries as options for improving time to market and reliability. We also discuss how the use of sequential code on the GPU can help prevent data movement. Finally we examine options for testing our code from both C++ and Python.

To get the most out of this book

You should be comfortable writing computer programs in C++, and basic knowledge of operating systems will help to understand some of the more advanced concepts, given that we have to manage device communication.

Software / hardware covered in the book	Operating system requirements
NVIDIA GPU or access to a Cloud-based VM with NVIDIA GPU	Ubuntu Linux 20 or later with NVIDIA Video Driver
CUDA Toolkit 12	
Docker 27.0	
VS Code 1.92	
CMake 3.16	
g++ 9.4	
Python 3.8	
Nsight Compute 2023.3	

In *Chapter 2* we discuss options for configuring the development environment. Some of the software that we need is installed automatically if you elect to use the Docker-based development environment.

If you are using the digital version of this book, we advise you to type the code yourself or access the code from the book's GitHub repository (a link is given in the next section). Doing so will help you avoid any potential errors related to the copying and pasting of code.

Download the example code files

The code bundle for the book is hosted on GitHub at `https://github.com/PacktPublishing/GPU-Programming-with-CPP-and-CUDA`. We also have other code bundles from our rich catalog of books and videos available at `https://github.com/PacktPublishing`. Check them out!

Download the color images

We also provide a PDF file that has color images of the screenshots/diagrams used in this book. You can download it here: `https://packt.link/gbp/9781805124542`.

Conventions used

There are a number of text conventions used throughout this book.

CodeInText: Indicates code words in text, database table names, folder names, filenames, file extensions, pathnames, dummy URLs, user input, and Twitter handles. For example: "Notice that each thread has a thread ID (`threadIdx.x`), a block ID (`blockIdx.x`), and a block dimension (`blockDim.x`)."

A block of code is set as follows:

```
__global__ void vectorAddKernel (int *a, int *b, int *c, int N){
    int idx = threadIdx.x + blockIdx.x * blockDim.x;
    if (idx < N) {
        c[idx] = a[idx] * b[idx];
    }
}
```

Any command-line input or output is written as follows:

```
cmake -DCMAKE_BUILD_TYPE=Debug ..
make
```

Bold: Indicates a new term, an important word, or words that you see on the screen. For instance, words in menus or dialog boxes appear in the text like this. For example: "Since we have a breakpoint set inside our kernel, we can click on the **Continue** button of the Debug Toolbar and our code will run until that point."

> Warnings or important notes appear like this.

> Tips and tricks appear like this.

Get in touch

Feedback from our readers is always welcome.

General feedback: If you have questions about any aspect of this book or have any general feedback, please email us at customercare@packt.com and mention the book's title in the subject of your message.

Errata: Although we have taken every care to ensure the accuracy of our content, mistakes do happen. If you have found a mistake in this book, we would be grateful if you reported this to us. Please visit http://www.packt.com/submit-errata, click **Submit Errata**, and fill in the form.

Piracy: If you come across any illegal copies of our works in any form on the internet, we would be grateful if you would provide us with the location address or website name. Please contact us at copyright@packt.com with a link to the material.

If you are interested in becoming an author: If there is a topic that you have expertise in and you are interested in either writing or contributing to a book, please visit http://authors.packt.com/.

Share your thoughts

Once you've read *GPU Programming with C++ and CUDA*, we'd love to hear your thoughts! Scan the QR code below to go straight to the Amazon review page for this book and share your feedback.

https://packt.link/r/1805124544

Your review is important to us and the tech community and will help us make sure we're delivering excellent quality content.

Part 1

Understanding Where We Are Heading

In this part we take the first steps towards understanding parallel programming. We learn how to set up our environment, and we execute our first CUDA programs. These first programs will be very simple; the priority is on making sure that our environment is working properly and that we understand how execution in the GPU takes place.

This part of the book includes the following chapters:

- *Chapter 1, Introduction to Parallel Programming*
- *Chapter 2, Getting Started*
- *Chapter 3, Hello CUDA*
- *Chapter 4, Hello Again, but in Parallel*

1

Introduction to Parallel Programming

Welcome to the world of **graphics processing unit (GPU)** programming!

Before we talk about programming GPUs, we must understand what **parallel programming** is and how it can benefit our applications. As with everything in life, it has its challenges. In this chapter, we'll explore both the benefits and drawbacks of parallel programming, laying the groundwork for our deep dive into GPU programming. So in this first chapter, we'll be discussing a variety of topics without developing any code. In doing so, we'll establish the foundations on which to build throughout our journey.

Apart from being useful, the information provided in this chapter is fundamental to understanding what happens inside a GPU, as we'll discuss shortly. By the end of the chapter, you'll understand why parallelism is important and when it makes sense to use it in your applications.

In this chapter, we're going to cover the following main topics:

- What parallelism is in software, and why it's important
- Different types of parallelism
- An overview of GPU architecture
- Comparing **central processing units (CPUs)** and GPUs
- Advantages and challenges of GPU programming

Getting the most out of this book — get to know your free benefits

Unlock exclusive **free** benefits that come with your purchase, thoughtfully crafted to supercharge your learning journey and help you learn without limits.

Here's a quick overview of what you get with this book:

Next-gen reader

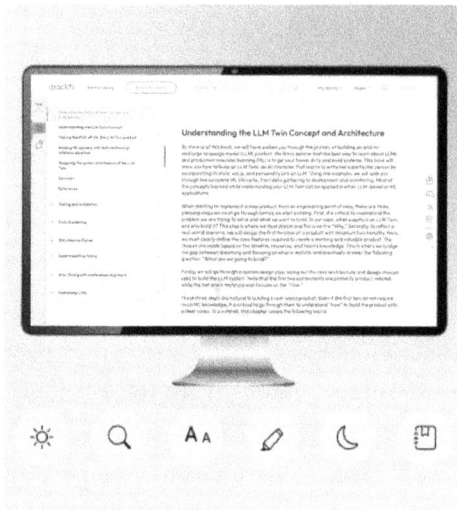

Figure 1.1: Illustration of the next-gen Packt Reader's features

Our web-based reader, designed to help you learn effectively, comes with the following features:

⌣ Multi-device progress sync: Learn from any device with seamless progress sync.

📑 Highlighting and notetaking: Turn your reading into lasting knowledge.

🔖 Bookmarking: Revisit your most important learnings anytime.

🔅 Dark mode: Focus with minimal eye strain by switching to dark or sepia mode.

Interactive AI assistant (beta)

Figure 1.2: Illustration of Packt's
AI assistant

Our interactive AI assistant has been trained on the content of this book, to maximize your learning experience. It comes with the following features:

✦ Summarize it: Summarize key sections or an entire chapter.

✦ AI code explainers: In the next-gen Packt Reader, click the Explain button above each code block for AI-powered code explanations.

Note: The AI assistant is part of next-gen Packt Reader and is still in beta.

DRM-free PDF or ePub version

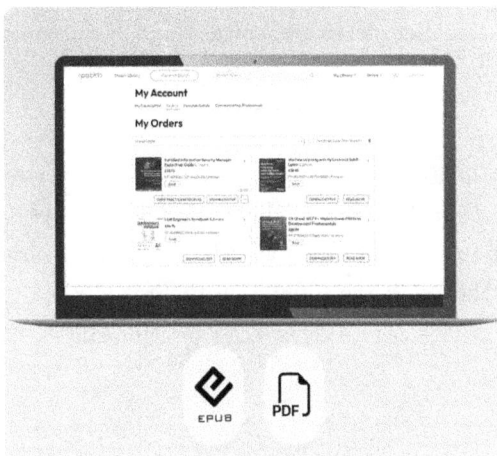

Figure 1.3: Free PDF and ePub

Learn without limits with the following perks included with your purchase:

⊞ Learn from anywhere with a DRM-free PDF copy of this book.

⊡ Use your favorite e-reader to learn using a DRM-free ePub version of this book.

Technical requirements

For this chapter, the only technical requirement that we have is the goodwill to keep reading!

What is parallelism in software?

Parallel programming is a way of making a computer do many things at once. But wait – isn't this what already happens daily? *Yes and no.* Most common processors today are capable of executing more than one task at the same time – and we mean *at the same time*. However, this is only the first requirement for parallel software. The second is to make at least some of the processor cores work *on the same problem* in a coordinated way. Let's consider an example.

Imagine that you're taking on a big task, such as sorting a huge pile of books. Instead of doing it alone, you ask a group of friends to help. Each friend takes a small part of the pile and sorts it. You all work at the same time, and the job gets done much faster. This is similar to how parallel programming works: it breaks a big problem into smaller pieces and solves them at the same time using multiple cores.

Of course, this example was chosen because it has a special characteristic: it's easily parallelizable in the sense that we can perceive how to break the big tasks into smaller ones. Not all problems can be easily broken down for parallel processing. One of our first challenges is finding ways to decompose problems into smaller tasks that can be executed simultaneously. Sometimes, there are parts of our **algorithm** that need to be executed on a single core while all others sit idle before we can separate the parallel tasks. This is usually called a *sequential part*. It's time for a different example.

Let's suppose you're having a movie and games night with your friends. You all decide to prepare some food and for that, you go to the supermarket. To make things faster, your friends come along so that, once there, everyone can select multiple ingredients at the same time – this is the parallel part. However, since you're all going in a single car, only one person can drive at a given time, no matter how many licensed drivers there are in the vehicle. You can always argue that they could take turns driving a part of the way, but in this scenario, it would only take longer to get to the supermarket.

Upon arriving, each person heads to a different aisle to gather the pre-defined ingredients. Once everything is collected, another crucial decision arises: should each person go to a separate checkout line to pay with their credit card, or should they all queue together if they only have one card? Opting for the parallel payment method reveals another interesting aspect of parallel processing.

Even when tasks are processed in parallel (each person is on a different checkout line), the execution times can vary unpredictably. This means that at any given moment, different lines move at different speeds, and those who have already paid for their ingredients may end up waiting for their friends (processors) to finish their payments.

Once all the payments are complete, a new sequential part is followed: driving back home. This time, a different driver might be executing this task while the other people – I mean, processors – sit idle waiting for the next task to execute. Some algorithms have sequential parts to synchronize data or to share intermediate results, and that's why only one processor is working. Here, we're collecting the data that each processor – I mean, friend – got from the supermarket and we have to move this from one location to another. There's no use for parallelism in this small part.

Why is parallelism important?

There are many situations in which the size of the problems we want to solve increases dramatically. And this is the moment when we have to start talking about more 'serious' real-world applications, such as weather forecasting, scientific research, and artificial intelligence.

Remember when we were driving to the supermarket and we mentioned that we could switch drivers for each part of the way? Wouldn't this only end up taking us more time? This was due to **context switching** – we would have to find a place to park, then switch drivers, then drive the car until the next stop. But why are we talking about this again? Because most of the time, we need a 'serious' real-world application to make it worthwhile working through all the details of parallel programming.

One exception could be using parallel programming to accelerate graphics and physics processing in video games; although these applications may not be critical for human life, they're pretty serious. We could always classify video games within the 'serious' simulation category. Let's understand some of the benefits we get by using parallelism in our software.

Speeding up tasks

Splitting tasks into smaller parts that can be done simultaneously dramatically speeds up the overall process. We now have multiple processors working on different parts of the problem at the same time.

Efficiency in resource use

Let's revisit our supermarket example. If all our friends sit idle inside the car waiting for one of us to get all the ingredients, we aren't using our resources efficiently. However, when each person is gathering a part of the list, we're better utilizing the resources that were already available. This is the same with our computer processor and its multiple cores – they're already there. Of course, most modern processors are capable of decreasing their clock speeds to reduce energy consumption, but that doesn't eliminate the waste of having an idle component.

Handling large datasets

In fields such as data science, video processing, and scientific research, it's very common to find problems that grow in size very fast. Many of these problems use matrices to represent data; when the size of the matrices increases, the time required to process them is impacted. By using parallelism, we can ensure that we're executing as much as possible at any given point in time, which makes the time to process large amounts of data acceptable.

Enhancing performance

When we reduce the time needed to process our dataset, this is perceived by the user as a performance gain. However, there's another aspect to this. Even when the time isn't reduced, the user may perceive a performance enhancement by having a more detailed simulation – one that uses more parameters (and thus a larger amount of data, as we discussed previously). Either way, this results in better performance and more responsive applications.

Enabling advanced technologies

By using parallelism, our capacity to perform simulations allows scientists to test more hypotheses than was possible before. Only when simulations seem to point in a viable and promising direction do we try them with concrete materials. This dramatically decreases the costs of discovery and accelerates the discovery process.

A quick start guide to the different types of parallelism

So far, we've only been talking about parallelism. In this section, we'll quickly discuss the different types of parallelism before we dive into GPUs – which is what we're all waiting for!

Data parallelism

The process of performing the same operation on different pieces of data so that data is processed equally at the same time by different processor cores – for example, processing an image to apply some change to each of its pixels – is called **data parallelism**. If one of the ingredients that we bought at the supermarket was a huge box of carrots that needed to be peeled, we could do that on our own, or we could distribute a peeler to each of our friends and perform the same process on the same data together, with each person working on an individual carrot.

Task parallelism

Sometimes, we have multiple steps that aren't dependent on each other and that could be executed by different processor cores. Often, one larger task is divided into smaller sub-tasks, each with its own very clear objective, which contributes to the larger task but has nothing to do with its sibling tasks. If we revisit our friends who have just returned from the supermarket, we can break the larger task of preparing dinner into sub-tasks, such as preparing some appetizers, preparing the main dish, and preparing a dessert. The data are the ingredients that were brought home; the processors will perform different operations.

However, to be technically accurate, we need to consider that the same data is used as input for the parallel sub-tasks, so for the sake of fairness, let's consider that we have two menus tonight but all with the same set of ingredients. That way, we could input the same data and have it processed by different functions (cooking methods).

Pipeline parallelism

There's another arrangement for parallelism we can utilize. Sometimes, we have some data processing that depends on the results of some previous processing. If we have multiple processor cores to work with, we could assign each processing step to a core and create a pipeline that leverages the benefits of parallelism as new data becomes available. In a fruit processing factory, we can witness this kind of parallelism as new fruits, let's say apples, arrive for processing and packaging. First, the apple truck delivers a large quantity of fruit that's dumped in an artificial water stream. The fruits get washed while being pushed through the water stream; once cleaned, a series of workers inspect the fruits to remove bad apples. After selection, the apples are separated by size and moved to different conveyor belts, after which they're packed and sealed, and then boxed and distributed.

This is exactly analogous to what happens with video processing as well, where each video frame is equivalent to a small set of apples. Each frame passes through a processing step and moves to the next processing component.

An overview of GPU architecture

After all that cooking, it's time for a change. Let's talk about GPUs.

First, let me say that I've decided to explain GPUs first before comparing them with CPUs. I'm doing this on the assumption that you're already somewhat familiar with the (basic) architecture of a modern CPU.

GPUs were originally used to accelerate the output of graphics processing, since modern computer usage takes place almost exclusively in graphical environments. This differs from computing in the past, where the character-based interfaces that were used weren't graphically demanding. However, a shift occurred when it was noticed that a processing unit that was capable of dealing with the computations necessary for computer graphics could also be used for anything that could be expressed in terms of matrix computations, which is what linear algebra is all about.

In the next chapter, we're going to focus specifically on NVIDIA GPUs, but, for now, we'll consider a general device. In this scenario, a GPU has several components that enable parallel tasks to be executed. The first important thing to note is that a GPU core is capable of performing arithmetic and logic operations, such as calculations. A GPU core can't be used for program control; for that, we can organize many cores within a **streaming multiprocessor** (**SM**), which is responsible for controlling instruction execution among the many cores.

As shown in *Figure 1.4 (a)*, a streaming multiprocessor has one control unit that works with the **CUDA cores**, whereas in *Figure 1.4 (b)*, we can see that a single GPU can have many streaming multiprocessors, which promotes its high throughput:

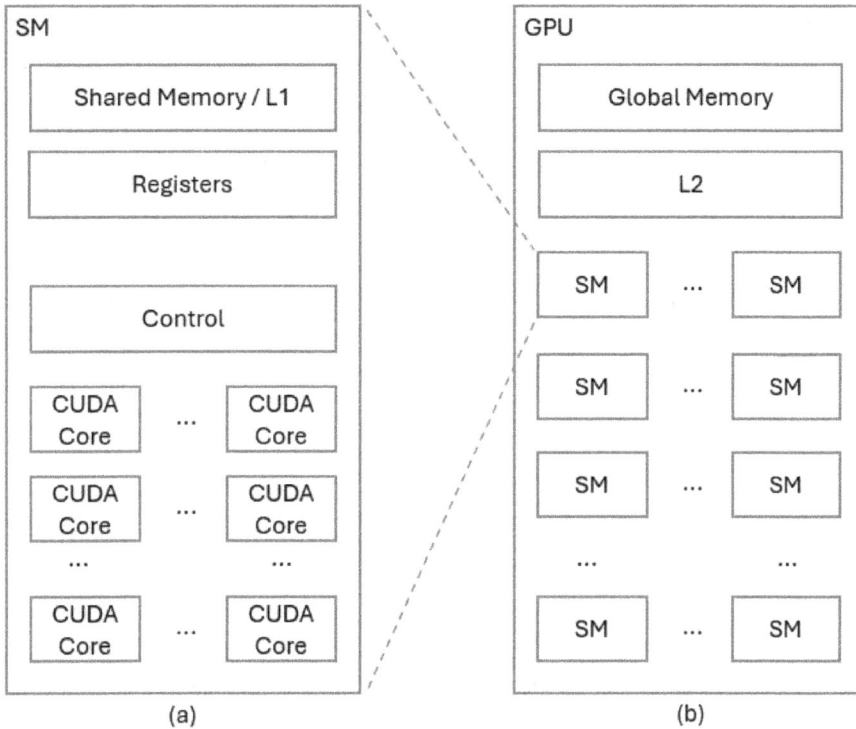

Figure 1.4: (a) a streaming multiprocessor with CUDA cores and (b) a GPU device with many streaming multiprocessors

An interesting difference between a streaming multiprocessor and a CPU core is that the streaming multiprocessor has a single control unit for many processing cores, while the CPU core has one control unit for each processing core. This is shown in *Figure 1.5*:

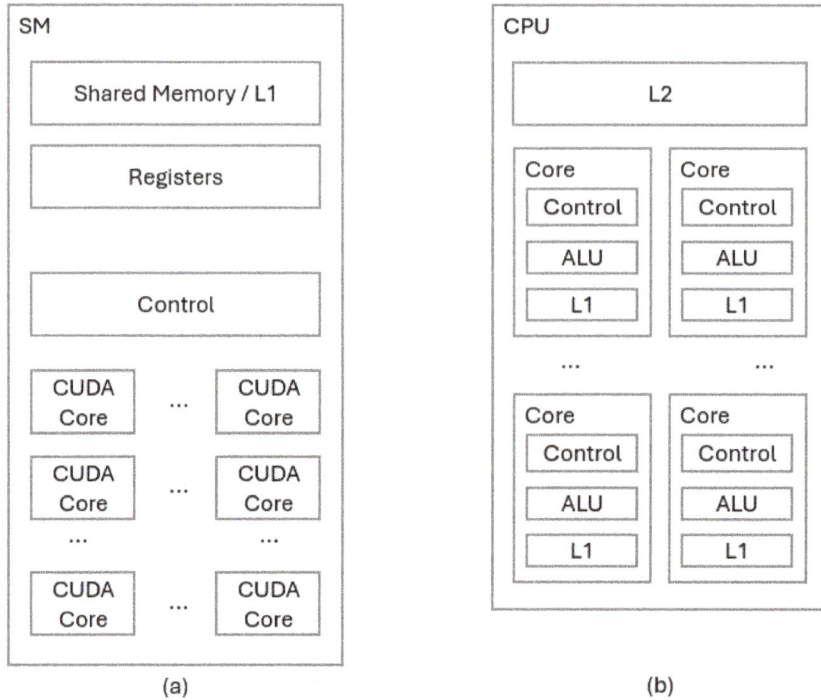

Figure 1.5: (a) streaming multiprocessor and (b) CPU

We also rely on a memory hierarchy with different amounts of space available at the different levels. As shown in *Figure 1.6*, there is a large amount of **global memory**, which is relatively slow when compared to the other memory components like L1/L2 cache and **shared memory**. This is usually the number that you see listed on your GPU box. Then, we have the cache levels. Close to the cores, we have two special types that are faster to work with: shared memory, which is shared among multiple cores, and registers, which are specific to each core. We'll learn how to handle this memory later in the book; for now, we just need to know that these are the components that will make up our solutions:

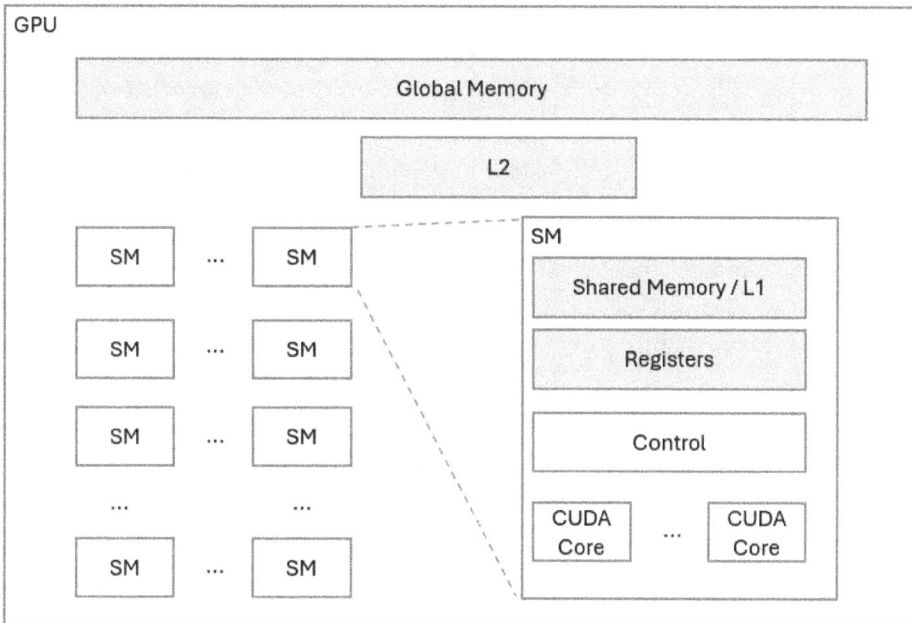

Figure 1.6: Memory hierarchy of a GPU

We also count on a scheduler that organizes and manages the execution of our software (and configuration) within the real hardware.

Finally, to make sure that everything is capable of communicating efficiently, we have a high-speed interconnection between the memory and the streaming multiprocessors.

Single instruction, multiple data (SIMD)

To understand why GPUs are designed the way they are, we need to think about the problem they were created to solve: *graphics processing*. Vector operations and **matrix multiplication** are the protagonists here, and one way to handle these efficiently is to have multiple pieces of data being processed with the same instruction by different cores at the same time. Thus, we have a single instruction and multiple pieces of data (**SIMD**) – this is one of the common patterns for parallelism. Of course, most of the time, we don't have enough cores to execute *all* the data points we need to process at once, so the scheduler will allocate a set of logical units of data to be processed first, and then the next lot, and so on, until all the data has been processed. But it's up to us to figure out whether our data is larger than the amount that can be held in global memory. This is a problem we'll cover later in this book.

Another interesting aspect of this design is that when we have multiple cores executing code and the program reaches a conditional statement, it drastically affects the overall performance. This is because the group will execute the first branch and then the second branch. Not all cores will execute both, resulting in some cores sitting idle while others are processing. We can overcome this by rethinking our solution. Let's consider an example (not a cooking one).

Let's suppose we have a huge quantity of integers that we need to separate into evens and odds so that they can be computed differently. We'll require a branch to figure out whether an integer is odd or even, which we know will have a performance impact. However, to rethink the way we provide the numbers, we could use a for loop with an increment of two at a time. We could also have one group of cores that starts at the first odd integer and another group that starts at the first even integer. This small change allows processing to occur without interruption, thereby delivering better performance.

Memory management and access

As we mentioned previously, GPUs have their own internal memory, the consequence of which is that we have to be mindful of how we access data. Something we also mentioned was that global memory is the slowest, so if we perform operations that load and store directly to global memory, this will impact performance. So, let's talk about how we can manage memory access to unleash our device's full potential.

The first thing to know is that the device's memory is separate from the system's main memory, so we need to copy memory from our computer's memory to the device's global memory, after which it can be used by our programs. *Figure 1.7* shows this memory separation and its connection via the system bus:

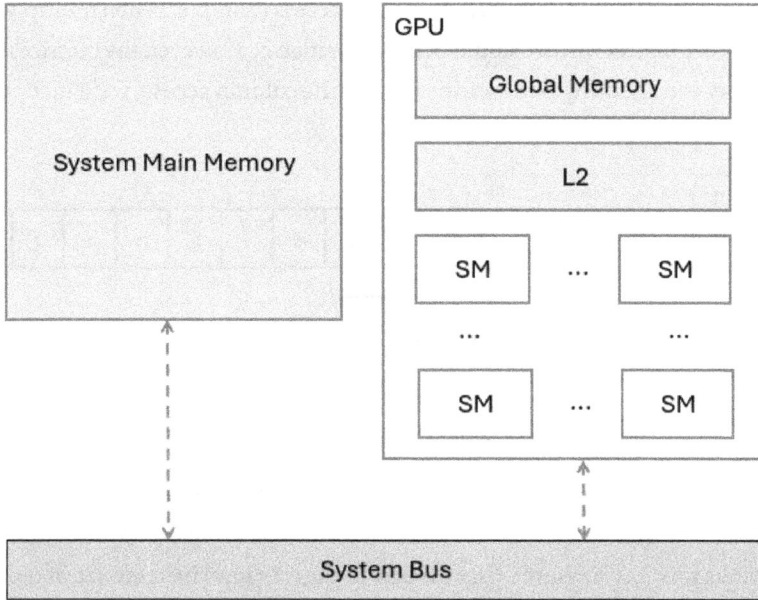

Figure 1.7: System main memory and GPU global memory

Global memory is the easiest to access because it's used in the same way that we access main system memory – by simply referring to the variable that was allocated to global memory by our main program.

On the other hand, when you declare local variables with a limited scope, they are typically allocated to registers (except for large arrays, which wouldn't fit anyway).

In between we have shared storage, which is a faster form of memory with a limited capacity that's shared by multiple execution threads. Usually, we use this to compute intermediate steps as much as possible, to postpone the final access to global storage, which holds the final computation result.

Before we leave this section, let's consider a memory access example. When multiplying matrices, we process a row of a matrix with a column of the other matrix. However, the matrices are allocated to global memory contiguously. This means that for the column access, we'll incur cache misses for all accesses:

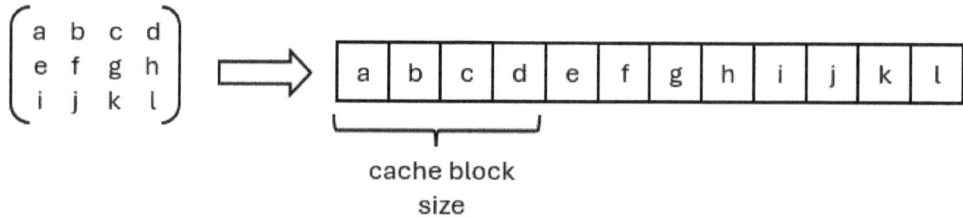

$$\begin{pmatrix} a & b & c & d \\ e & f & g & h \\ i & j & k & l \end{pmatrix}$$

cache block
size

Figure 1.8: A matrix in contiguous allocation

Considering that the matrix is stored in memory in row orientation – the way C and C++ store this type of data – the first element of the second row will be immediately after the last element from the previous row. Let's assume that the size of the row matches the size of our cache block. When we need to access the elements of a row, they may not be in the cache at first, but after the first load, we'll be able to access the other elements directly from there. This isn't the case when we want to access the rows since each element is in a separate location in the main memory and is a cache block apart from row-neighbour elements.

A simple approach would be to load the column (or at least a part of it) to shared memory so that we can perform the operations for all the rows from the other matrix against this preloaded chunk of data.

The upshot is that by carefully managing memory access patterns we can avoid bottlenecks, which is crucial for maximizing **memory bandwidth** and minimizing latency.

Comparing CPUs and GPUs

Now that we know a little more about how GPUs are organized, we can compare them with CPUs to understand the impact of using these devices.

Modern CPUs are typically composed of many cores, so they're capable of executing parallel applications by using threads. But while they're capable of handling tens of threads, a single GPU can handle thousands of threads.

As mentioned previously, the fact that GPU cores execute the same instruction on many pieces of data simultaneously is an interesting difference from CPU cores. On a CPU, each core is a complete processor that can execute either different applications or different threads of the same parallel application. This means that branch execution on a CPU core doesn't affect the performance of other CPU core executions.

Another important distinction is that CPUs can switch between tasks quickly, while GPU cores are controlled by their streaming multiprocessor.

Regarding memory management, most of the time we don't need to change the way we access our variables. Although this may affect program performance, the impact is proportionally much smaller than it is in the case of GPUs.

Advantages and challenges of GPU programming

So far, we've learned why parallelism matters, considered the various GPU device components, and compared GPUs with CPUs. Now it's time to understand how GPUs can enhance the performance of our solutions and how to overcome the challenges that come with these benefits.

Since we've already talked about some of the benefits, let's start with the challenges that come with **GPU programming**.

GPU challenges

The most obvious challenge is that we can't change the device's components, so we can't upgrade its memory, for example. Hardware limitations will directly restrict what we can do and how we'll need to break down our data for processing.

We also talked about memory transfers, something that can easily become an overhead if we have to move data to and from the device constantly. Typically, we try to move data to the device and compute as much as possible before having to move more data.

Another challenge is that some types of computation aren't fit to be executed within the GPU, such as code that has too many branches or that isn't parallelizable (remember driving to the supermarket?). We may choose to execute sequential code on the device if that's an alternative to moving data away from the device's memory. Moreover, memory management considerations are a constant factor during development, because the wrong memory access pattern can have a performance penalty that nullifies the benefits of using a GPU in the first place.

These limitations make it obvious that developing for GPU devices is more complex than writing traditional sequential software for CPUs, and developers must invest some time to learn what's necessary.

GPU advantages

Although there are challenges with developing GPU software, the benefits far outweigh them.

The most immediate benefit is their massive parallelism; even with the simplest GPUs, we gain access to hundreds of processing cores. If we can model our solution to a linear algebraic method, that's even better as it will allow us to achieve high throughput in our processing, especially if we pay due regard to memory transfers.

Also, there are many specialized libraries today that make it easier to develop applications – most numerical methods necessary for mathematical modeling are already available in thoroughly tested libraries, for example. If it's possible to use one of those libraries, it will not only accelerate the development time but also increase its quality.

Additionally, the direct effect of high data throughput using GPUs is better use of energy – another benefit of performing many operations simultaneously.

Summary

In this chapter, we learned about various concepts regarding parallel software and its main variants. We learned about the architecture of GPUs, and we compared GPUs with CPUs in order to understand the differences in developing software for each. Finally, we discussed the challenges and the benefits of using GPUs in our applications.

At this point, armed with this new knowledge, a practical side-benefit is that we can organize a meeting with our friends much more efficiently, with trips to the supermarket and preparation of appetizers becoming faster!

In the next chapter, we'll learn how to configure our environment so that we can start programming. There are a few steps we must take to get everything in place ready for that. We'll discuss two alternatives: using Docker or installing the CUDA Toolkit directly on our machine.

Unlock this book's exclusive benefits now

UNLOCK NOW

Scan this QR code or go to packtpub.com/unlock, then search this book by name.

Note: Keep your purchase invoice ready before you start.

2

Setting Up Your Development Environment

When working with any development tool, it is crucial to have a functional environment for experimentation.

When working with GPUs, it becomes even more important to set up the device correctly. However, there are many details that can vary between different operating systems and distributions.

We will learn about some of the tools that can help with program construction and the roles they play, and also about where to get the official documentation for our operating system. As a reference, we shall be using **Ubuntu**.

The chapter starts by showing how to make things a little easier in terms of configuration management by using **Docker**, and then moves on to discussing the direct installation of development tools on our system.

These then are the chapter's main topics:

- Development environment setup
- Where to get official documentation
- How to use Docker to simplify things

Technical requirements

In this chapter, we are going to work on our computer to configure the environment in order to use our GPU.

For the operating system, we will be using Linux. Although any distribution could be used, it's best to select one that is officially supported by NVIDIA. We have a lot of choice when it comes to open source distributions for Linux, but we will go with Ubuntu as it is easy to find and install, with numerous online posts addressing common issues. It is also officially supported by NVIDIA. At the time of writing, Ubuntu 24.04 LTS is available, but it is not yet listed as supported by the NVIDIA installer for CUDA 12.4 (the current version). Instead, we have Ubuntu 20.04 and 22.04, either of which is suitable for our purposes.

We need to have a computer with an NVIDIA GPU: it could be a virtual machine on your preferred cloud service, a laptop, or a desktop, but to take full advantage of the information presented in this book, it is mandatory to have an NVIDIA GPU.

Another alternative may be to use a cloud platform service which does not have a dedicated full virtual machine but provides support for GPUs, as does Google Colab, which provides a hosted Jupyter Notebook service and which, after some configuration, supports CUDA C/C++ programming. The service may be accessed at `https://colab.research.google.com/`, but its configuration is beyond our scope.

Configuring your development environment

A fundamental requirement is to have NVIDIA's proprietary graphic driver installed. This is important because the default driver that works with NVIDIA GPUs in Linux installations is the nouveau open source driver, which can execute graphics but is not capable of running CUDA code.

We are going to learn about two possible configurations. We will follow an order that is less intrusive to our machines; you will have an opportunity to experiment with CUDA before committing to installing it directly. In the first configuration, we will discuss execution through Docker, and in the second configuration, we will see the installation of everything directly on our system. Each configuration has pros and cons, which we will also discuss.

Just to make our strategy clearer, let's summarize it:

1.   Installing the CUDA proprietary device driver is mandatory, regardless of the **CUDA Toolkit** – so we are going to deal with that first.

2. Regarding the development environment (a.k.a. CUDA Toolkit), we have two paths: Docker-based installation or installing it on our system directly.

3. To make sure that we consider both alternatives before deciding on one of them, we are presenting the Docker path first because it is less intrusive.

4. After taking a brief look at Docker and its pros and cons, we will see how to configure and use it to our advantage.

5. After all this, we will learn how to install the CUDA Toolkit directly onto our system.

Now that we have outlined our strategy, in the next section we will learn how to configure the video driver required to run our CUDA programs.

Getting the correct video driver

There are several ways to determine which driver version you should use. The simplest method is to visit NVIDIA's website (`https://www.nvidia.com/en-us/drivers/`) and fill in the form with your GPU and operating system details. The form will return the correct driver to use:

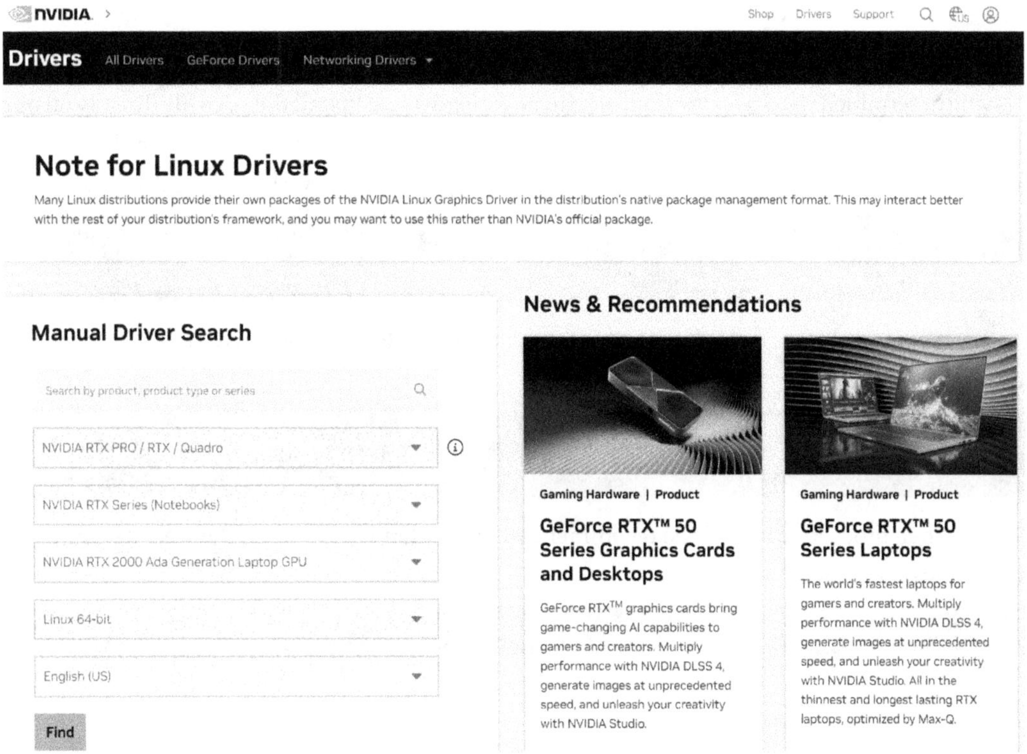

Figure 2.1: NIVIDA page for device driver selection

For the example configuration, we have the following result:

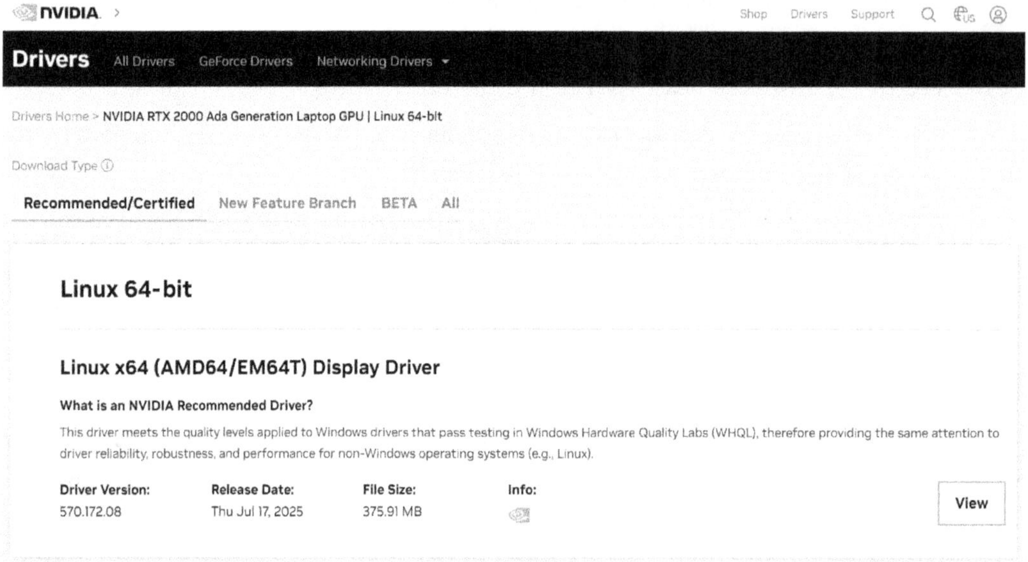

Figure 2.2: NVIDIA site with device driver result

Having determined the driver version, we can download it and install the `.deb` file directly on our system or we can use the information in this page to help us select the driver from the Ubuntu repositories as we show below. The first thing to do is update our system with the following:

```
sudo apt update
sudo apt upgrade
```

To get the latest drivers, add the official Ubuntu **Personal Package Archive (PPA)** for graphics drivers:

```
sudo add-apt-repository ppa:graphics-drivers/ppa
sudo apt update
```

We can then proceed to install the recommended driver that we found on the website using the following command:

```
sudo apt install nvidia-driver-<version>
```

In our example, it would be like this. Note that for apt packages, only the major version number is used:

```
sudo apt install nvidia-driver-570
```

It is also possible to try to auto-detect the best driver for your system. Instead of the previous command, you could use this:

```
sudo ubuntu-drivers autoinstall
```

Both ways are fine.

Now, we have to prevent the open source driver from loading. We do this by editing a special file – using the **nano** CLI text editor – with the following command:

```
sudo nano /etc/modprobe.d/blacklist-nouveau.conf
```

And adding the following lines:

```
blacklist nouveau
options nouveau modeset=0
```

After copying those lines, press *Ctrl + S* to save and *Ctrl + X* to leave the nano editor.

Then, execute the following:

```
sudo update-initramfs -u
```

It is necessary to reboot our system since we need to remove the open source driver from memory and load the new one. We can verify that our configuration works fine by using the following command:

```
nvidia-smi
```

This command will present some information about the current GPU and any processes that are using resources, similar to the following:

```
+-----------------------------------------------------------------------------------------+
| NVIDIA-SMI 570.133.07              Driver Version: 570.133.07       CUDA Version: 12.8   |
|-----------------------------------------+------------------------+----------------------+
| GPU  Name                 Persistence-M | Bus-Id          Disp.A | Volatile Uncorr. ECC |
| Fan  Temp   Perf          Pwr:Usage/Cap |           Memory-Usage | GPU-Util  Compute M. |
|                                         |                        |               MIG M. |
|=========================================+========================+======================|
|   0  NVIDIA GeForce RTX 2060        Off | 00000000:01:00.0   Off |                  N/A |
| N/A   41C    P8             1W /   80W  |    11MiB /    6144MiB  |      0%      Default |
|                                         |                        |                  N/A |
+-----------------------------------------+------------------------+----------------------+

+-----------------------------------------------------------------------------------------+
| Processes:                                                                              |
|  GPU   GI   CI            PID   Type   Process name                         GPU Memory  |
|        ID   ID                                                              Usage       |
|=========================================================================================|
|    0   N/A  N/A          1357     G    /usr/lib/xorg/Xorg                        4MiB   |
|    0   N/A  N/A          2064     G    /usr/lib/xorg/Xorg                        4MiB   |
+-----------------------------------------------------------------------------------------+
```

Figure 2.3: Result of nvidia-smi program execution

In this section, we've seen how to identify the correct driver for our device and how to prepare Ubuntu for its installation, but this is only part of the story. Now we need the development tools that use the GPU through this driver. The next section will present the first path of the strategy we mentioned earlier.

Docker at a glance

If you have used Docker before, you may want to skip this section. If not, let's stick together for an overview of this technology.

Dealing with multiple versions of libraries creates a myriad of problems and difficulties. Creating an isolated environment is a great alternative, and this is exactly what Docker does for us.

We use **Docker images** as a controlled environment where we can have our own specific versions of libraries – even if they already exist on our base system. It is possible to have multiple images for different software versions. Another important concept is that of a **Docker container**, which is a running process based on a Docker image.

When we run a Docker container, it is possible to mount a folder from the user system, and this feature allows us to have a development environment with all its toolkits and build source code from the user system without having to install all the build tools directly.

Pros and cons of using Docker for build

Before we decide on which path to take, let's find out the magnitude of the challenges ahead. Among the plethora of arguments about containerization technologies, the two most important pros and cons are listed here. Let's start with the cons.

Challenges in GPU support configuration

Setting up GPU support in Docker containers involves additional configuration steps, which can be challenging for those unfamiliar with the process. (Fortunately, all the steps are described in this chapter.) Unlike CPU-based containers, enabling GPU acceleration requires the **NVIDIA Docker runtime**, which must be correctly installed and configured on the host system.

Moreover, not all Docker hosts support GPU pass-through, which can limit the environments in which CUDA-based Docker containers can be run. This limitation can be particularly problematic in cloud environments or on shared infrastructure, where GPU resources might not be readily available or properly configured. Although it may not be a problem on most laptops, it is important to make sure that the host system can support GPU-accelerated containers, and this can require additional steps, such as verifying hardware compatibility and updating drivers.

Challenges in debugging

Debugging issues within a Docker container can be more complex than on a native system, which can present challenges for developers. Containers add an abstraction layer that can obscure the root causes of issues, making it harder to diagnose and resolve problems. This is particularly true if an issue is related to containerization itself or to interactions between the container and the host system. However, as we will see in the next chapter, we can overcome this by running our environment inside the container with **Visual Studio Code** (a.k.a. **VS Code**).

Furthermore, the ephemeral nature of containers can complicate the debugging process. Containers are often designed to be stateless and can be easily recreated, which means that any changes or configurations made during debugging sessions can be lost when the container is restarted. For this reason, it can be a good idea to persist logs to mounted volumes; these can then be analyzed even after container execution has terminated.

Debugging GPU-related issues within containers adds another layer of complexity. GPU drivers and CUDA libraries need to be correctly configured and accessible within the container, and any misconfigurations can lead to subtle and hard-to-trace issues.

Now, let's consider the strengths of using this approach.

The benefits of isolation

Docker containers provide a highly effective way to isolate the development environment from the host system. This isolation ensures that the various dependencies of different projects do not conflict with each other. For CUDA-based projects, this is particularly helpful because the versions of CUDA and the other libraries can be tightly controlled within the container. This isolation helps maintain a clean host system, free from multiple installations and potential version conflicts.

Moreover, this container-based isolation is great for collaborative environments. Developers working on the same project can have identical development environments, eliminating the common 'well it works on my machine' scenario. By using Docker, every team member can use the same container image, ensuring that the code behaves consistently across all development setups. Another interesting aspect is that by running the development tools within containers, the risk of harmful code affecting the host system is minimized. Docker containers operate with restricted permissions, adding an extra layer of security by limiting the potential impact of security vulnerabilities within the development environment. The only issue we face with these restrictions is that they block the profiling of CUDA applications, but, as we will see in *Chapter 4*, it is possible to configure a different runtime for specific moments when we need to run the profiler.

Ease of setup

Setting up a CUDA development environment can often be a daunting task, especially for those who are new to GPU programming or the CUDA ecosystem. Docker simplifies this process significantly by allowing us to use pre-configured Docker images from repositories such as **Docker Hub**. These images come with CUDA and all necessary dependencies pre-installed, circumventing the need for complicated installation procedures.

The convenience of Docker is not limited to beginners. Even experienced developers can benefit from this simple setup process. Instead of spending valuable time configuring the environment for each new project or ensuring compatibility across different machines, we can simply pull a Docker image and start programming almost immediately.

Additionally, Docker's ease of setup promotes a more agile development workflow. When starting a new project or testing out new technologies, the time saved on environment setup can be significant.

Readying our development environment

Many websites provide information on using and configuring Docker, including the official website, which is the authoritative resource for the latest information, as well as the NVIDIA Docker support site. The NVIDIA Container Toolkit is the key piece which allows our containers to 'see' our GPU device. This is important, because one of the main objectives of containers is to provide isolated execution environments, so by default they do not allow direct access to the hardware. (URLs are given at the end of this section.) However, to help you get started, we 'll quickly run through the process for setting up the development environment. Note that this list may change in the future.

> **Motivational note**
>
> Although the set-up process outlined here may seem rather complicated, it will be done only once, so stick with me because it will be worth it!

As always, let's begin with an update to make sure our system is up to date:

```
sudo apt update
sudo apt upgrade -y
```

After that, we need to install some required packages. We've broken this into two lines for readability:

```
sudo apt install -y apt-transport-https ca-certificates
sudo apt install -y curl software-properties-common
```

Now, we need to add Docker's official GPG key. This command will not display any message:

```
curl -fsSL https://download.docker.com/linux/ubuntu/gpg | sudo gpg
--dearmor -o /usr/share/keyrings/docker-archive-keyring.gpg
```

Add the Docker repository to our system. This will also display no message:

```
echo "deb [arch=$(dpkg --print-architecture) signed-by=/usr/share/
keyrings/docker-archive-keyring.gpg] https://download.docker.com/linux/
ubuntu $(lsb_release -cs) stable" | sudo tee /etc/apt/sources.list.d/
docker.list > /dev/null
```

Our system now knows that there is something out there called Docker, but we need another update to make sure we refresh our local information of available packages and versions.

To do that we need a new update, like this:

```
sudo apt update
```

Finally we have got to the point where we are ready to install Docker!

```
sudo apt install -y docker-ce docker-ce-cli containerd.io
```

For a quick test, we execute the following command. It will download a Docker image and run it, printing something on the screen:

```
sudo docker run hello-world
```

Notice the sudo command. This is necessary because our current user is not in the correct execution group, which didn't exist until now. To remove the need to use sudo, we need to configure our user as follows:

```
sudo usermod -aG docker $USER
```

For this change to take effect, we need to log out and log back in.

We can now run hello-world again without using sudo:

```
docker run hello-world
```

One more thing to understand is that Docker runs as a service of our operating system. It is a good idea to let it start automatically every time the computer turns on. We configure that using the following commands:

```
sudo systemctl enable docker
sudo systemctl start docker
```

Now take a breath, for we have achieved an important milestone: our system is capable of executing Docker. It can be used also for other types of systems. Well done! But now we need to get back to work because there is more to do if we want to enable Docker to use GPUs.

We have to install the software from NVIDIA that will allow us to use the GPU inside our container. To do that, we need to add a new repository to our system, rather as we did for Docker:

```
curl -fsSL https://nvidia.github.io/libnvidia-container/gpgkey | sudo gpg
--dearmor -o /usr/share/keyrings/nvidia-container-toolkit-keyring.gpg \
   && curl -s -L https://nvidia.github.io/libnvidia-container/stable/deb/
```

```
nvidia-container-toolkit.list | \
    sed 's#deb https://#deb [signed-by=/usr/share/keyrings/nvidia-
container-toolkit-keyring.gpg] https://#g' | \
    sudo tee /etc/apt/sources.list.d/nvidia-container-toolkit.list
sudo apt-get update
```

After that, we can install the package:

```
sudo apt install -y nvidia-container-toolkit
```

We also need to define the NVIDIA runtime:

```
sudo nvidia-ctk runtime configure --runtime=docker
```

Now we need to restart the Docker service to use the new capability:

```
sudo systemctl restart docker
```

Let's run a test to make sure that all the installations work fine:

```
docker run --rm --runtime=nvidia --gpus all ubuntu nvidia-smi
```

What we did here was inform Docker that it should make all the GPUs on the system available to the container. The Ubuntu image is downloaded from Docker Hub (where all major software companies make their software available for us) and the nvidia-smi command is executed inside the running container. We get something similar to this:

```
+-----------------------------------------------------------------------------------------+
| NVIDIA-SMI 570.133.07              Driver Version: 570.133.07      CUDA Version: 12.8    |
|-----------------------------------------+------------------------+----------------------+
| GPU  Name                 Persistence-M | Bus-Id          Disp.A | Volatile Uncorr. ECC |
| Fan  Temp    Perf         Pwr:Usage/Cap |           Memory-Usage | GPU-Util  Compute M. |
|                                         |                        |               MIG M. |
|=========================================+========================+======================|
|   0  NVIDIA GeForce RTX 2060        Off | 00000000:01:00.0 Off   |                  N/A |
| N/A  42C    P8              1W /  80W   |     11MiB /  6144MiB   |      0%      Default |
|                                         |                        |                  N/A |
+-----------------------------------------+------------------------+----------------------+

+-----------------------------------------------------------------------------------------+
| Processes:                                                                              |
|  GPU   GI   CI          PID   Type   Process name                          GPU Memory  |
|        ID   ID                                                             Usage       |
|=========================================================================================|
+-----------------------------------------------------------------------------------------+
```

Figure 2.4: Result of nvidia-smi execution inside a Docker container

The result is very similar to before; the only difference is that no processes are executing, and this is related to the running container context. For the container, no processes are using the device.

This is our second milestone: having a working Docker installation capable of running CUDA software.

Official websites

Here are the (current) addresses of the websites that contain all the information about what we just did, and which may be necessary for future reference:

- Official Docker website – `https://www.docker.com/`
- Official NVIDIA Container Toolkit – `https://github.com/NVIDIA/nvidia-container-toolkit`

Wow, that was a lot of information! We have learned not only why Docker is very helpful, but also how to configure and validate the installation. After that, we learned how to use an image specifically targeted at CUDA that uses the device driver we installed before, and all without adding the CUDA Toolkit directly into our system! Now it's time to learn how to configure the CUDA Toolkit directly. Remember that regardless of the approach, the installation of the NVIDIA driver is needed. Let's jump in!

CUDA Toolkit installation

Now that we know how to use the CUDA Toolkit in an isolated fashion, let's learn how to install it directly on our machine. This option provides a greater level of flexibility, but also entails having to manage the possibility of different versions of libraries spreading through our systems. This can become a problem when we want to update the version or if we want to test our software with multiple versions of the CUDA Toolkit.

First we need to download the Toolkit from the official NVIDIA website at `https://developer.nvidia.com/cuda-toolkit`, selecting our operating system, hardware architecture, distribution, and version. In our case: Linux, x86_64, Ubuntu, 20.04.

After that, we are presented with three options: deb (local), deb (network), and runfile (local). The easiest is to use a local .deb file and, when selecting this option, we are presented with the following commands:

```
wget https://developer.download.nvidia.com/compute/cuda/repos/ubuntu2004/
x86_64/cuda-ubuntu2004.pin
sudo mv cuda-ubuntu2004.pin /etc/apt/preferences.d/cuda-repository-pin-600
wget https://developer.download.nvidia.com/compute/cuda/12.5.1/local_
installers/cuda-repo-ubuntu2004-12-5-local_12.5.1-555.42.06-1_amd64.deb
sudo dpkg -i cuda-repo-ubuntu2004-12-5-local_12.5.1-555.42.06-1_amd64.deb
sudo cp /var/cuda-repo-ubuntu2004-12-5-local/cuda-*-keyring.gpg /usr/
share/keyrings/
sudo apt-get update
sudo apt-get -y install cuda-toolkit-12-5
```

The CUDA Toolkit page mentions CUDA driver installation, but that was the first thing we installed, so we can skip that step.

After running the installation steps, it is recommended that we reboot our system and, following that, we can test our installation with nvidia-smi, as we did before with Docker. However, it is a good idea to use the following command, which prints the version of the NVIDIA CUDA compiler:

```
nvcc -V
```

This will present the NVIDIA compiler version.

When directly installing the CUDA Toolkit there were fewer steps because we did not need to install Docker. Keep in mind though that having the CUDA Toolkit directly installed on our system means we may have to deal with different versions of some libraries, depending on our projects' needs. This version management is not a huge concern with the Docker approach because everything gets packed inside the Docker container image. If we want to switch between versions, we just need to run a different container image.

Summary

In this chapter we've learned about the options for running the CUDA Toolkit. The first approach was based on Docker, and after considering some of its pros and cons we outlined the steps involved in its configuration. Once configured, we were able to query the GPU system inside a running container. The second approach was to install the CUDA Toolkit directly onto our system. This is a little more intrusive, and we may have to deal with multiple versions in the future, but is also important to be aware of it as a possibility.

With all that done it's time to fasten our seat belts, because in the next chapter we'll be writing our first CUDA program!

Unlock this book's exclusive benefits now

UNLOCK NOW

Scan this QR code or go to packtpub.com/unlock, then search this book by name.

Note: Keep your purchase invoice ready before you start.

3

Hello CUDA

Every programming journey starts with a simple 'Hello World' program, and with all the features that GPUs provide to the developer, it is the best approach to explaining how things really work. As with any intricate topic, there is a myriad of detail that complicates GPU programming. If we had to know it all before writing any code it would be tiresome and boring. To avoid this, we will adopt an incremental approach. We will learn a little about how to program our GPU devices, and we will have to believe in a little magic here and there until we grasp all the concepts.

We'll start with a superficial understanding of what makes a GPU program, and then move on to a fully functional toy program as a milestone in terms of using our GPU device. At the end of the chapter, we will wrap up with a section on how to use the default NVIDIA example of querying a device and some discussion of the main details that can be inspected from the execution environment.

In this chapter we're going to cover the following main topics:

- What a kernel is
- A first running program
- Inspecting devices
- A better working environment

Technical requirements

Now it is time to build something, so we are going to use the environment we prepared in the last chapter together with the text editor of your choice. Of course, using a programming IDE is better because it provides support for language highlighting and even code completion, so we will cover how to install and configure Visual Studio Code (`https://code.visualstudio.com/`), which is capable of connecting to a running Docker container and even to remote machines through SSH. Remember to download all the code from the chapter's GitHub repository `https://github.com/PacktPublishing/GPU-Programming-with-CPP-and-CUDA/tree/main/ch3`.

The kernel and some terminology

With the risk of being overly simplistic, we can say that the **kernel** is the key concept of GPU programming. We can also start by saying that it is a function. Specifically, a kernel is a special function written in C or C++ that runs on the GPU instead of the CPU. It's designed to be executed by many threads in parallel, and as we mentioned previously, each thread runs each line of code in parallel, allowing highly efficient computation. Kernels are fundamental to CUDA because they enable the GPU to process large amounts of data simultaneously, leveraging its parallel processing capabilities.

Kernels operate within a hierarchical structure of threads, blocks, and grids. A **thread** is the smallest unit of execution in CUDA, and multiple threads are grouped together into **blocks**. Each block runs independently and can be scheduled on any of the GPU's processing units.

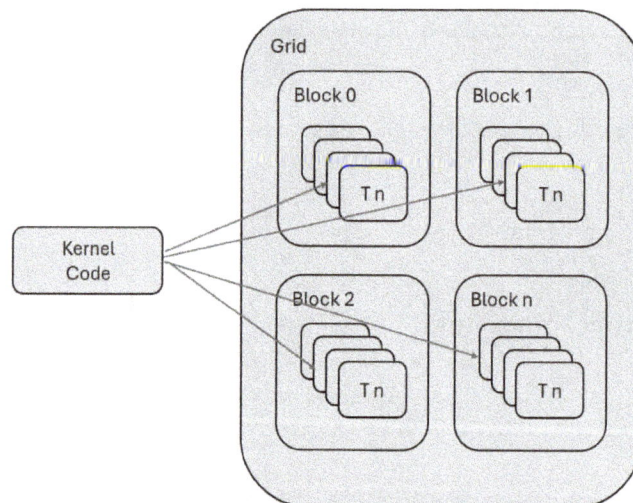

Figure 3.1: Thread, block, and grid hierarchy

As we can see in *Figure 3.1*, blocks are organized into grids. The **grid** is the overall structure that contains all the blocks and represents the entire workload to be executed by the kernel. When we launch a kernel, we need to specify the number of blocks in the grid and the number of threads in each block.

> **Some numbers to illustrate**
>
> According to the Ada Architecture Document (`https://images.nvidia.com/aem-dam/Solutions/geforce/ada/nvidia-ada-gpu-architecture.pdf`), the RTX4090 GPU has 144 streaming multiprocessors with 128 CUDA cores, to give a total of 18,432 CUDA cores on the board.

To make this a little clearer, let's consider the preceding GPU architecture for a moment, again simplifying it a bit. The GPU device has multiple streaming multiprocessors (SMs), each of which contains several cores. When a kernel is launched, blocks are assigned to SMs, and the threads within those blocks are distributed across the cores. This means that SMs can execute multiple blocks concurrently, taking advantage of the GPU's parallel processing capabilities.

Each SM has a limited number of resources, such as **registers** and shared memory. The configuration of threads and blocks affects how these resources are allocated. If there are too many threads or blocks, the GPU might run out of resources, leading to reduced performance or even failure. If there are too few threads or blocks, on the other hand, the GPU won't be fully utilized.

This may seem like too much information at the moment, but let's recall our deal to believe in a little magic here and there on occasion. Now is a good time for such a belief. Just keep in mind that kernels are special functions: they are executed by threads that run on CUDA cores. Cores are grouped in SMs, which are mapped to blocks.

Now that we have a schematic overview of the concepts involved in GPU programs, let's take a look at a complete, yet super-simple, first program that makes use of our device.

A first running program

An old curse that haunts programmers says that if, when learning some new programming language or technology, we do not start with a simple 'Hello World' example, everything we do afterward with that technology will not go well.

Of course, this is just a joke, but let's start with a 'Hello World' example just in case.

Here is the code listing:

```
1 #include <cuda_runtime.h>
2 #include <iostream>
3 __global__ void hello_world() {
4   int tid = threadIdx.x + blockIdx.x * blockDim.x;
5  printf("Hello, World! Thread %d\n", tid);
6 }
7 int main() {
8  hello_world<<<1, 10>>>();
9  cudaDeviceSynchronize();
10  return 0;
11 }
```

💡 **Quick tip**: Enhance your coding experience with the **AI Code Explainer** and **Quick Copy** features. Open this book in the next-gen Packt Reader. Click the **Copy** button **(1)** to quickly copy code into your coding environment, or click the **Explain** button **(2)** to get the AI assistant to explain a block of code to you.

```
                                              Copy      Explain
function calculate(a, b) {
  return {sum: a + b};                         1          2
};
```

🔖 **The next-gen Packt Reader** is included for free with the purchase of this book. Scan the QR code OR go to packtpub.com/unlock, then use the search bar to find this book by name. Double-check the edition shown to make sure you get the right one.

We are going to work together here to make the code navigation as smooth as possible.

There are four things to note about our Hello World code:

- There is a special keyword on line 3, `__global__`, that informs the compiler that `hello_world` will run on the device.

- In line 4, we refer to special environment variables that allow us to identify which thread is running. Notice that each thread has a thread ID (`threadIdx.x`), a block ID (`blockIdx.x`), and a block dimension (`blockDim.x`). This is necessary because, usually, we have many blocks with many threads. For each block B we have threads from 0 to T. This means that block 1 will have a thread 0 and block 2 will also have a thread 0, and thus the numbers repeat – so it is the combination of these three dimensions that uniquely identifies a thread.

- In line 8, we call our function, but we add the configuration of the number of threads and blocks. This configuration is passed into the runtime environment with triple angle brackets before the list of arguments (which is empty in our example). We can see the numbers 1 and 10, meaning that we will have one block with ten threads.

- On line 9, we have a special command that makes the main program wait for our kernel to complete its processing. This is necessary because the kernel call is asynchronous, but do not worry about that for now.

The rest of our simple program is the same as a traditional Hello World C/C++ program.

To compile the code, assuming that our program is in a file called `hello_world.cu`, we use the following command:

```
nvcc -o hello_world hello_world.cu
```

But wait! What if we want to use the CUDA Docker image that we saw in *Chapter 2*? Well, then we will need to do the following. Assuming we have cloned the book's GitHub repository, we have a local folder containing all our code. Let's open a terminal in the folder that contains our `hello_world.cu` program.

In the terminal prompt, we will enter a Docker command that is very similar to the one we saw in *Chapter 2*, but now, instead of running `nvidia-smi` to display some information, we'll request an interactive session so that our terminal prompt will be running *inside* the container. We can do this with the following command:

```
docker run -it --rm --gpus all -v ./:/code nvidia/cuda:12.0.0-devel-ubuntu20.04 bash
```

This command deserves an explanation. We added the `-it` and `--rm` parameters; this means open an interactive session and remove the running container when we are done. The `-v` parameter allows us to map a folder on the host machine to a given folder inside the running container. In this case, we are mapping the current folder, `./`, to `/code` in the running container. Since we opened the terminal in the repository folder, we will be able to see, edit, and use our files inside the container. Then comes the image that we are going to use, `cuda:12.0.0-devel-ubuntu20.04`, which is the CUDA development environment based on **Ubuntu 20.04**. Lastly, we indicate what to run. In this case, we want `bash` so that we can get a terminal to interact with in our interactive session. What we removed from our previous command was the `--runtime=nvidia` option, since it is the default.

What we can do now is run that compiled program inside our `/code` folder and get an executable called `hello_world` for our program that we can call as follows:

```
./hello_world
```

This will present the following result:

```
Hello, World! Thread 0
Hello, World! Thread 1
Hello, World! Thread 2
Hello, World! Thread 3
Hello, World! Thread 4
Hello, World! Thread 5
Hello, World! Thread 6
Hello, World! Thread 7
Hello, World! Thread 8
Hello, World! Thread 9
```

Now that we have seen a simple CUDA program, let's reflect on it. To run a CUDA program on a GPU device, we must always have at least one kernel, because the `main` function will run on the CPU. But we have to remember that we are actually asking for a separate device to execute some code, instead of the CPU. It is also important to notice that, although our result here is presented in the order of the execution calls, it may not always be the case because the blocks and threads are scheduled for execution without a predefined order. With a program as simple as this, and considering that we are scheduling only ten threads, results may be in execution call order, but for any program with more than one block and with many threads, there is no guarantee of scheduling order.

At present we are dealing with very simple programs, but later on we will be using more advanced features, and it is always a good idea to check whether our environment is capable of executing what our program is defined for. To do that, we can inspect the **runtime properties**. Let's take a look at those in the next section.

Consulting devices

We can programmatically find out the capabilities of our installed device, but we do so using a different program. This is a program that does not run a kernel, and so does not use the device; it finds out about the capabilities through the device driver. We can use this approach to guarantee that our programs have all that is needed for correct execution, and since GPU hardware evolves so quickly, it is a good idea to have some verification of this sort.

For the sake of simplicity, we are going to look at a shortened version of the code that comes with the CUDA SDK. We will also suppress the error-checking code. The original device query program from the CUDA code samples is a much more complete version but it includes many #ifdefs which make the code more confusing. We just want to explore some of the possibilities for now; we will revisit error-checking in *Chapter 6*.

```
#include <cuda_runtime.h>
#include <iostream>
int main() {
    cudaDeviceProp deviceProp;
    int dev = 0;
    cudaGetDeviceProperties(&deviceProp, dev);
    std::cout << "Device " << dev << ": " << deviceProp.name << std::endl;
    std::cout << "  CUDA Capability Major/Minor version number: " <<
        deviceProp.major << "." << deviceProp.minor << std::endl;
    std::cout << "  Total amount of shared memory per block: " <<
        deviceProp.sharedMemPerBlock << " bytes" << std::endl;
    std::cout << "  Maximum number of threads per block: " <<
        deviceProp.maxThreadsPerBlock << std::endl;
    return 0;
}
```

To compile our program, we use the same interactive Docker session that we were using and enter the following command:

```
nvcc -o device_query device_query.cu
```

There are many more properties than those we are inspecting here, but this small set relates to what we discussed earlier about threads, blocks, and memory. We will get a result similar to this:

```
Device 0: NVIDIA GeForce RTX 2060
  CUDA Capability Major/Minor version number: 7.5
  Total amount of shared memory per block: 49152 bytes
  Maximum number of threads per block: 1024
```

Note that the **CUDA Capability** specification is not the same thing as the CUDA Toolkit that we have installed on our system. For now, all we need to say is that the CUDA Capability defines the hardware capabilities that are present and we can use it to check whether the hardware we're trying to run our program on is compatible with what the program is trying to accomplish.

The shared memory per block tells us the amount of memory shared by all threads within the same block. We will learn how to use this information to our benefit in a future chapter. Finally, we can check the maximum number of threads per block, on the basis of which we can calculate the best configuration to use for our kernels. This is important because CUDA will not automatically define the optimal launch configuration for us; it depends on many factors, including the amount of resource we plan to use. For example, if we set a larger block for shared memory there will be less space for L1 cache.

Since the programs that we just saw were really simple, we compiled them directly on the command line, but as applications grow bigger, you might be wondering about how confusing things could get.

If only there was a way to manage all these complications... Well, there is! In the next section we'll learn how to configure our environment.

A better working environment

In this section, we are going to go through the installation and configuration of Visual Studio Code (VS Code) (`https://code.visualstudio.com/`), a free IDE from Microsoft that uses extensions to help with different working scenarios and programming languages. It has a simple yet functional interface, so let's dive straight in.

VS Code installation

From the VS Code website, we can download the appropriate version of VS Code. Following the convention for the book of using Ubuntu, it is the .deb file.

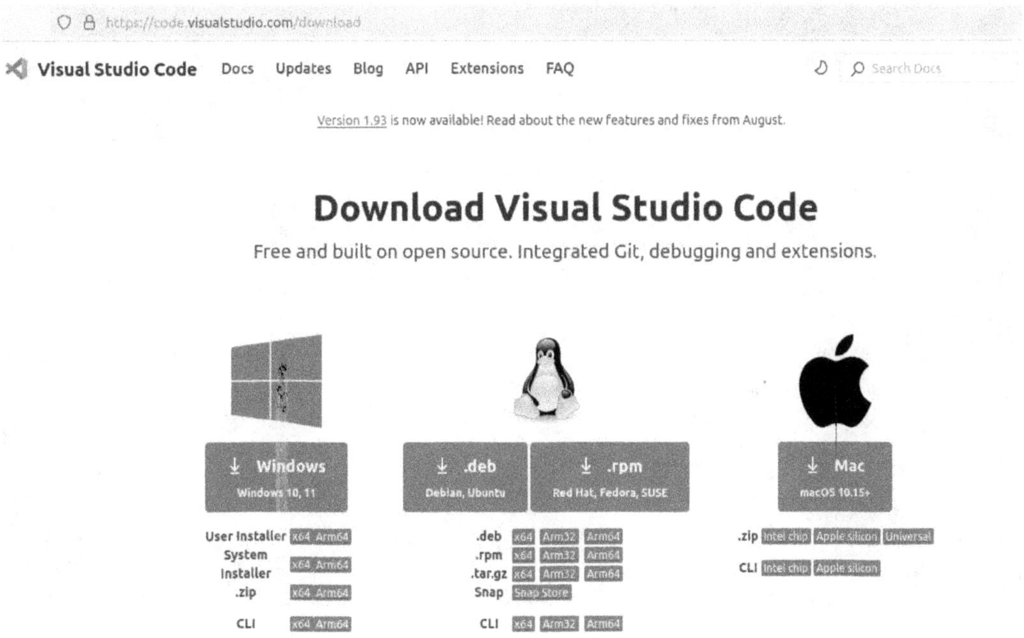

Figure 3.2: VS Code download site

After downloading VS Code, we install it by running the following command. We need to select the file that corresponds to the right version:

```
sudo apt install ./Downloads/code_[version]_amd64.deb
```

After installation, we will find the VS Code icon within our applications.

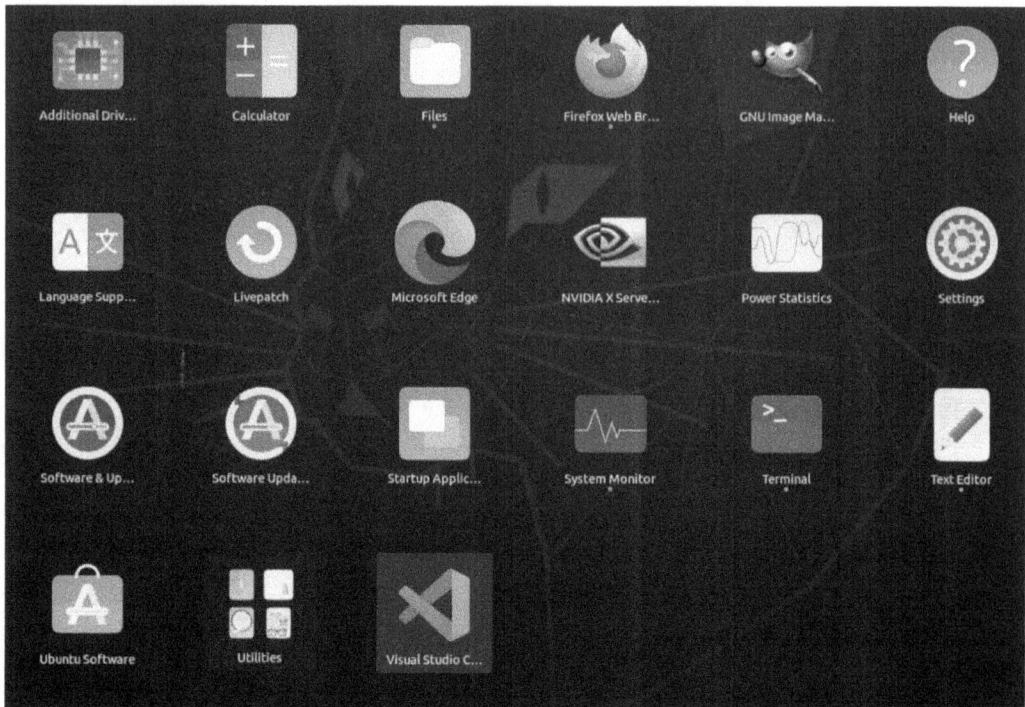

Figure 3.3: VS Code is installed!

VS Code configuration

When opening VS Code for the first time, we are presented with a list of steps to complete to configure it to our environment. We are not going to cover all the details, but we are going to talk about the extensions that we will need. VS Code is the base tool, but we can add functionality with different extensions.

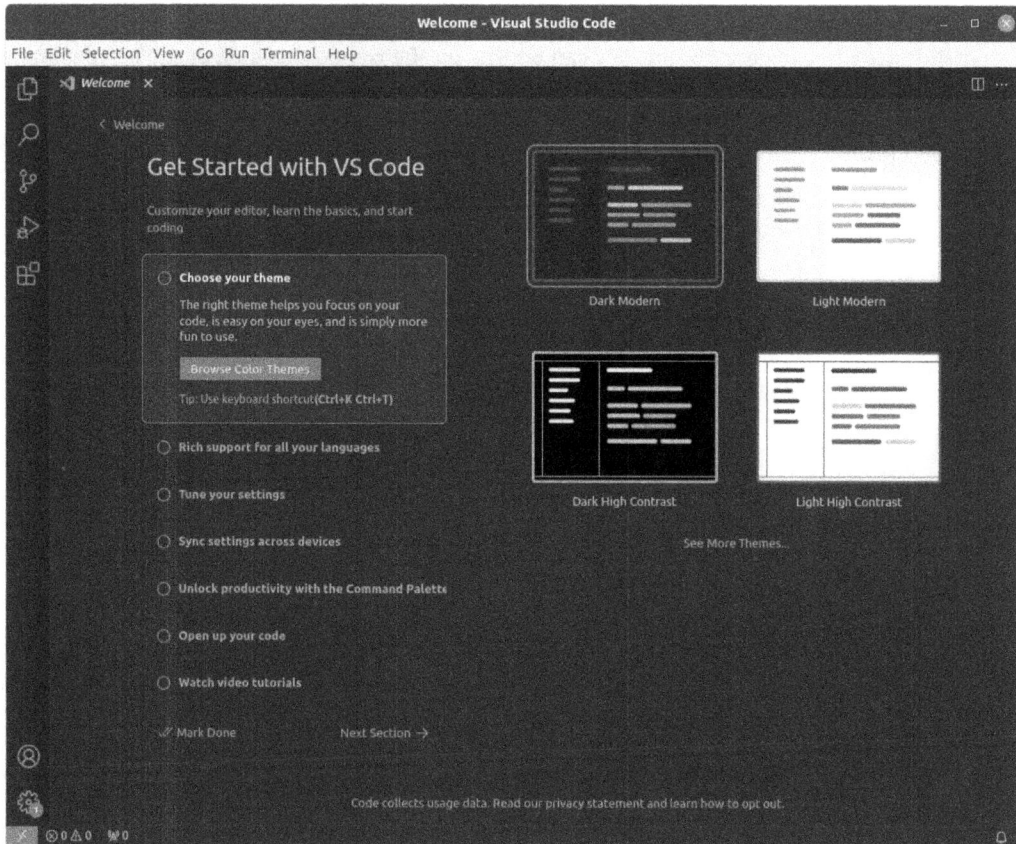

Figure 3.4: VS Code welcome screen

🔍 **Quick tip:** Need to see a high-resolution version of this image? Open this book in the next-gen Packt Reader or view it in the PDF/ePub copy.

🔒 **The next-gen Packt Reader** and a **free PDF/ePub copy** of this book are included with your purchase. Scan the QR code OR visit packtpub.com/unlock, then use the search bar to find this book by name. Double-check the edition shown to make sure you get the right one.

The steps are listed on the left with a radio button on the left side of each one. (See *Figure 3.4*.) The first one is **Choose your theme**. We can do this on the right-hand side of the screen. **Dark Modern** is pre-selected.

After selecting the theme that we are most comfortable with, click on **Next Section** at the bottom of the screen to move to **Rich support for all your languages**, where we can select the programming languages that we will be using. In our case, we need C/C++, so let's click on **Browse Language Extensions**.

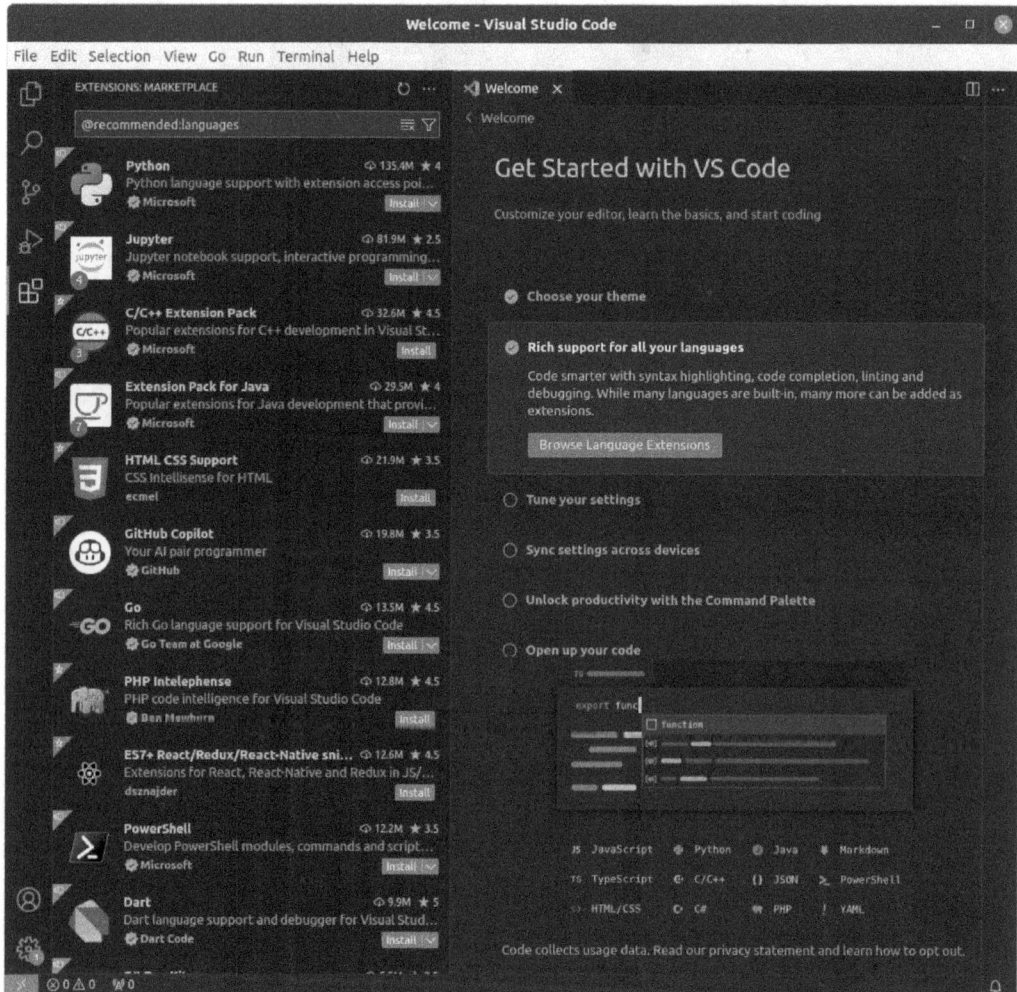

Figure 3.5: Popular programming language extensions

When we do that, a list of popular programming languages appears on the extensions sidebar. Click **Install** on the **C/C++ Extension Pack** from Microsoft.

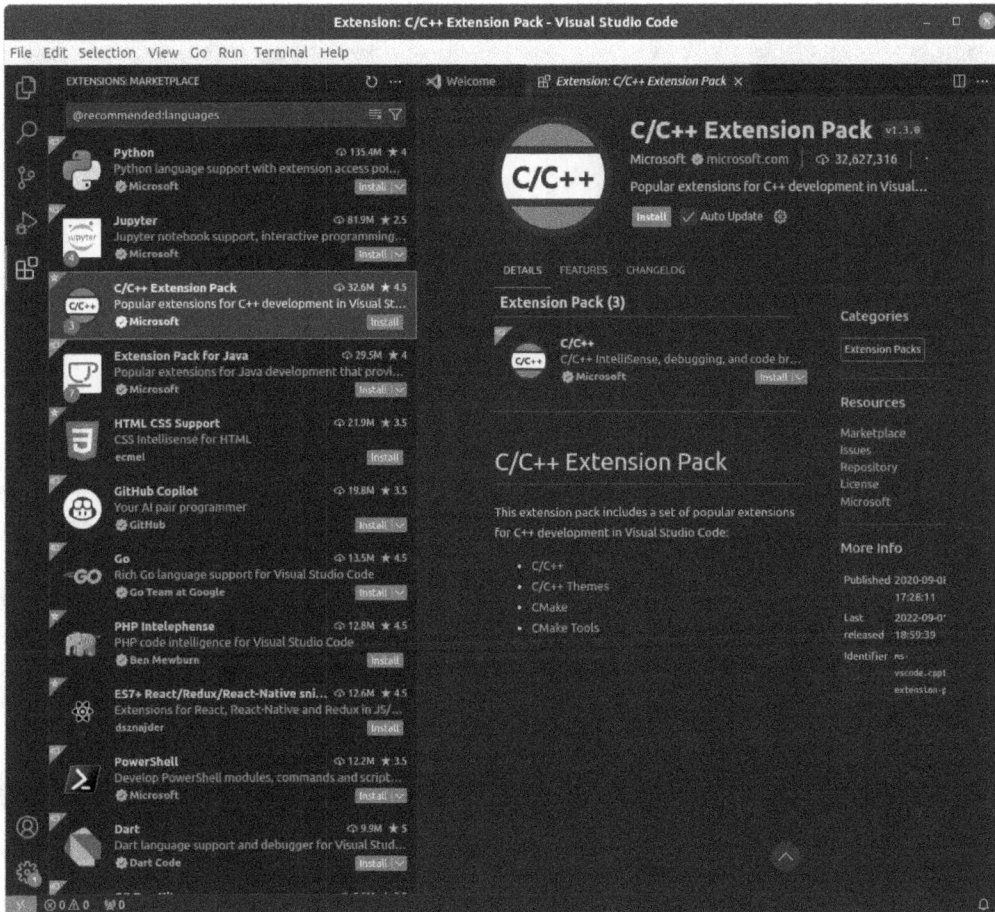

Figure 3.6: Installing C/C++ extension

After installing our programming language support, we can now install **Nsight Visual Studio Code** from NVIDIA, which will help us with our CUDA-specific code (and actually much more). Type `nsight` in the search bar of the extensions pane and get the following result:

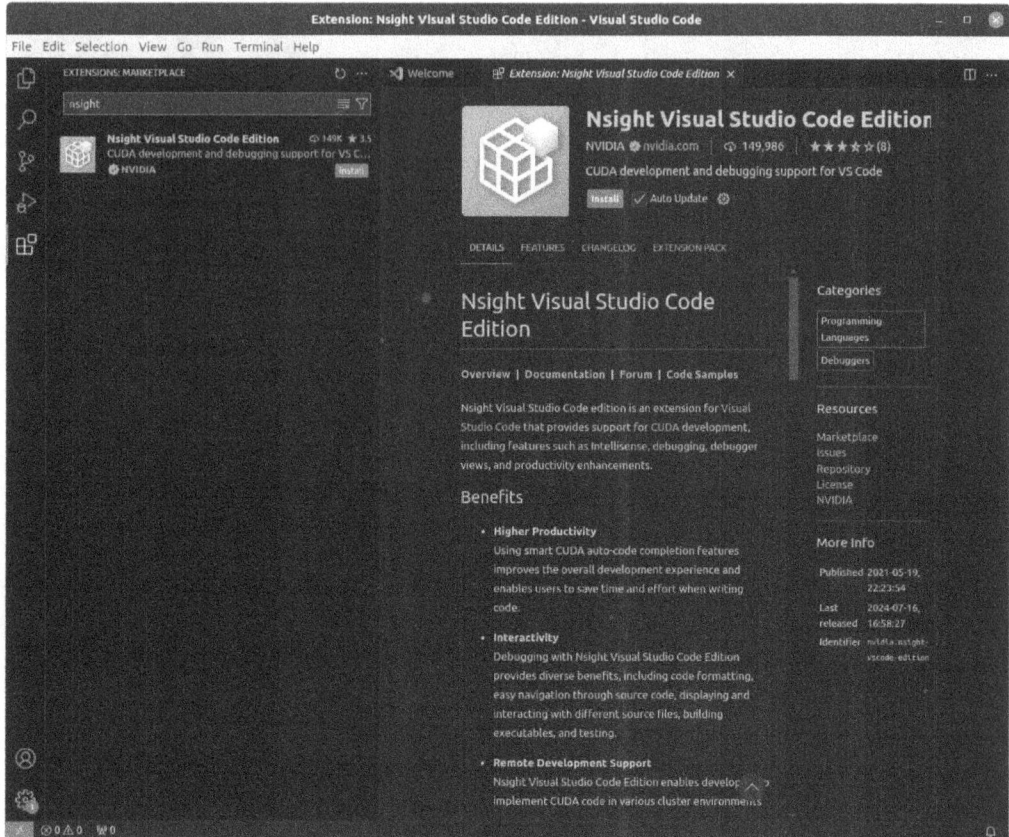

Figure 3.7: Nsight Visual Studio Code Edition extension

There are several other extensions that will help us a little bit more. The first is **Dev Containers** (we need to type this in the search bar). Like many of the previous extensions, this one is also from Microsoft, and it allows us to connect to a running container (or start a session to do that) and use VS Code as the IDE with the tools that are present *inside* that container. How cool is that?

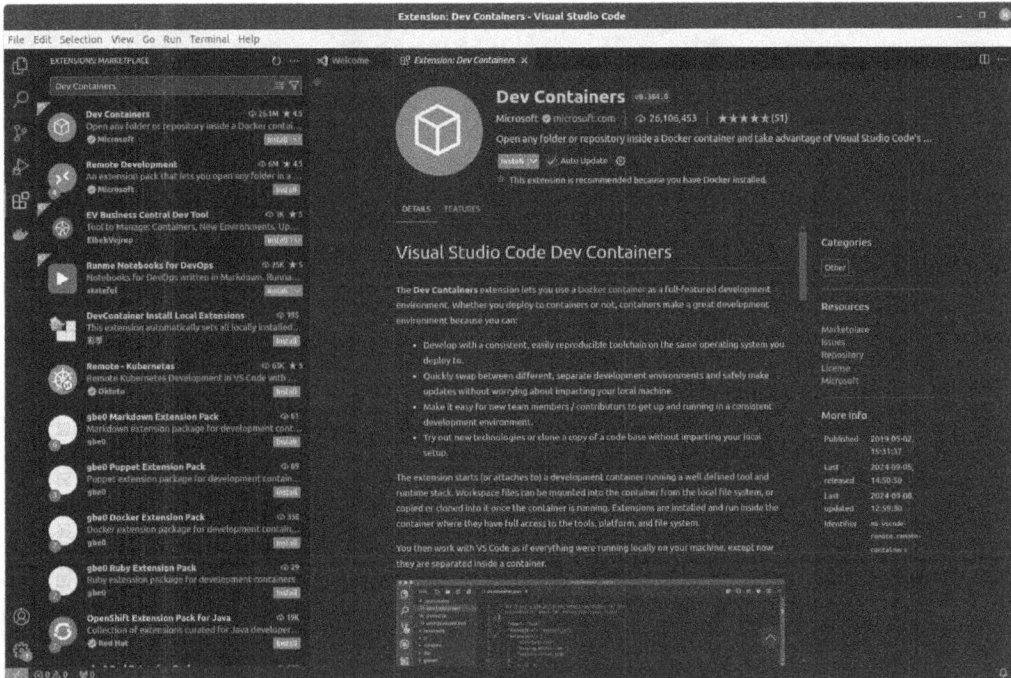

Figure 3.8: Dev Containers extension

The other is the Docker extension, which helps us manage everything Docker-related that we have, such as images and containers. Just type docker in the search bar, and then we will install the Microsoft extension.

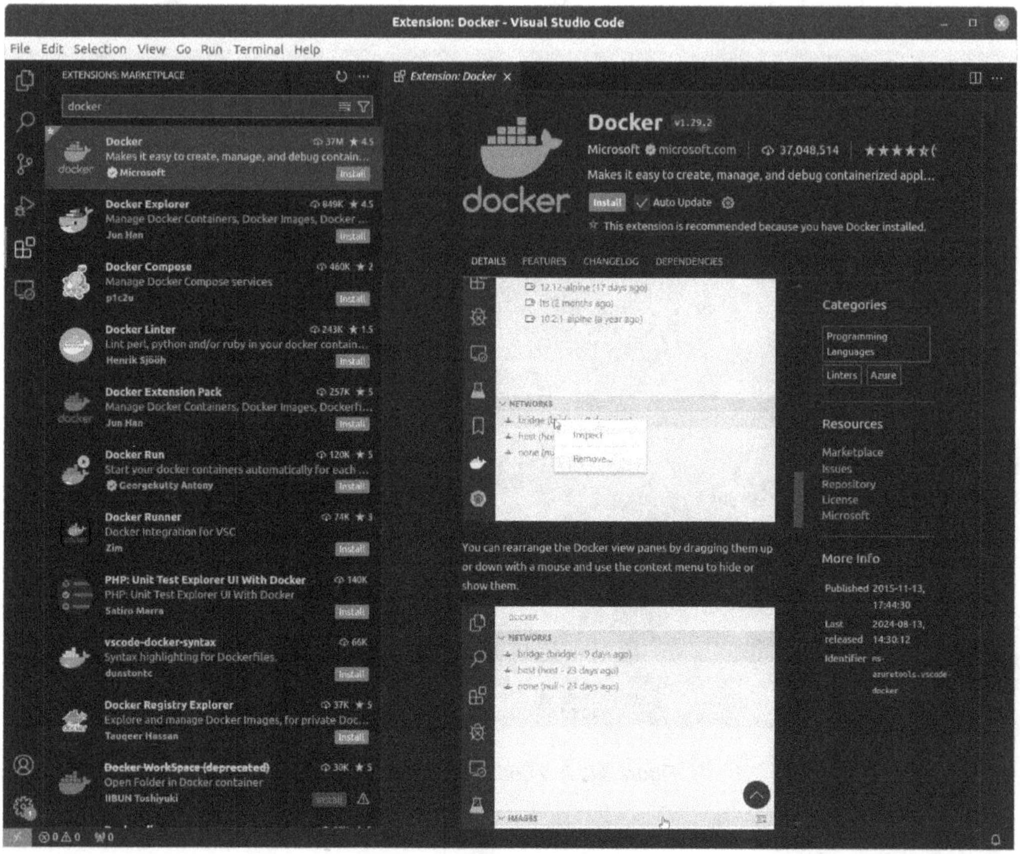

Figure 3.9: Docker extension

With that, we are almost ready to go, but let's take a quick pause to summarize what we have done so far. We have downloaded VS Code and installed all the extensions that are going to make our CUDA programming journey more effective and, if not simple, then at least simpler (after all we are talking about GPU development, which is an advanced topic).

Our installed extensions are as follows:

- C/C++ Extension Pack from Microsoft
- Nsight Visual Studio Code extension from NVIDIA
- Dev Containers extension from Microsoft
- Docker extension from Microsoft

How to use VS Code with the CUDA container

Assuming you have closed the previous Docker session from the `hello_world` program, let's run this command again:

```
docker run -it --rm --gpus all -v ./:/code nvidia/cuda:12.0.0-devel-
ubuntu20.04 bash
```

Now, if we select the Remote Explorer icon on VS Code, we will see that our running Docker container appears as an option for connection (*Figure 3.10*).

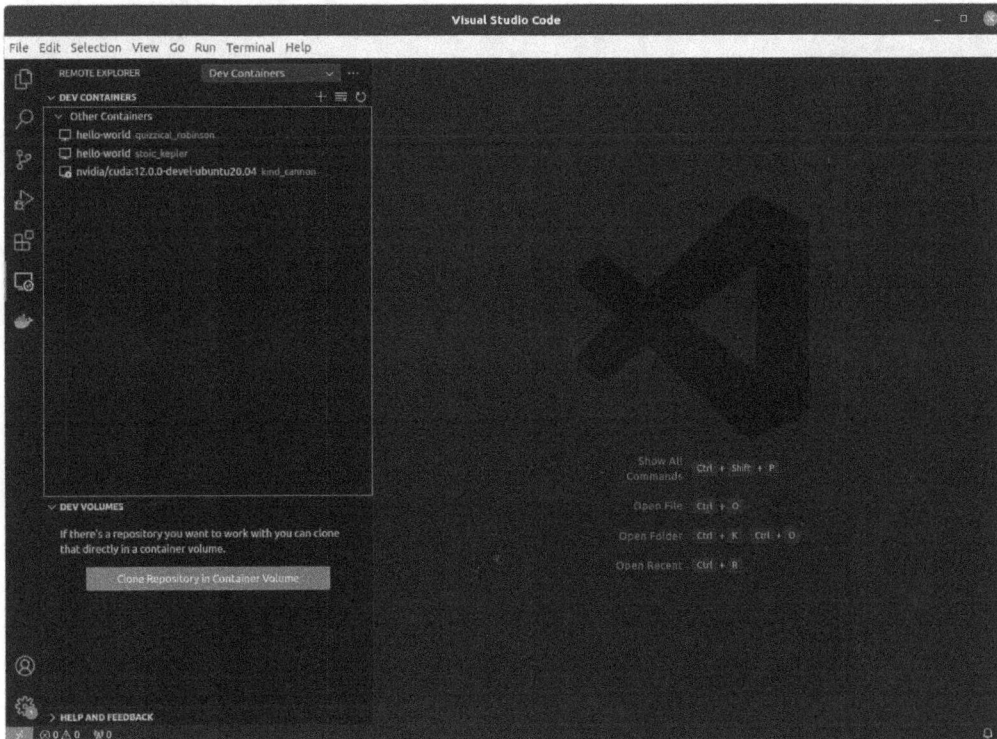

Figure 3.10: Our running Docker container is there!

If we right-click on our running container, we get a new menu that presents the option to attach to our container either in this VS Code window or in a new one. We will attach it in a new window for now. A dialog will appear, indicating that attaching to a container may execute arbitrary code. Choose **Got it** so that it may continue.

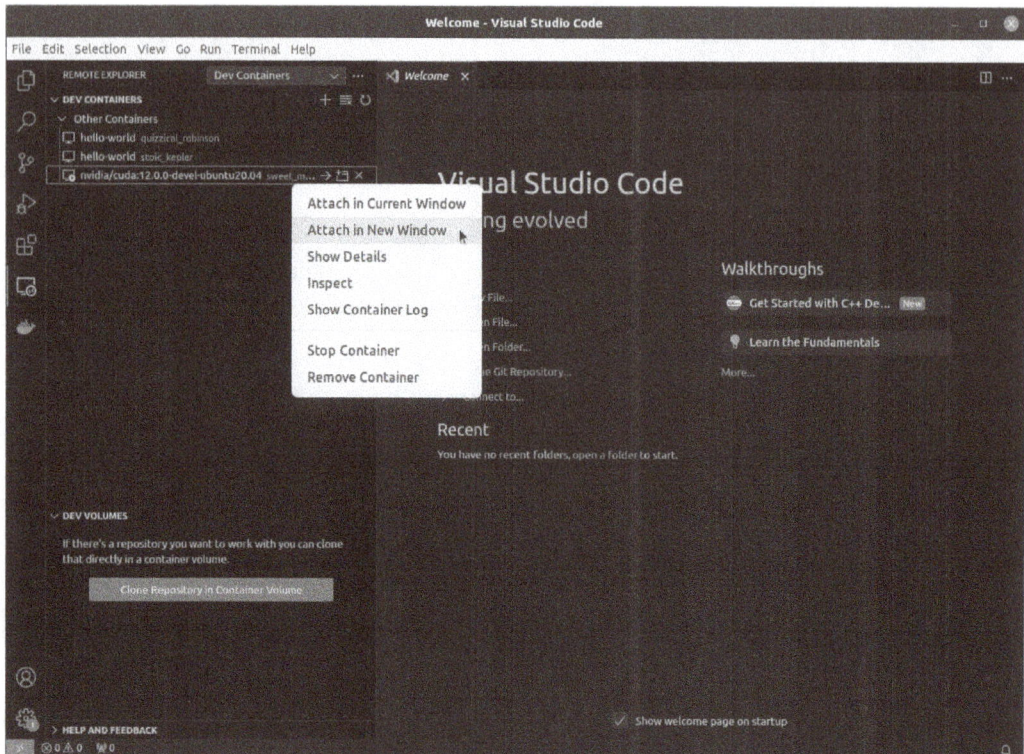

Figure 3.11: Attaching to the container

In the bottom-left corner, we see a status bar indicating that our window is connected to the container.

Figure 3.12: The connected VS Code window

We can now select **Open Folder** on the main screen and select the /code folder, which is the one we mapped from our host machine.

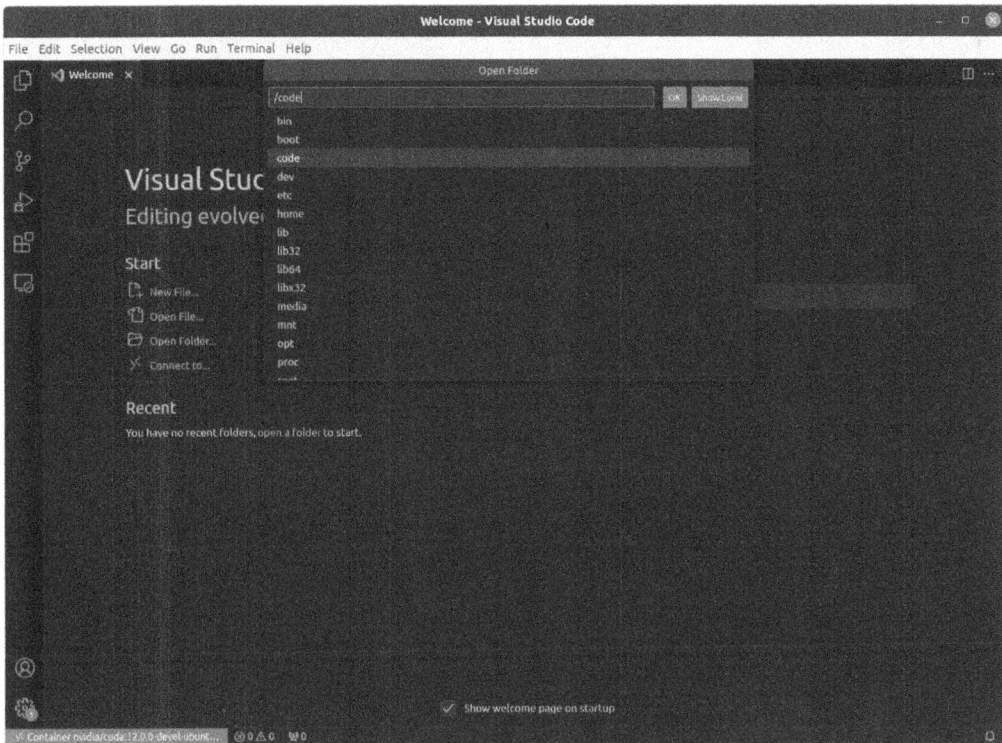

Figure 3.13: Opening the /code folder

Once the folder has been opened, we will see the explorer sidebar with our repository. VS Code will complain that this container does not have Git installed on it. We will customize our environment by using the base Docker image to construct our own environment in which we will have Git installed. This will be performed by a Dockerfile provided together with the code on the repository. Another interesting thing to notice is that our extensions are not active. This is because the extensions are not installed on this container. This will be configured in the next section.

Another great tool that VS Code provides is the terminal, which allows us to execute the same commands that we could execute in our interactive Docker session.

One thing to keep in mind is that the Docker container session is a volatile environment. This means that everything you install on the container to help with the build process will be lost the next time you start your container. If only there was a way to keep those changes... Well, there is! We'll now see how to configure VS Code to start a specific container with everything we will use in the coming chapters installed on it.

Using dev containers

We can configure a special folder called .devcontainer to contain the configurations that will help us. Inside this folder, we have the configuration file that manages our container's startup, and the Dockerfile that is used to build our custom image for execution. Some in-depth documentation about this process is available (`https://code.visualstudio.com/docs/devcontainers/` `containers`), but we will provide the necessary files in our GitHub repository to simplify the process. Now we need to use the command palette (accessed with *Ctrl + Shift + P*) and select **Dev Containers: Rebuild and Reopen in Container**.

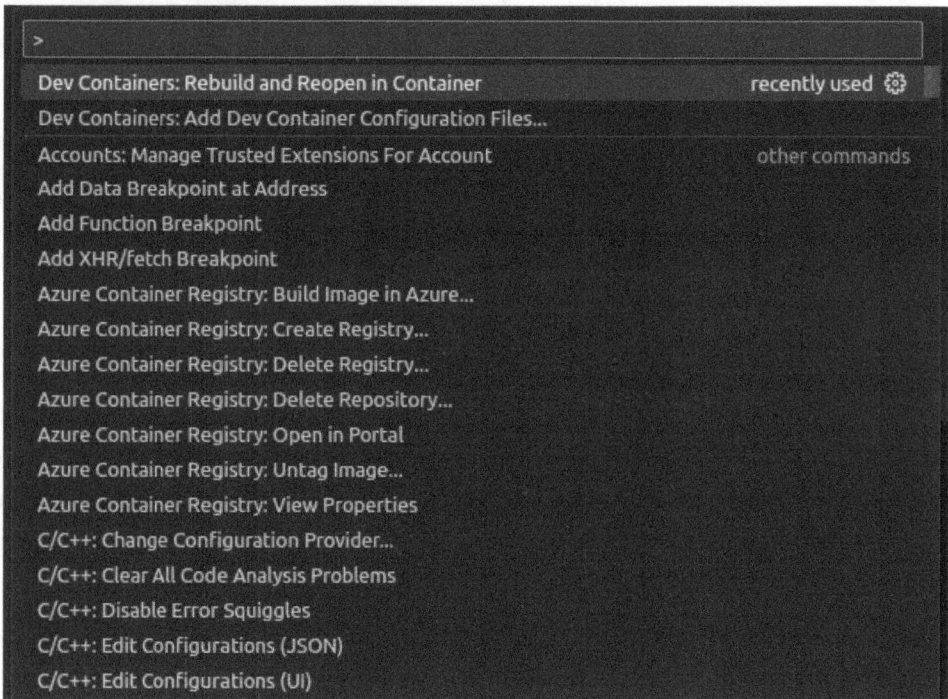

Figure 3.14: Rebuilding the container

This will build a new image, based on the original CUDA image but with some customizations that we need to fully use our environment. The last step is to install our VS Code extensions inside the new container. You can see on the **EXTENSIONS** sidebar that they are all listed as not installed.

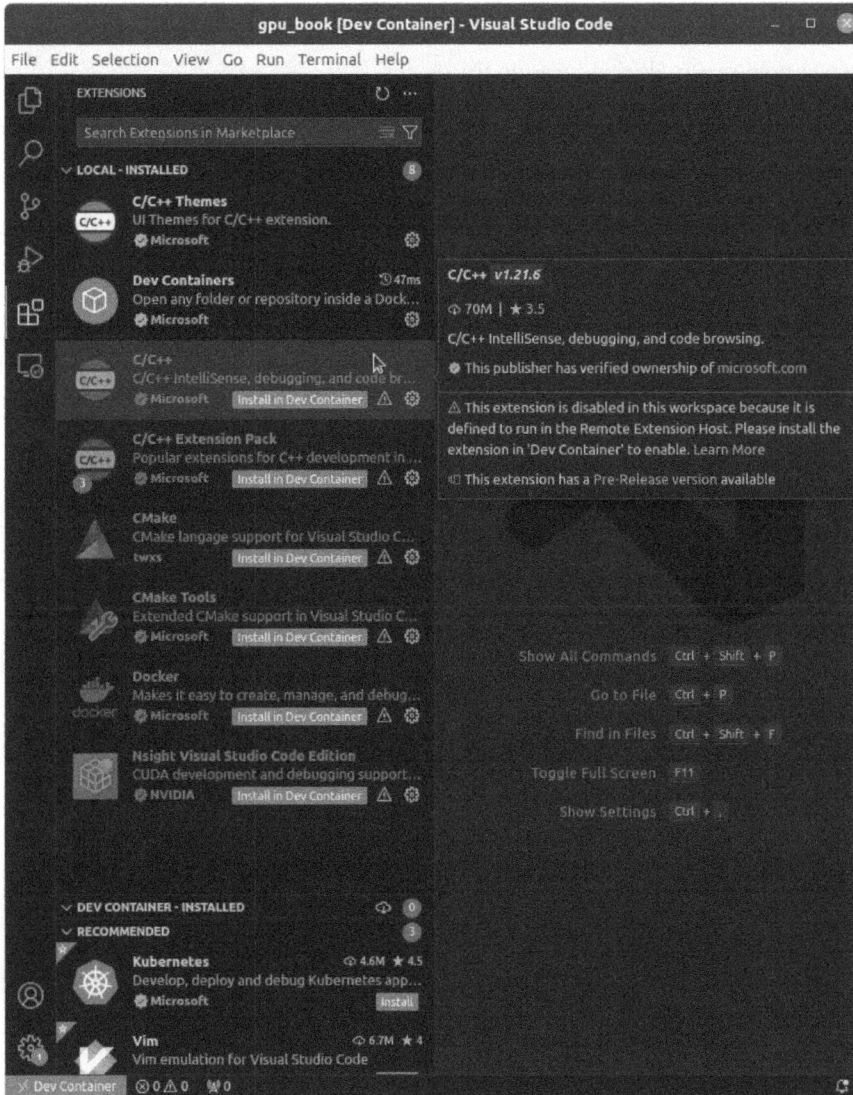

Figure 3.15: Extensions not installed

We can easily solve this by clicking on the **Install in Dev Container** button for each of the tools we have previously installed, and then we are ready to roll!

Summary

In this chapter, we took our first steps to running code on our device. We learned about the concepts that govern thread execution and how that maps to our hardware, and we dodged the programmers' curse by creating and running our 'Hello World' program to learn how this awesome technology actually executes on the device.

Next, we executed a simple program to query some of the device's properties that we can use to our benefit, since they enable us to dynamically configure the execution of our applications.

Finally, we learned how to configure VS Code and prepare it with extensions that allow us to access our Docker CUDA container and get ready for development.

In the next chapter we will build on what we've learned so far and round out our knowledge of foundational topics in GPU programming, so that we're ready to harness the power of the GPU in *Part 2* of the book.

4

Hello Again, but in Parallel

The objective of using GPUs is to exploit parallelism to accelerate the execution of our programs. For that, we must understand the parallel model that GPUs make available. In this chapter we'll first learn about the SIMD execution model and discuss a simple program to test number primality in parallel, but using an approach which makes it almost like a CPU application. Then we will learn more about moving data to and from the GPU, since its memory is separated from the main system. The chapter closes with a section presenting a simple program that fully benefits from the use of GPUs.

Thus in this chapter we're going to cover the following main topics:

- SIMD execution model
- Primality test with a not-so-parallel program
- Moving memory
- Vector addition in full parallel

Technical requirements

We will use the environment configured during *Chapter 3* with VS Code and our development container. If you have chosen to install the CUDA Toolkit on your machine, you can simply run the build commands on a terminal. The code is provided in the GitHub repository `https://github.com/PacktPublishing/GPU-Programming-with-CPP-and-CUDA/tree/main/ch4`.

The SIMD execution model

Having first encountered the Single Instruction Multiple Data execution model in *Chapter 1*, it is now time to revisit the concept and use it in real programs.

A quick recap: the idea is that we execute the same instruction on many pieces of data at the same time. This makes things faster because we are computing many items together.

However, keep in mind that not all problems can map directly to this kind of processing; this is one of our challenges. Another important point is that we need data to be arranged contiguously in memory in order to optimize access to it.

Remember that threads will execute in groups that share a little memory, but more than that, these groups will execute at the same instruction level, which means that if we have a branch in the code some threads will execute first while the others will be idly awaiting their turn to be executed. We have to carefully think about our code and try to minimize these kinds of situation to achieve better performance.

Bit twiddling

It is possible to use the same instruction at once on a vector of numbers, say four floating point numbers inside a kernel. For that, we have to provide our data in such a way that it can be loaded as vectors. The execution is very similar to what happens in CPUs that provide vector instructions capable of executing the same instruction on two large registers loaded with multiple numbers.

When it is possible to reduce the precision needed for a computation, say by using a float instead of a double or by using a byte instead of an integer, this can also lead to a performance improvement because it will give one more level of data crunching to our code.

It should be clear by now that programming GPUs requires us to be much more aware of what is going on with our program and our device than when we are programming with a CPU. This does not mean it is necessarily harder, but it does require more thought. Among the main points to be aware of are the following:

- Where our data is and how it is stored in memory; is it contiguous even for matrices?
- Our code executes in many cores at the same time, but we cannot control the scheduling of that.
- Memory transfers take a lot of time.
- Once we're working with GPU memory, accessing global memory still can hold us back.

We often say that we need problems to be data-parallel for GPUs to shine. I think that is only part of the story, however. We can have thousands of processing cores in a GPU, and when we have a problem that is not totally data-parallel it is still possible to achieve *some* performance increase. We just have to determine whether the performance improvement we are achieving, considering the time necessary to copy data to and from the device, is worth the cost in terms of device acquisition, energy consumption, and increased programming effort.

When discussing parallel programming, there are two reasons why data-parallel problems are typically the first to be considered:

1. They are problems that *really* exist and occur in many areas of science
2. They are the problems that show the use of parallelism in the simplest and most direct way

So, let's talk about the simplest problem of them all: **vector addition**. A vector is an ordered tuple of numbers, and this means we can use an array to represent a vector. Here we are talking not about the C++ Vector data structure, but rather the mathematical concept. The addition of two vectors will have to iterate over all the elements and add the corresponding elements.

In **sequential programming**, it is easy to see that we have to wait while we add the current pair of elements before we can move to the next pair. With parallel programming, however, we can add multiple pairs at the same time. If we are using a GPU for this task, the number of cores we have determines the number of elements that we are able to add at the same time.

To better understand this, let's use a graphical representation:

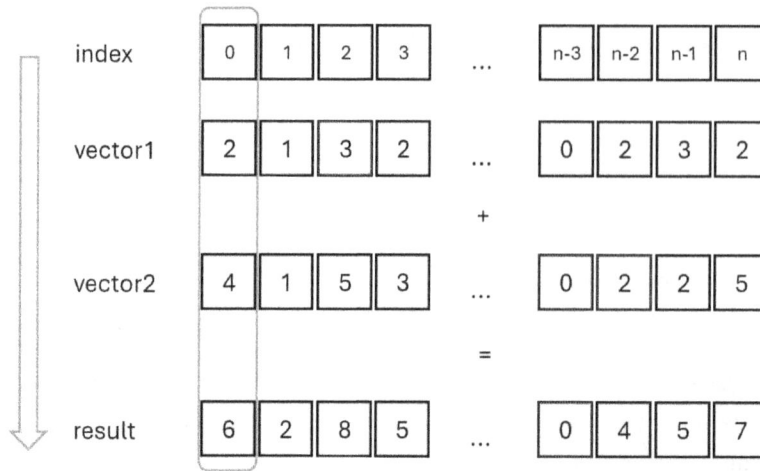

Figure 4.1: Vector addition, one pair of elements at a time

As we can see in *Figure 4.1*, for each index we have a pair of elements that the sequential algorithm must add, and it must then store the result in the final vector. The time increases according to the number of elements that the arrays store.

In *Figure 4.2* we observe a different situation: potentially all our element pairs could be added at the same time – of course depending on the number of available cores and elements – and this increases performance dramatically.

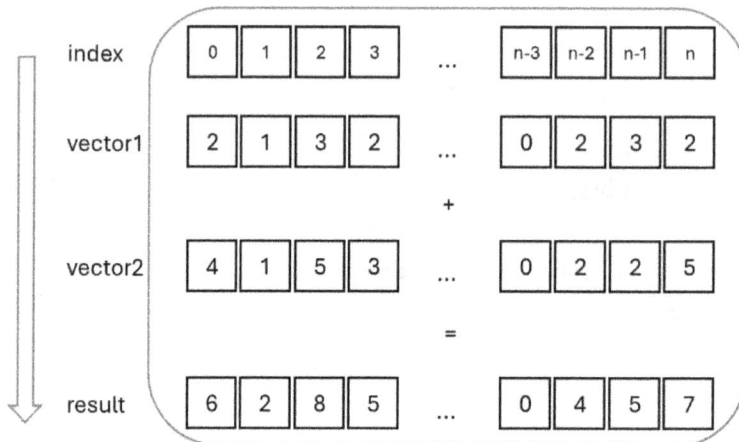

Figure 4.2: Vector addition, multiple pairs of elements at a time

If all elements were copied from the main memory to the device (i.e. GPU) memory contiguously, then access to data will also perform better on the device side because the access patterns will make better use of memory hierarchy.

This example is a great place to start talking about SIMD because it does not have any branches; it is as simple as accessing two memory addresses, adding them together, and saving the result to a third address.

Actually, this example is so simple that even changing some aspects of configuration, for example the number of threads per block, will not affect its performance significantly.

But wait, if the simplest parallel example is vector addition, why are we starting with **prime numbers**? Simple: because with prime numbers we can execute our function without the need to first allocate and copy data. After exploring some details of kernel execution with the prime numbers application, including how to measure its performance, we have a section dedicated to **memory transfers**, and after that it will be easier to explore the details of our parallel example.

Not-so-parallel prime number verification

Testing for primality is one of the first programming assignments most programmers encounter at school, almost after writing their 'Hello World' program. OK, maybe not exactly that early, but you get the point.

What is a prime number?

Let's first understand why we are so interested in testing whether an integer number is prime. An integer number is considered prime if its only divisors are 1 and itself. Here we are talking about integer division, of course; you can always divide an integer if the expected result is a real number, but that is another mathematical argument.

> **Warning!**
>
> We are NOT using any mathematical formality or rigor here, and we are just discussing certain properties of prime numbers. So for all the mathematicians out there, we would like to request some artistic license (if that is even possible when dealing with honorable mathematics!).

This is a fundamental characteristic because it makes it possible to write any non-prime number as a product of prime factors. OK, I know, an example please.

Take the non-prime number 10. It is easy to list its divisors: 1, 2, 5, and 10. We can test a little later, but being sure that 2 and 5 are prime numbers, it is also easy to see that the number 10 can be written as the product of prime numbers 2 and 5. OK, but so what?

Well, suppose I have a certain message that I want to encrypt. This product of primes is used to create private and public keys. Of course, it is trivial and very fast to decode a key that was created with primes 2 and 5, but if the numbers were large enough it would take so long that the security of the message would be guaranteed.

Great, so how are we going to test these numbers? We are trying to balance the amount of information necessary to understand our topic and the use of examples that are simple enough to not become an obstacle, so we'll use the simplest of all possible algorithms: testing the numbers that could divide a given prime candidate until we find a divisor or none. Of course, as programmers, we are going to improve its performance here and there a little, which will be a great source of discussion as well! But again, we will present a simple algorithm in the next section.

How to test if a number is prime

When we talked about the number 10 in the previous section it was easy to find its divisors due to two things:

- It is really small, which makes the calculations easy
- It is even, which means it is divisible by 2

If we take an odd number, it is automatically more challenging. We have to stop for a moment and think, and as the number gets larger it becomes more difficult – to the point where some people even try to memorize as many primes as possible just for fun!

But even when you take a relatively small odd number like 127 it can be hard to say off the top of your head whether it is prime. (It is, I have tested it before.)

> **Fun fact about 127**
>
> The number 127 is the largest odd integer that fits a single signed byte and it is also a prime number. As we all know – since we are in a GPU programming book – a byte has 8 bits and if we use one bit for the sign then 7 bits remain, which can accommodate the number 127.

Our simple algorithm will test all the numbers between 1 and the number itself, and if we find any integer divisor the candidate number is not prime. Is this what we do for cryptography? Of course not, but it is perfect for our GPU example!

But that's enough talk, let's see some code. For now, we will show only the function that performs the prime calculation; the rest of the program is available in the GitHub repository (in the ch4 folder).

```
1 bool checkPrimeCpu(long long num) {
2     if (num <= 1) return false;
3     if (num == 2) return true;
4     if (num % 2 == 0) return false;
5     for (long long i = 3; i * i <= num; i += 2) {
6         if (num % i == 0) { return false; }
7     }
8     return true;
9 }
```

In this function, we test whether a given number passes the conditions of being a prime number. The first thing we might notice is that for num = 2 we immediately return true. This is because 2 is the only even number that is a prime number; and that is why we also return false for any number that is divisible by 2, right on line 4.

Fun fact about 2

Although it fits perfectly the definition of a prime number, since it is divisible only by 1 and itself, this happens with 2 *just because* it is right next to number 1! What are the odds of that? It is 'odd' how all the other even numbers are divisible by 2 – an amazing fact!

After removing the even numbers from our discussion, the real processing happens in lines 5 and 6. Our for loop is constructed in a special way to improve performance a little bit: since all the prime numbers (except for 2) are odd, a good way to decrease the amount of processing is to cut the number of candidate divisors in half simply by starting at 3 and using an increment of 2. That way we are always getting odd numbers in our variable i.

An interesting characteristic of this algorithm is that it assumes upfront that the number num is prime, and what it tries to do is then prove that it is *not* prime. It does so by trying to find a divisor for number num among all the i numbers tested one by one. It is exhaustive – perhaps even exhausting! This is why we try to find as many optimizations as possible. The first was the trick of incrementing by 2, but another one is a little more subtle and deserves a quick explanation.

The test condition of the for loop we are testing is:

```
i * i <= num
```

This is the same as:

$i^2 \leq num$

Or:

$i \leq \sqrt{num}$

What happens here is that divisors occur in pairs, and because of that, we may reach a point where we no longer need to look for divisors as we have not already found any up to that point. Let's use a concrete example.

If our candidate prime number is 21 – small enough for anyone to analyze using pen and paper calculations – our first impulse would probably be to carry out calculations up to the number 21 like the following:

- 21 / 3 = 7 and 21 % 3 = 0 (3 is a divisor for 21 because the remainder of the integer division is 0)
- 21 / 5 = 4 and 21 % 5 = 1 (5 is not a divisor for 21)
- 21 / 6 = 3 and 21 % 6 = 3 (6 is not a divisor for 21)
- 21 / 7 = 3 and 21 % 7 = 0 (7 is a divisor for 21)

So we see that 3 divided 21 with 7 as the result, which of course means that 7 multiplied by 3 will yield 21. Thus if we have already found that 3 divides 21 we do not need to test 7, its product counterpart.

But where should the line be that separates the divisor pairs? Well, this is interesting; let's try something. If I have many pairs of numbers that when multiplied together result in a candidate prime number, there may be a number in these pairs that, when multiplied by itself, yields the candidate prime number. That would mean this number pairs with itself, such as:

i * i (have we seen this before?)

And that is exactly the point at which we should stop trying to look for divisors, because after this point any possible divisor would be a pair with a previous number; and if no divisor has been found, one will not be found after this point.

The name of this is the square root of a number, and we might ask why we are using i * i over and over again. Well, actually it is a programming thing, and it will be much more important on the GPU side than it is on the CPU side. It is faster to multiply a number by itself than it is to calculate the square root of the number.

Going back to our code, in line 6, if any number is capable of dividing our candidate prime with zero remainder, then we immediately return false. Again, it is all about performance: this function is targeted only at testing whether a number is prime or not, not at counting all the divisors of a given number, so a single divisor is enough to return the result. However, to return true at line 8 we need to test until our limit is reached, to make sure we find any divisors if they exist.

A kernel to test for prime numbers

As we have seen before, a kernel is a special function that can be executed by our device. So our kernel to test if a number is prime or not is slightly different from our CPU function, even though the essence is just the same, as we will see below. One thing worth noting is that, to make better use of the GPU, we pass in a range of numbers to be tested for primality, each thread calculating whether its number is prime or not while other threads test different numbers.

```
__global__ void checkPrimeKernel(long long start, long long end){
    int tid = threadIdx.x + blockIdx.x * blockDim.x;
    long long num = start + (tid * 2);
    if (num > end) return;
    bool isPrime = true;
    if (num <= 1){
        isPrime = false;
        return;
    }
    if (num == 2){
```

```
            isPrime = true;
            return;
    }
    if (num % 2 == 0){
            isPrime = false;
            return;
    }
    for (long long i = 3; i * i <= num; i += 2) {
        if (num % i == 0) {
            isPrime = false;
            break;
        }
    }
}
```

At the start of the code are three special lines. The first calculates the unique `tid` that identifies the current GPU thread, and this is then used to calculate which number this unique thread has to test as a prime candidate. By adding, in the second line, the start of the range with its unique identifier we see that every thread will compute a different number in the range.

The other curious line is the third line, which tests to see whether our number is out of range. This can happen because the threads execute in blocks, and as they move forward there may not be enough numbers to be processed. A thread that is out of the range must abort execution and sit idle waiting for its siblings to complete.

After that we have three decision blocks, just as we had for our CPU implementation. Remember that using branches will make the code run sequentially, but notice that every time the branch is executed it simply sets a variable and returns, so this has no real impact on overall performance.

The `for` loop in this case is the same as our CPU implementation, with the same optimizations. One thing that's different is that we are not returning anything. Instead, we are setting a boolean variable, `is_prime`, to be true or false depending on what is found out. One possible solution would be to return from the GPU all the primes identified for the executed range, but remember that at this stage we are not worried about how to move data to and from the GPU. We could also print the prime numbers we find, but this would interfere with execution performance so we have left this out for now (although the line to print the values is left commented out in the repository code, for you to test).

But enough talk! Now it's time to see how to compile and run our code. We are using **CMake** to build our code, so we move to our build folder inside the primes project and execute the following:

```
cmake ..
```

This will configure our project and after that, we will issue the following:

```
make
```

This will build the primes program, and then we can execute it with:

```
./primes
```

This will execute both the CPU and the GPU versions of our functions and print the times taken for each version to complete.

Our baseline reference was executed on an Intel Core i7-10750H CPU and a NVIDIA GeForce RTX 2060 GPU. We ran the program with different ranges of numbers, with the results that can be seen in the table below. Note that all times are in milliseconds.

	Range of numbers to test		
	100,001- 101,001	100,001- 110,001	100,001- 190,001
CPU	0.1643	1.3839	15.6056
GPU	0.1335	0.1433	0.2298
Speedup	1.23	9.66	67.91

As we can see, as the data size increases the GPU starts improving, to at least two orders of magnitude away from the CPU implementation. Of course, this is a really simple example which does not involve memory transfers – something that as we will see can really affect overall performance – but that is exactly the point, to present simple things so that we can gain a foundational understanding of the components of GPU programming. Another amazing thing is that the GPU times, although increasing, remain of the same order of magnitude.

OK, but how did we get these numbers? In the next section we'll learn how to measure the execution times of certain events on the GPU device, and how to compare them with the execution of CPU code.

How to measure execution time on the GPU

What we are really interested in is how to measure things on our device, but for the sake of completeness the CPU times were measured using `<chronos>` from the standard library; the example code is pretty straightforward.

On the GPU side things are not as simple, even though the idea is similar: record the starting point, record the end point, and subtract one from the other. Unfortunately, simply timing the call to the kernel will not work because it will send the call to the device and will return control almost immediately to the main program – it is a non-blocking call. So we have special commands to help us with that, called **CUDA Events**. For now, we are only going to talk about their use to measure the time elapsed since recording an event's starting point.

In the code below, we can see how that wraps our kernel call:

```
cudaEvent_t startEvent, stopEvent;
cudaEventCreate(&startEvent);
cudaEventCreate(&stopEvent);
cudaEventRecord(startEvent, 0);
checkPrimeKernel <<<blocksPerGrid, threadsPerBlock>>>(start, end);
cudaEventRecord(stopEvent, 0);
cudaEventSynchronize(stopEvent);

float gpuDuration = 0;
cudaEventElapsedTime(&gpuDuration, startEvent, stopEvent);
std::cout << "Time taken on GPU: " << gpuDuration << " ms" << std::endl;
cudaEventDestroy(startEvent);
cudaEventDestroy(stopEvent);
```

First, we declare the events with the type `cudaEvent_t` and create them within our execution context using the `cudaEventCreate` command. Before kernel execution, we call `cudaEventRecord(startEvent, 0)` to mark the first event. This 0 means we are tracking the default stream (which is something we are going to talk about in *Chapter 5* and use in *Chapter 8*).

We are ready to call our kernel execution, but again this call is non-blocking – an old way of saying that it's asynchronous – meaning that it will return control after completing the call, not after its execution. That is why, after calling the `cudaEventRecord(stopEvent, 0)`, we have to call `cudaEventSynchronize(stopEvent)`. This is a **blocking call** that waits for our device to complete the kernel execution, so enabling us to track the amount of time spent.

The calculations also need a special function `cudaEventElapsedTime` which returns the difference in time between the two events.

Finally we have to clean up the events, and we do that with `cudaEventDestroy` for each of the event variables previously created.

One important thing about measuring execution times is that we normally run our code many times to allow what we call a warm-up phase. This allows us to prepare the system to take more accurate readings: GPU initialization may need to take place, or the overall system might be busy with other things during execution which could interfere with our data. So the point is to execute a part of the test and discard those results, then focus on the middle executions.

Great, now we know how to execute a real program and even how to measure its execution time. But let's be honest, a program that cannot receive data and cannot return any data is not really that useful to anyone. So our next stop is the Memory Management Station!

Memory: bring me some data!

It is hard to think of a useful computer program that does not need to process some data. In the previous section, we tested to see whether a number was prime or not, and we could print it, but then would lose this information! The GPU device has a separate memory dedicated to it, however, so now let's discuss how we can move memory around.

With great power come great leaks!

We will see in a moment that we have instructions to allocate, copy, and free memory on the device, and this means that we can also have memory leaks! But we will see how to minimize the risks.

We have already talked about how vector addition is a good example of parallelism, but it is obvious that we need at least two vectors to add, and that we need to persist the result somewhere that can be retrieved from the GPU memory.

Remember that we also mentioned how a mathematical vector could be represented by a memory array, and that is exactly what we are going to examine now. The first three commands that we are going to use are `cudaMalloc`, `cudaMemCpy`, and `cudaFree`. These are analogous to their C counterparts `malloc`, `memcpy`, and `free`. The curious aspect is that `cudaMemCpy` needs an indicator to say whether the copy is being performed from the host to the device or from the device to the host.

It is easy to infer that we are going to have pairs of arrays, typically one on the host and one on the device representing this array (or at least a part of it, if the original array is too large to fit into the device memory).

Suppose we have a float array like:

```
float *h_A = (float *)malloc(1000);
```

Typically we prefix host memory with h_, which may seem silly now, but believe me it will be important when it is 2:47am and you are trying to figure out why (oh why) something is not the way it should be.

Before copying any data, we have to create our device counterpart for this array, and we do that with the following code:

```
float *d_A;
cudaMalloc((void **)&d_A, 1000);
```

As cudaMalloc works with void *, we need to type cast our float array first. Typically we also prefix device memory, but with d_, which may seem silly now, but yeah, you get it.

Pausing for a moment, we have two arrays, and this means we are now able to copy data between them. Remember, however, that since they are physically allocated in separate memories we also have to indicate the direction of the memory copy.

Our command for this will be:

```
cudaMemcpy(d_A, h_A, 1000, cudaMemcpyHostToDevice);
```

Since we are executing on the default stream – a topic we won't reach until *Chapter 8* – we may assume for now that cudaMemcpy will be a blocking call, so calling a kernel right after this will not pose any specific problems.

Once execution is complete we may call cudaMemCpy again but in the other direction, like this:

```
cudaMemcpy(h_C, d_C, 1000, cudaMemcpyDeviceToHost);
```

Notice that we have now used a different pair of arrays. Just assume for now that they were correctly defined and initialized, because they will be in our upcoming example in the next section.

Finally, we should remove all allocated memory from our device, especially for programs that will be running for long periods of time, or we may incur memory leaks. We can use the following to return the memory to the system:

```
cudaFree(d_A);
cudaFree(d_B);
cudaFree(d_C);
```

We do that only for our d_ prefixed arrays, because they are on the device; for our host arrays we may use good old free().

Right, now we have all we need to jump into a real-world parallel example of a GPU program! In the next section we introduce the long waited vector addition.

Vector addition

Now comes the time for some real parallelism (although still simple): we are going to process vector addition using everything we have learned so far.

Once again we are going to have CPU and GPU code in the same program so that we can compare execution times, and the hardware remains the same as before: an Intel Core I7-10750H and an NVIDIA GeForce RTX 2060 GPU.

This time let's jump right into the code:

```
__global__ void vectorAddKernel(
    float *A, float *B, float *C, int N) {
    int i = threadIdx.x + blockIdx.x * blockDim.x;
    if (i < N) {
        C[i] = A[i] + B[i];
    }
}
void vectorAddCpu(
    float *A, float *B, float *C, int N) {
    for (int i = 0; i < N; ++i) {
        C[i] = A[i] + B[i];
    }
}
```

We created the CPU version in a similar fashion to our kernel, passing in the number of elements in the array, so that it would be easier to compare the functions. Maybe the only thing that really catches our attention is the fact that the CPU version has a for loop to process all the elements, while the GPU version has none. This is because, in this scenario, control is shared with the GPU device. When we configure the kernel execution we define how many blocks and threads we will be using, and this is done in accordance with the number of elements we have to process.

This brings us to another interesting piece of code to analyze. In the main program, right before the call to the kernel, we have the following code:

```
int threadsPerBlock = 256;
int blocksPerGrid = (N + threadsPerBlock - 1)
                    / threadsPerBlock;
```

The number of threads is arbitrarily defined, although it is hardware-dependent and most architectures limit it to 1024, but the number of blocks per grid is defined based on the number N of elements we have to process. Combining the number of threads per block and the number of blocks per grid yields a large number of threads, capable of handling all the data elements for our problem, and this is where our for loop becomes unnecessary. We just define the number of processors that are needed for our computation, and the CUDA runtime and its internal hardware structure will allocate the resources necessary to both compute and schedule the new blocks and threads – assuming we don't have enough cores to compute all at once (as is typically the case).

Now we have a great opportunity to understand one more detail that appears, and will always appear, in our kernels.

We have to use a guard clause that checks to see if the thread id of the current thread is within the limits of our computation, but why is that? Well, because of the configuration we just saw. We have to define a certain quantity of threads per block and blocks per thread to be able to compute our problems. However, rare is the case in which our problem size exactly matches the computing resources we have. If we have ten thousand elements in our array, which is exactly the example that we will compute in a moment, we would have the following numbers:

blocksPerGrid = (10000 + 256 – 1) / 256 = 40.0664

This value will be cast to integer, becoming 40. Now, if we go the other way around we have:

40 * 256 = 10240

Which is *larger* than our problem size. This means that 240 – almost an entire block – will be idle because the threads will have an id that is out of the range of our array. Those calculations are not magical – even if they seem so – and we will discuss how to get to these numbers in *Chapter 5* as well. But for now, it is enough to understand that it has to do with accommodating the problem size and taking care not to extrapolate beyond the array limits.

In terms of code, those are the parts that really catch our attention for now. The entire listing can be accessed in this book's GitHub repository, so we do not need to get distracted by entire listings for now.

The execution times are also very interesting, as seen when we examine the following table.

	Number of array elements				
	10,000	100,000	1,000,000	10,000,000	100,000,000
CPU	0.021	0.280	2.142	24.806	218.270
GPU	0.089	0.123	0.134	0.577	4.955
Speedup	0.24	2.27	15.91	42.95	44.04

Again, all times are in milliseconds.

Now we should note that those numbers consider *only* the time needed to compute the vector addition. Why is this important? Because now we have to *move* data around! Here are the numbers when we take into account the time needed to copy data to and from the GPU:

	Number of array elements				
	10,000	100,000	1,000,000	10,000,000	100,000,000
CPU	0.021	0.280	2.142	24.806	218.270
GPU	0.145	0.445	2.398	21.855	212.297
Speedup	0.15	0.63	0.89	1.14	1.02

When we compare the times from both tables we notice that data movement easily dominates the total time of GPU computing, and that is why we will be learning strategies that enable us to take advantage of the incredible processing power we have at hand.

One simple improvement would be to move data once and compute many times. Of course, for our vector addition example that is difficult to imagine because we need both arrays, but suppose that one of them could be loaded once and only the second array needed to be copied.

Relevant to this focus on performance, in the next section we are going to learn about a more sophisticated way to gather information about program performance.

Measuring the Euclidean distance between two points

Now that we know how to compute vector addition let's use a slightly different mathematical concept.

The **Euclidean distance** is the length of the straight line between two points in space and it is useful in many fields, from robotics to statistics. We are not going to discuss why it is important for now, but suffice it to say that it has many applications.

Given two points with coordinates x, y, and z we can calculate the Euclidean distance as follows:

$dx = x' - x''$

$dy = y' - y''$

$dz = z' - z''$

$$dist = \sqrt{(dx)^2 + (dy)^2 + (dz)^2}$$

Assuming that we have a structure to represent our point, our kernel will be as follows:

```
struct Point {
float x;
float z;
float y;
};

__global__ void calculateEuclideanDistanceKernel(Point *lineA,
  Point *lineB, float *distances, int numPoints) {
  int idx = threadIdx.x + blockIdx.x * blockDim.x;

  if (idx < numPoints) {
    float dx = lineA[idx].x - lineB[idx].x;
    float dy = lineA[idx].y - lineB[idx].y;
    float dz = lineA[idx].z - lineB[idx].z;
    distances[idx] = sqrtf(dx * dx + dy * dy + dz * dz);
  }
}
```

The rest of the code is available on the GitHub repo and follows the same pattern that we saw before: allocate memory, copy memory, execute the kernel, then copy results back.

What we are going to explore now is the use of NVIDIA's **Nsight Compute** tool to collect profiling information from our kernel execution. We are not going to undertake a deep dive into its usage, but rather, resolve a situation that arises from the use of Docker in this equation.

Up until now we have been using Docker to isolate execution of our development environment, and fortunately all the tools we need are inside our container image. However, when it comes to profiling, the execution needs to have some special privileges – and this is something we try to avoid when using Docker. When we want to profile our applications we need to add another configuration to our Docker command to make sure we have these permissions.

Here is the revised Docker run command:

```
docker run -it --rm --gpus all --cap-add=SYS_ADMIN -v ./:/code nvidia/
cuda:12.0.0-devel-ubuntu20.04 bash
```

The only difference is the `--cap-add=SYS_ADMIN`, which allows the running environment to access the system information necessary for profiling.

Now we can use `ncu` to launch NVIDIA Nsight Compute with our program:

```
ncu -o ./report.rpt ./euclidean_distance
```

And we will see a result similar to this:

```
==PROF== Connected to process 2318 (/euclidean_distance/build/euclidean_
distance)
==PROF== Profiling "calculateEuclideanDistanceKer..." - 0:
0%....50%....100% - 8 passes
Time taken: 0.177925 seconds
==PROF== Disconnected from process 2318
==PROF== Report: /3_euclidean_distance/build/./report.rpt.ncu-rep
```

This means that the information has been collected and stored in the file we designated: `report. rpt`. We may now import this to observe the results as follows.

```
ncu --import ./report.rpt.ncu-rep
```

We will see a summary of the execution like the following:

```
[2678] euclidean_distance@127.0.0.1
  calculateEuclideanDistanceKernel(Point *, Point *, float *, int) (4, 1,
1)x(256, 1, 1), Context 1, Stream 7, Device 0, CC 7.5
    Section: GPU Speed Of Light Throughput
    ----------------------- ------------- ------------

    Metric Name            Metric Unit Metric Value
    ----------------------- ------------- ------------

    DRAM Frequency          cycle/nsecond          5.18
    SM Frequency            cycle/usecond        911.87
    Elapsed Cycles                  cycle          2980
    Memory Throughput                   %          3.41
    DRAM Throughput                     %          3.41
    Duration                      usecond          3.26
    L1/TEX Cache Throughput             %         12.18
    L2 Cache Throughput                 %          2.22
    SM Active Cycles                cycle        205.20
    Compute (SM) Throughput             %          0.57

    ----------------------- ------------- ------------

    WRN   This kernel grid is too small to fill the available resources
  on this device, resulting in only 0.0 full waves across all SMs. Look at
  Launch Statistics for more details.
```

Notice the warning, which indicates that the program is too small to fill our device. This is to be expected, since the execution used only one thousand points to calculate the distances.

There will be time to process each of these numbers in detail in *Chapter 7*, but for now it is enough to note that they are not really that good. Although our human perception of the calculations is that they seem pretty fast, the device is not being fully utilized and this results in energy wastage, for example. But let's pause for a moment and celebrate a new milestone: we now know how to collect execution data about our programs, which will help us improve them in the near future.

At the end of the chapter is a list of exercises to help consolidate all this information in our brains. They are optional in the sense that no grading is provided, but going through them is highly recommended, and they are actually quite straightforward.

Summary

In this chapter we've learned a lot: how parallelism takes place when executing kernels, how to move memory around, and even how to collect execution data that can be used for performance analysis. These are very important concepts that will form the basis for future discussions in which we go into details. The why and how are going to become clearer.

And with that we have completed the first part of the book. In the next chapter, the first of *Part 2*, we'll see what makes the GPU so powerful!

Exercises

It is very useful to practice variations on the code we have just discussed.

1. Create a program based on the prime number testing program but updating two arrays: the first with the number tested by the thread and the second, on the same index position, to hold the test result (whether or not the number is prime). Copy the results back to the host and print only the prime numbers.

2. Create a program that performs the scalar multiplication of a vector. It receives as input parameters a float number and a float array, and executes the multiplication of each element of the array by the given number. Remember to copy the result back to the host.

3. Now, with two input arrays calculate the element-wise (corresponding elements on each index):

   - Vector multiplication
   - Vector division
   - Vector absolute difference
   - Vector maximum – the result array should receive the maximum of the two input elements
   - Vector minimum – the result array should receive the minimum of the two input elements
   - The modulus of the element from the first array and the second array
   - The absolute difference between the two elements

4. Now, with a single input array calculate and return the results on a different array:

   - The exponentiation of the array elements to the power of 2
   - The square root of the elements of the array

Unlock this book's exclusive benefits now

UNLOCK NOW

Scan this QR code or go to packtpub.com/unlock, then search this book by name.

Note: Keep your purchase invoice ready before you start.

Part 2

Bring It On!

In this part we deep-dive into the details of GPU programming. First we get to grips with the concepts needed to control our GPUs and understand how programs interact with the hardware. Then we look at parallel algorithms that appear in many scenarios and examine how to analyze performance so that we can apply optimizations.

This part of the book includes the following chapters:

- *Chapter 5, A Closer Look into the World of GPUs*
- *Chapter 6, Parallel Algorithms with CUDA*
- *Chapter 7, Performance Strategies*

5

A Closer Look into the World of GPUs

Now that we've had a glimpse of GPU programming with slightly larger applications it is time to learn in more detail what enables GPUs to confer such speed advantages. First, we are going to learn about several concepts relating to the GPU cores and how we address them.

After that, we will go through more advanced concepts concerning how modern GPUs execute much more at the same time. Finally, we will take a first look at how to improve memory access times in the GPU environment, and consider why it matters.

With the solid foundation of the previous chapters to build on – we've seen how to compile and run CUDA programs, and have learnt about the effects of memory transfers on performance – we are well placed to understand in more detail what is required in order to create a high-performing GPU application. By the end of this chapter, you will have mastered the abstractions that represent GPU execution, some more advanced techniques to speed up performance measurement, and how to think about memory usage.

The main topics of this chapter are these:

- Thread, block, and grid concepts
- Asynchronous data transfer
- Streams
- Events
- Shared memory

Technical requirements

This is going to be a more conceptual chapter, in which we dive deep into topics governing the realm of GPU. But fear not, more code is on the way!

Understanding the thread, block, and grid concepts

In *Chapter 4* we finally executed truly parallel CUDA programs, and we saw that a configuration is needed for launching the kernel. More than that, this launch configuration forms part of the program itself. Taking a closer look at the vector addition program, we saw that the CPU version has a for loop while the GPU version has a configuration in place of this for loop. Thus we need to discuss the concepts that determine how execution takes place. Threads, blocks, and grids work together, but let's get to know them individually first.

Threads

A thread is the basic unit of execution in CUDA, with each thread having its own unique ID that allows it to independently access a specific portion of the data. For a given problem, we define a set of threads that can handle the requisite amount of data. Thread IDs can be one-dimensional, two-dimensional, or three-dimensional (threadIdx.x, threadIdx.y, threadIdx.z), depending on the block configuration defined.

Every thread has some local memory and registers. Each local variable is allocated to registers, but the number of registers per thread is limited, so if we define too many local variables we may incur **register spilling**, when it is necessary to allocate variables to local memory that is slower to access.

Hidden from our sight, the **thread scheduler** on each streaming multiprocessor (SM) manages the execution of **warps** – which is a fancy word for a low-level group organized and controlled by the hardware. The scheduler switches between warps that are waiting on memory and warps that are ready to execute, so that this can hide memory latency as much as possible.

Blocks

A block is a high-level group of threads that execute a kernel together, and which can synchronize and share memory. We may think of blocks as containers for threads. Just like threads, blocks can be organized in one, two, or three dimensions (blockIdx.x, blockIdx.y, blockIdx.z). This provides a flexible way of mapping the threads and blocks to multidimensional problems like image processing or scientific simulations, reflecting our data structures.

Blocks and warps are not the same!

Keep in mind that although both are groups of threads, blocks are defined by us when we call for kernel execution. On the other hand, warps are a low-level grouping defined by the hardware to organize thread execution. Warps have 32 threads that execute the exact same instruction at the same time.

As of the time of writing, each block contains a maximum number of 1024 threads, which is a limit imposed by the hardware. This affects how we structure our problems. Remember that the amount of memory we have is limited, so the more threads we allocate to a block the less memory will be available for them, both to share as well as to define local variables.

An important characteristic of blocks is that they allow threads to cooperate via shared memory. They can use this special memory to share intermediate results or to communicate with each other, as long as they reside on the same block.

Shared memory is a power-up!

Shared memory is a special kind of on-chip memory that is close to the cores and which is shared among the threads of a block. Since it is dramatically faster than global memory, it is essential to use it to improve performance.

What difference does it make to organize things like this? Well, the system may schedule blocks to execute in any order across the available streaming multiprocessors, the only restriction being that threads in separate blocks will not be able to communicate with each other.

Within their block, threads can synchronize by using the `__syncthreads()` function, which makes all the threads wait on that call point until all threads have reached it. We will use this in a concrete example in *Chapter 6*.

Grids

A grid, not surprisingly, is a collection of blocks used to execute a kernel. The grid organizes many blocks that can be executed independently across the streaming multiprocessors. Once again, like threads and blocks, a grid can be one-dimensional, two-dimensional, or three-dimensional, depending on the problem structure (`gridDim.x`, `gridDim.y`, `gridDim.z`).

But what is this fixation with levels of organization? Let's remember that one way in which our hardware accelerates our computations is to parallelize the execution of parts of our code as much as possible. In *Chapter 4* we saw how the vector addition program did not have a loop to go over all data points exactly because the *hardware took care of that for us*. By using these three layers of organization with three dimensions each, we guarantee that we can assign a unique thread id to each execution thread that will directly map to the data it has to process, making it ready for execution at any time.

> **The right sizes**
>
> The number of threads per block is called the **block size**, and the number of blocks in the grid is called the **grid size**. This can be a little confusing at the beginning but these sizes matter. The numbers that go in the block dimensions define the number of threads, and this can be at most 1024 (as of this writing). However, the number of blocks will be defined by the dimensions of the grid!

It is worth stopping for a moment to remember that the original objective of GPUs was to process *graphical* problems. This helps us understand why having three-dimensional structures makes total sense. The fact that we are using GPUs for general purposes should not blind us to their origins.

Putting it all together

Before we move on to discuss how to define the number of threads and blocks we should use, it is worth recapping how these configurations work together.

We use the `blockDim` to define the number of threads and how they are arranged within the blocks. For example:

```
dim3 blockDim(1024, 1, 1)
```

as well as

```
dim3 blockDim(32, 32, 1)
```

will give us the same number of threads because `blockDim.x` * `blockDim.y` * `blockDim.z` = 1024. However, the first example is a good approach to working with vectors while the second is better suited to working with matrices.

So, what we should note is that the values that define the block dimensions are used by the scheduler to allocate the threads, and thus we have for each `threadIdx.x`, `threadIdx.y`, and `threadIdx.z` the different values.

In a 1D situation we have the global index for a thread given by:

```
int globalIdx = threadIdx.x + blockIdx.x * blockDim.x;
```

Whereas in a 2D situation we will have two global indices for the thread given by:

```
int globalIdx_x = threadIdx.x + blockIdx.x * blockDim.x;
int globalIdx_y = threadIdx.y + blockIdx.y * blockDim.y;
```

The same holds true for how gridDim defines the number of blocks; this is why we have used `blockIdx.x` and `blockIdx.y` in the previous calculation for global indices.

Launching configurations

Understanding threads, blocks, and grids is key to understanding the configuration we use to launch a kernel execution. When we were adding vectors in *Chapter 4*, we chose to use 256 threads per block, and after that we had to calculate how many blocks were needed to accommodate all our data points. For the case of vectors of size 100,000,000 we would have:

100,000,000 / 256 = 390,625 blocks needed

However, we do not always have easy numbers, and in that case we use a more general formula to find the required number of blocks:

We use the integer value so as to ignore anything after the decimal point. This is equivalent to using the `floor` function, but that function still returns a floating-point value which would need to be converted to an integer. And with that, comes the need to calculate inside our kernel what our unique thread id is. We do this by getting the current block and thread ids (which are given to us by runtime) and performing a simple calculation like:

```
uniqueId = threadIdx.x + (blockIdx.x * blockDim.x)
```

Here we use the `.x` to refer to the dimension of the block or grid that was specified during kernel launch configuration. Since our vector addition example is a one-dimensional problem, it makes sense to launch the kernel with both block size and grid size using just one dimension.

256 threads per block is a common choice for balancing performance and **occupancy**, occupancy being a key concept that refers to the ratio of warps executing to the maximum number of warps that a streaming multiprocessor can support. The larger the occupancy value the higher the performance, up to a certain point. This is because high occupancy can help hide memory latency by swapping the waiting warp with a ready warp. If we have too many waiting warps or too many ready warps, however, we will see a performance decrease.

> **Big enough problems**
>
> It is a curious fact that if you measure the execution of a program that is processing a piece of data that matches the number of CUDA cores on your GPU, the numbers will be worse than those seen for a larger problem that exceeds the number of available processors. This is a little counterintuitive at first, but a lot of things are happening to make a CUDA program execute on the device. For example, we have to copy data in and out, and we have to launch the execution. If the problem is too small it is in effect not worth all that work.

Now that we understand all the indexing we need, and how to define the configuration for our kernel executions, we are ready to learn in the next section how CUDA can help us improve performance when dealing with memory transfers.

Asynchronous data transfers

As we saw in *Chapter 4*, when copying data to and from the device, we need to specify the direction in which we are moving data. However, in our first examples, we waited to copy our entire dataset before starting to process the data. After processing we waited for the results to be copied back to the host, where our main program could use them. We saw, when considering the time necessary to move data, that total runtime increased significantly. Luckily there is something we can do to improve on this.

Actually, there are two things that work together to improve performance: **asynchronous data transfers** and **streams**. We will look at asynchronous data transfers first.

Being asynchronous means that once data transfer starts, control returns immediately to the CPU which is then free to run other code, for example, to gather another part of our large dataset. The function that we use for this is `cudaMemcpyAsync`, which conveniently is named in a way that's already familiar since we previously learned how to use `cudaMemcpy`, the synchronous version.

For the sake of clarity let's consider a more concrete example. If we have to read data from storage, it can take a while (depending on our equipment). Even with modern solid state drives (SSDs) (as of writing NVMe memory is the fastest consumer-available storage), it is still slower than main memory. This means we could load part of our data and start transferring it to our device with an asynchronous data transfer, and after scheduling the transfer we could start loading the next chunk from disk. By *overlaying* the operations in this way we can make the data transfer time invisible. Pretty clever, right?

Exploring our example a little further, let's put the times needed to process our fictitious data together.

Scenario 1 – the naive approach:

1. load data from disk

2. transfer data to the device

3. process data on the device

4. transfer data back to the host.

This scenario is represented in *Figure 5.1*, where we see that the only performance gains we might achieve are if we use a large number of processing cores, but only during the processing phase.

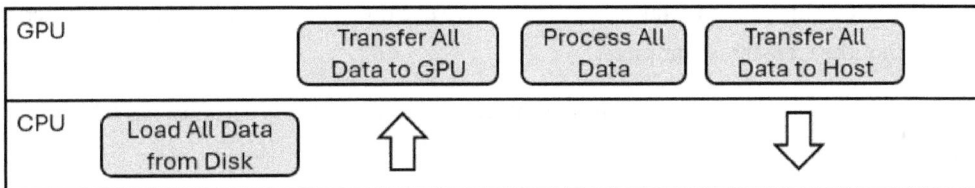

Figure 5.1: A naive approach

Scenario 2 – the asynchronous approach:

1. load a chunk of data from disk

2. start an asynchronous transfer with the loaded data

3. check if data is transferred with a blocking call

4. process data on the device with an asynchronous call to the kernel

5. start loading the next chunk of data from disk

6. transfer the partial results from device to host

7. repeat until all data is processed

In this scenario, shown in *Figure 5.2*, we explore other features of the GPU to achieve higher gains.

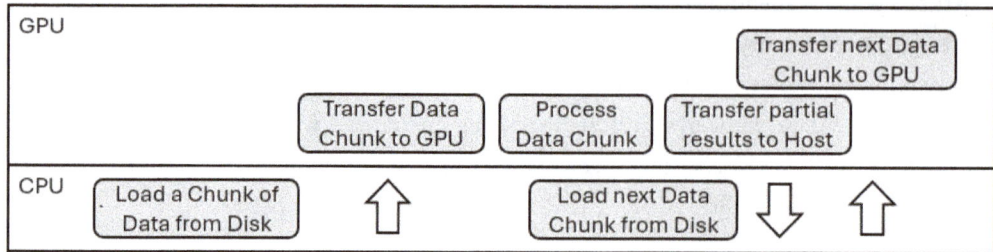

Figure 5.2: Overlapping data transfer and processing

With this second scenario, which is a little more sophisticated, we achieve greater overlapping, and this improves the overall performance. One more thing we can do in this scenario to improve performance even more is perform an asynchronous data load from disk. This has nothing to do with GPUs, and is outside our present scope, but basically we could have a pool of CPU threads waiting for data to be loaded to some shared array, which the main thread could use once fully loaded from disk.

However, there is a catch – isn't there always?! – in that if we use an asynchronous data transfer we have to check whether it has completed *before* using the data, otherwise we might end up using incomplete or corrupted data. Makes sense right? We use the `cudaStreamSynchronize` function to ensure that the transfer is complete.

There is one more thing that is present in every text related to GPU programming, which reads something like this:

"Thou shall diminish the amount of data transfer in thy computations"

And as GPU programmers, we struggle and suffer and battle this, thinking how can we achieve any results if we do not copy data to and from the device? So let us free our hearts from such a curse by understanding that we will use as many data transfers as needed. However, we will be very careful and mindful about how to optimize things to the last byte. This means, for example, that we will not copy data recklessly, like copying an array of arrays one array at a time, because copying a single large array performs better than copying the same amount of bytes via many smaller operations. However, we will not deprive ourselves of copying data when necessary. Another factor to consider is whether it is possible to keep part of the data already copied to the device for as long as possible, and simply copy other parts of the data to process against the existing data; this also improves performance when it is possible.

The other concept that we mentioned before was streams. We have a full section dedicated to it later in this chapter so, for now, it is enough to say that we can have data transfers *and* computation occurring at the same time if we separate them carefully.

Since we are talking so much about memory and performance, now is a good time to remember that in the majority of cases, the memory we allocate in RAM is *pageable*, which means that the operating system may claim that memory, save data to disk and let other applications use the resource. This also means that if we want to transfer a piece of data that was located in a memory page that was sent to disk, the operating system will have to move that data back to RAM before we can start our transfer.

To avoid this situation, it is possible to use **page-locked memory** (a.k.a. **pinned memory**), which is a special type of memory that cannot be swapped to disk, meaning that when we need to transfer the data allocated in that region of memory to a device, it will be readily available. Furthermore, page-locked memory supports a special feature called **Direct Memory Access (DMA)** which allows data transfers to happen without involving the CPU – and that means speed.

To use this special memory, we need to allocate our memory on the host using the CUDA functions `cudaHostAlloc` or `cudaMallocHost` that allocate pinned memory. This memory may be used for both synchronous and asynchronous memory transfers.

Remember, however, that with great power comes great responsibility (and I think we will see this many times throughout the book). Overusing pinned memory has the drawback that it restricts the amount of memory available to the system as a whole, so it may affect overall performance.

Before we move to the next section there are two more special features to discuss:

- **Unified memory** – this is a memory management feature from CUDA that abstracts away all the memory handling that we've been talking about. It exposes a unified memory space to the program, such that when we need to use memory, the CUDA runtime will guarantee that the memory page is present on either the device or the host as needed. The drawback is that it may incur numerous memory transfers of varying granularity, and as we know by now, this is not the best way to achieve good performance. However, it is true that it simplifies the memory management tasks.

- **Zero-copy memory** – in a simpler way, zero-copy targets those times when we need to access data within the GPU space. Instead of performing a copy, you access the host memory directly. This is better when the dataset is small so that waiting for memory transfers would result in greater performance penalties.

In the next section we resume our conversation about CUDA streams and discuss how we can use them together with all the memory resources we've just learnt about to improve execution times even further.

Parallelizing with streams

Now we will talk about the second feature that helps improve performance of CUDA programs: streams.

We can think of a stream as a queue in which we enqueue kernel executions and memory transfers, which are then executed sequentially on the GPU in the order in which they were added. There is a **default stream** which receives index 0, used when we don't define a specific stream for execution. One important characteristic of the default stream is that it is synchronous, meaning that each operation completes before the next one starts. This simplifies behavior but limits performance improvements.

However, we can define our own non-default streams and execute different operations on different streams so that we end up overlapping memory transfers and computations. Since streams are not tied to any streaming processor or memory channel, anything available will execute the requested operations.

We must keep in mind that the number of streams is not directly hardware dependent, although it depends on two things that *are* hardware dependent. The first is the number of connections allowed to the GPU, which is controlled by the environment variable CUDA_DEVICE_MAX_CONNECTIONS. This is usually set to 8 and refers to the number of PCI connections that we will be using. The second is the number of async engines present; high-end GPUs typically support up to seven concurrent streams while consumer-level GPUs may support around three concurrent streams.

Another great feature of streams is that they support two memory transfers at the same time. The condition is that one must be from host to device and the other from device to host. This means that we can have one memory transfer from host to device on stream 1, a kernel execution on stream 2, and a memory transfer from device to host on stream 3 all at the same time. Unfortunately, we cannot have multiple memory transfers on different streams from host to device in parallel (as of the time of writing).

Notice that we used 1, 2, and 3 as the streams in our example. This is because stream 0 is the default one that synchronizes executions; when we want to maximize performance asynchronously it is important to use non-default streams.

To create non-default streams, we use cudaStreamCreate(), to handle specific operations, while cudaStreamDestroy() is used to free the resources associated with a stream once no longer needed.

It is important to note that when using those great non-default streams, things happen asynchronously, and this means we have to check to see whether the previous operation has been completed before we start trying to use anything that is part of that previous operation. There are specific resources to control this, including what are called *events*. Although we looked at CUDA events superficially in *Chapter 4* when measuring execution times, we will learn much more in the next section. For now, it is enough to know that we can use them to guarantee our execution sanity when it comes to asynchronous streams.

Synchronization is an essential part of working with CUDA streams because it ensures that tasks which depend on each other are executed in the correct order. In CUDA, synchronization refers to controlling when a particular stream should start executing a task relative to other streams or when the CPU should wait for a stream to finish. Without proper synchronization you can end up with race conditions, where data is read or modified before an operation is fully completed, leading to incorrect results.

The primary function for synchronizing streams is cudaStreamSynchronize(). This function blocks the host (CPU) until all the tasks in the specified stream have been completed. It's useful when you need to ensure that a stream has finished all its tasks before proceeding to the next part of your program. For example, after launching a kernel in one stream and performing memory transfers in another, you may want to synchronize them to ensure that the data is available before attempting further computation.

Another commonly used function is cudaDeviceSynchronize(), which forces the host to wait for completion of all previously launched operations on the GPU, across all streams. While cudaDeviceSynchronize() is a more global synchronization point compared to cudaStreamSynchronize(), it is often considered less efficient because it halts the entire device instead of just a specific stream. As a result, it should be used carefully and only when necessary.

In the next section, we continue to talk about events and how they can help us with CUDA programming and synchronization.

Following the events

The two main purposes of CUDA events are to measure performance and to help with synchronization. They make this possible by providing mechanisms for tracking the execution times associated with certain operations. Specifically for synchronization we can wait on an event to complete, and with that we have the possibility for a task running in a stream to wait on the completion of another task in a different stream.

Events are created using the cudaEventCreate() function, which allocates the resources necessary for the event.

When creating an event, we can specify certain flags to modify the event's behavior. For example, the cudaEventBlockingSync flag ensures that the event will block the CPU thread that waits on it until the event is complete. Conversely, the cudaEventDisableTiming flag allows the event to be used only for synchronization without measuring timing.

Once an event is no longer needed, it is crucial to free the resources associated with it. This is done using the cudaEventDestroy function, which takes the event as a parameter.

With CUDA events we have a great mechanism for measuring the time which has elapsed between various operations on the GPU. The timing functionality is primarily accessed through the cudaEventRecord and cudaEventElapsedTime functions. When we call cudaEventRecord, the current GPU time is captured and associated with the specified event. This allows us to create time stamps for specific operations, such as kernel launches or data transfers, enabling precise performance analysis. What happens backstage is that the runtime captures what is in execution at the time we called cudaEventRecord, and monitors this to track event completion.

To measure the time elapsed between two events, we use the cudaEventElapsedTime function. This function calculates the time difference in milliseconds between two recorded events and returns it as a floating-point value.

One important aspect of event timing is the overhead associated with using events. Although the creation, recording, and querying of events are lightweight operations, they do introduce some level of overhead. We should be mindful of this overhead when carrying out performance measurements in performance-critical sections of code.

Events can also be used to measure the performance impact of different execution strategies. For instance, by placing events before and after different kernel configurations, we can analyze how changes to grid and block sizes influence execution times.

When you want to ensure that a specific operation has been completed before proceeding, you can use the cudaEventSynchronize function. This function blocks the calling thread until the specified event has been recorded, guaranteeing that any dependent operations will not start until the previous operations have completed. This is particularly useful when the host code relies on the results of GPU computations.

Remember that when we start recording the event, the runtime captures what is running, so, with our vector addition from *Chapter 4* for example, we recorded the startEvent when there was nothing executing, then we issued memory transfers, a kernel execution and a last memory transfer. After that we called another event recording, but this time a lot of things were going on, so when we called cudaEventSynchronize on stopEvent, the program waited for everything associated with this event to complete before resuming execution again. *This* is the magic behind an event: it understands what is associated with it and can track everything for synchronization.

One last speed booster that we have to explore is shared memory, a special memory that enables thread communication locally. It is the topic of the next section.

Accelerating with shared memory

As mentioned earlier in this chapter, in the threads section, there is special on-chip memory that (again, as of the time of writing) has only 48 KB per block that is visible to all the threads in that block. That 48KB is memory enough to keep, let's say, an array of float numbers to store the result of each thread's execution. That way, by the end of execution, one of the threads – typically thread 0 – can go over all of that shared array and sum all the values.

Another typical use for shared memory is pre-fetching data from global memory and processing it locally. Let's say we need to compute the dot product of a vector against many other vectors. We could load vector A to shared memory and reuse this against all the other global accesses, when accessing the elements of each row from matrix M. Although simple, this would save global memory access since the threads would benefit from cached values for the rows of matrix M, and the vector would remain in shared memory throughout the entire processing operation. Depending on the sizes of the data that we need to process, we can bring two vectors from global memory at once and load two shared arrays. After that our threads will process data locally – saving all the global accesses that would otherwise be performed – and at the end of our computation we store a single value to a given global memory address. When we extrapolate that to the amount of data we typically process with GPUs, we readily perceive that it will make for greatly improved performance.

The lifetime of data allocated to shared memory – which typically is an array of the block size (remember, the number of threads in a block) – is the same as that of the block. Once the block gets deallocated that shared memory is freed as well.

With that, we have learned about all the internals of the GPU realm, empowering us to write much more performant programs.

Understanding hardware capabilities

With each new hardware release, NVIDIA makes new features available for developers, and this brings the need to make sure that our hardware is *capable* of performing certain tasks. If our application depends on a specific hardware characteristic, we can test for that characteristic by looking at the properties retrieved by the program we used back in *Chapter 3*. If the specific capability we need is not present, we can inform the user and terminate execution.

If we create applications for different hardware versions, it may be necessary to create different versions of our kernels and compile them in different files, possibly loading the correct version dynamically at runtime.

Summary

In this chapter we've covered the internal details needed to write programs in a more considered way. It will be important to pay attention to these details, indeed rather more than is the case when writing single-threaded programs for CPUs. When dealing with GPUs, we have to consider things like having only 48KB of space to share between threads, and how to use these resources wisely in order to speed up our code a little bit more. We have seen that by using different streams, we can execute many things at once, and can even copy data to and from the device at the same time; but again, we have to be mindful of the relevant details. Rest assured that although this seems complicated now, it will become easier. Shortly we will be writing programs that use all these resources, and that will help the details stick in our minds.

In the next chapter we'll cover practical aspects of the concepts we've got to know here. We will discuss what makes a parallel algorithm, well, parallel. We will implement different versions of applications that solve some common problems in parallel programming, and which benefit greatly from the use of GPUs. In these versions we will use the various approaches discussed here and measure the effects on performance. We will perform a matrix multiplication which, just like vector addition, is an example of what we call embarrassing parallelism, on account of the way it is calculated. In addition we will tackle numerical integration, which has relevance to a wide variety of domains.

Unlock this book's exclusive benefits now

UNLOCK NOW

Scan this QR code or go to packtpub.com/unlock, then search this book by name.

Note: Keep your purchase invoice ready before you start.

6

Parallel Algorithms with CUDA

We can now better discuss and understand parallel programs and how to express them using CUDA, and how the hardware details and programming concepts affect and direct our programs. The next step on our learning path is to understand better what it is that makes a parallel algorithm parallel, and what the limits are to the degree of parallelization that can be achieved.

First we will discuss the principles that guide **parallel algorithms**, in more detail than we did in *Chapter 1* since we can now refer to the programs we wrote there. After that we will look at some common algorithms that illustrate different levels of parallelization, allowing us to see the challenges ahead. The chapter wraps up with a discussion of different implementations, to help you apply the knowledge gained to real situations.

Over the course of the chapter we will be covering the following topics:

- Design principles of parallel algorithms
- Parallel matrix operations: multiplication, addition
- Parallel integral calculation, reduction, and sort algorithms

Technical requirements

We will use the environment configured in *Chapter 3* with VS Code and our development container. If you have chosen to install the CUDA Toolkit on your machine, you can simply run the build commands on a terminal. The code is provided on the GitHub repository that can be accessed here: https://github.com/PacktPublishing/GPU-Programming-with-CPP-and-CUDA/tree/main/ch6.

Designing parallel algorithms

In *Chapter 1* we discussed what parallelism is and used a cooking analogy to present some ideas for executing multiple steps simultaneously, and to show how some steps would not benefit from changing the executor. We are now going to use a similar analogy as we explore in more detail the design of parallel algorithms.

A good starting point is the idea that a parallel algorithm is not simply a sped-up version of a sequential one. It involves a fundamental restructuring, such that tasks can occur simultaneously to take advantage of multiple computing units.

In *Chapter 1* we imagined a group of friends preparing a meal together – a small setup that gave us a glimpse of parallelism. They could cut and chop in parallel, but there was not massive parallelism. However, let's suppose that they had tremendous success in their endeavor and must now prepare not a few but some thousands of meals. Every step must now be carefully thought about to make sure that time and effort are not wasted. This is more like the scenario we have when using GPUs, where there are thousands of processors and we want to make sure they are used in the best way possible, and not left to sit idle.

But if we stop and think for a moment, a restaurant setting is more like a multicore CPU: it can handle any kind of meal with a few chefs and cooks. A GPU can be thought of as being narrowed down in terms of options on the menu, but offers massive throughput, rather like a catering service at a music festival. Remember that CUDA cores work in groups called warps that are step-controlled by a streaming multiprocessor, or SM for short. It is hard to imagine having one 'controller cook' issuing commands to other cooks like 'chop now', but we could think of an SM as the cook and CUDA cores as a tool that can dice vegetables all at once – like those seen on those old TV commercials.

However, to have a minimally interesting meal we will need more than a single vegetable diced in parallel: we should have multiple ingredients being prepared in parallel to become part of the final meal. For that we will need many cooks, using their groups of tools to work on different parts of the ingredients list until they reach a point where they need to synchronize with each other.

Hardware specialization impact

Here we have an interesting characteristic to consider. Consumer-level GPUs usually present three asynchronous engines, which means they can perform two data movements in different orientations – from Host to Device and from Device to Host – together with one kernel execution. On the other hand, high-end GPUs have more engines, enabling them to execute more kernels simultaneously. This is an important consideration because it may speed up algorithms in another dimension. Consider an algorithm that has two steps, the first performing a matrix multiplication to yield an intermediate result, the second performing a matrix addition of the intermediate result and another input matrix. If we used two separate result buffers, we could execute both kernel calls at almost the same time, if enough streaming multiprocessors were available.

Different from the relation of CUDA cores and SMs, the allocation of threads to blocks is 'thought ahead' to optimize occupation. In our analogy we can think of the number of cooks that we are allocating to a given workstation. We can even think of the access patterns to ingredients. Each time a cook needs more ingredients they request them from the shelves, but only in fixed-size boxes. This suggests that thinking about how we access our data can affect our achieved performance greatly.

Another important consideration is that rarely will our bigger application use a single kernel to perform all the steps necessary to obtain the outcome. We will usually have many kernels, one for each phase of the computation, but each acts on the same data that is already loaded into memory. Originally they were the raw basic ingredients, but as cooking takes place the ingredients change into the final dish.

Understanding how to spot and exploit parallelism

The idea of exploitable parallelism helps define which tasks can be executed independently. High parallelism occurs when many parts of an algorithm can proceed independently without a strict sequence, just as chopping different vegetables can happen simultaneously and in any order. In a parallel algorithm, high parallelism allows multiple threads to work independently, boosting speed and efficiency.

At first it does not occur naturally to humans to approach a problem or task in parallel. Usually we look for a solution and *then* we look for parts that are sufficiently independent. To continue with our cooking example, as we get increasingly experienced, it starts to become apparent right from the beginning that appetizers and desserts could be prepared in parallel.

Although parallelism is the key to increased performance, the level of independence among the steps of our algorithms directly influences the amount of parallelism we may achieve, and thus it limits the speedup that is feasible. In other words, throwing in more processing cores does not yield a proportional increase in speed!

Imagine we are going to prepare one hundred cupcakes. The ingredients for the cake mix must be mixed in a specific order, and for the sake of our analogy let us suppose that a single batch of cake mix will be used for the hundred units. Here are the steps to follow:

1. Combine the ingredients to create the cake mix – a sequential step here that requires an ordered execution.

2. Separate out small portions and pour them into cupcake tins. This can be parallelized, for we may have many cooks, each one getting a portion of cake mix, preparing the tin, and positioning that on the baking board.

3. The third step is baking, in which all the available cooks idly wait for the one who monitors the *single* oven. This is what we call a synchronization step, since we can only continue after everything is processed.

4. The last step is to distribute the cooked cupcakes to the cooks so that each one can create their own icing styles.

In this scenario, when we go through the description we see two things that could be optimized to increase parallelism. The first is that we could have many cooks preparing many portions of cake mix – but notice that this does not affect the need to mix the ingredients in the same given order. The other is that we could have more ovens, but if we are to provide an individual oven to each cook, we may confront space and energy limitations.

This is exactly analogous to what happens in our CPU versus GPU situation. Remember from *Chapter 1* how we discussed the idea that GPUs are specialized hardware and that CUDA cores are not the same type of processing cores as the ones we find in CPUs: it is as if GPUs do not have their own mini ovens while CPUs do have them!

We will see this difference of algorithms later in the chapter when we discuss matrix multiplication and a sorting algorithm. Sorting will have alternate steps that depend on the computation of the previous step, leading to the need for a **synchronization step**.

> **Amdahl's Law**: speedup limits
>
> Amdahl's Law highlights the limit of parallelism for tasks that must remain sequential. Imagine a dessert recipe with a final cooling step that takes 30 minutes. No matter how many cooks you add, the dish cannot be ready until the cooling step finishes. Similarly, in parallel computing, a task with unavoidable sequential steps will not speed up indefinitely, even with more threads. If a portion of the program remains sequential then doubling the number of threads can only improve the speed of the other parallelizable part of the program. Even if we could make the parallel part execute immediately, the total running time will remain the minimum time needed to execute the sequential part.

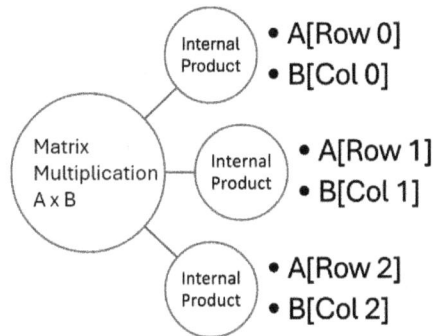

Figure 6.1: Task decomposition of matrix multiplication

Synchronizing steps to avoid problems

In the last section we mentioned having synchronization steps, but why are they necessary?

If we go back to the cupcake example for a moment, we might describe a cupcake as a small cake with some icing. (Although there could be some cupcakes without icing, let's assume for our discussion that *all* cupcakes have icing.) As humans, we tacitly expect, due to the many cupcake pictures we've seen before, that icing comes *on top* of the cupcake, but if you go back and read the description again, there was nothing saying that icing would be on top. This means that, without synchronization steps, the cooks who completed the icing preparation step could pour it onto the final plate before the prior step – baking – was completed. So, some cupcakes would end up sitting on the icing while others would have the icing on top.

In programming we want to spot and exploit parallelization as much as possible, but we must make sure that we obtain the correct results. It makes no sense to have super-fast but incorrect results!

Although sometimes necessary, synchronization delays results and so we try to avoid it as much as possible. Sometimes, by changing the algorithm or finding another mathematical property or identity to exploit, we can avoid a synchronization, but if that is not possible then we must live with the delay introduced. Dealing with incorrect results is much worse!

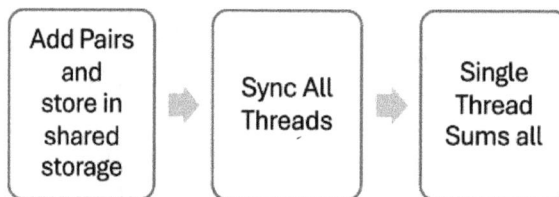

Figure 6.2: Wait for all local additions before summing all

Balancing the workloads

Given that the scheduling of processing is done automatically by SMs, it may seem a little peculiar to discuss **load balancing** for our applications. However, in the previous section we considered changes to algorithms that could decrease the need to synchronize. When we start looking to other algorithms to avoid the need for synchronization, we may reach situations in which some threads end up being overloaded, and that can lead to bottlenecks that affect overall progress even if there is no need to synchronize.

To illustrate this, let's consider the most common load balancer that we have used before: splitting the processing between odds and evens. We test whether a number is divisible by 2, and if it is so divisible that makes it even; otherwise it is odd. This works well because half the numbers are even and the other half are odd. However, if we want to process an array of numbers and apply some special processing only in the case of values divisible by 3, we have an imbalance, because only approximately 33.33% of numbers are multiples of 3. Assuming that we are processing a huge quantity of numbers, there is no way to tell upfront that we will have more multiples of 3 coming in for processing. Supposing we have a special kernel for multiples of 3 and another for all other numbers, then this implies that we may end up having cores idle when processing one group or the other. On the other hand, if we arranged the multiples of 3 to be interweaved with non-multiples on a stride of 3, we could dedicate the threads whose ids were multiples of 3 to the processing of those specific positions. That would work like pre-allocating one third of the threads to those numbers.

Of course this is just an arbitrary example, but it is useful for reflecting on the impact of load balancing our work.

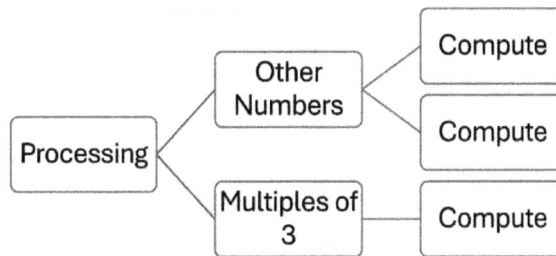

Figure 6.3: Load balance

Finding the critical path

We have been talking about how much parallelism we can find in an algorithm, but rarely will an application have just a single step as is the case in the multiplication of two matrices. (Unless we are creating a matrix multiplication library!) Usually, an application will have many steps or phases which may have differing levels of parallelization, but those steps will create a sequence that must be completed in a specific order. This is like a recipe in which we need to peel all the potatoes before chopping them – we may parallelize the peeling, but we still need to complete the peeling phase before continuing.

This sequence of dependent tasks forms what is known as the **critical path** for the application. Identifying this is important because it determines the minimum amount of time that can be achieved using parallelism on whichever steps may be parallelized. Remember that Amdahl's Law states that the speed-up we can achieve is limited by the portions of our applications that are inherently sequential, and we must consider that these will also be part of our critical path.

When designing parallel algorithms, identifying and minimizing **dependencies** is crucial for optimizing performance. The goal is to 'unblock' as many tasks as possible so that they can run concurrently. By rearranging tasks and managing dependencies we can reduce the time required to complete processing. In some algorithms, this is achieved by structuring data or steps to remove unnecessary dependencies, allowing the system to proceed in parallel wherever possible.

If data movement is a necessity, we may try to overlap memory transfers with GPU processing, and during that time we may have the CPU preparing other parts of data, to make full use of our hardware and asynchronous execution.

Let us consider an application in which we need to calculate the matrix multiplication of values from the user profiles of some system like a streaming service and metric weights for a set of movies. After that we reduce the values of each row to obtain each user's score. Lastly, we find the minimum and maximum values.

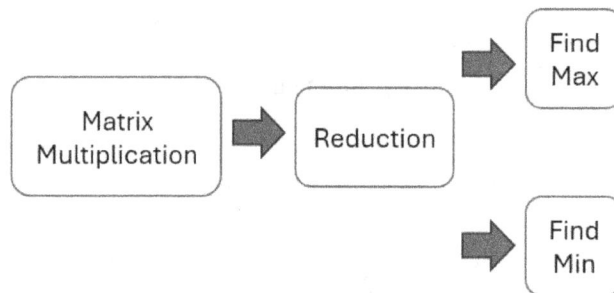

Figure 6.4: Critical path of the user ranking application

As we can see in *Figure 6.4*, there is no dependency between the final steps to find the minimum and maximum values, but we must wait for previous steps to complete.

GPU hardware – not so general, but massively parallel

GPU parallelism is different from general parallelism in that we are dealing with specific hardware which supports a specific programming model. Many times, we will catch ourselves trying to figure out a way to make an application fit in with the way the GPU processes data. Other hardware may offer various models of parallelism, but few approach the massive parallelism made available by GPUs. That is why it may be worth restructuring our applications in many ways to make them compatible with the GPU processing model: massive parallelism!

Designing parallel algorithms requires careful thought about task division, synchronization, and load balancing. It is not enough to break down tasks: they must be structured to minimize dependencies and maximize parallelism, making synchronization points rare and balancing workload among threads. This balance ensures that each thread can contribute equally to the outcome, enhancing the algorithm's overall speed and efficiency.

One thing worth mentioning is that, although sometimes necessary, if we overuse synchronization in our programs then we may end up degrading the performance gains provided by using parallelism in the first place. At its limits, using synchronization in unnecessary places will yield sequential execution of a parallel program.

In the next and following sections we will explore algorithms to perform some common computations that can be accelerated using parallelism. We will start with matrix processing due to its task-independent nature, but then we gradually move to more task-dependent examples to illustrate everything we have been talking about.

Computing matrix addition and multiplication

Let's dive into **matrix addition** and matrix multiplication, two operations that at first glance might look similar but which actually differ quite a bit, especially when it comes to how they are handled by computers – and particularly when programming with CUDA.

Matrix addition is straightforward. Imagine we have two matrices, say A and B, that are the same size. We just add each element in A to the corresponding element in B. So, $C[i][j]=A[i][j]+B[i][j]$ for every row i and column j. Since each element's addition happens independently of the others, this is an *embarrassingly parallel* task. That's a fancy way of saying that each calculation is independent of any others, so in theory we could compute them all at once without needing to coordinate or wait for results from other parts of the matrix.

On the GPU, matrix addition is highly efficient because there is no need for synchronization between threads. Each thread can just grab a single element from each matrix, add them, and store the result. And here's the cool part: if our matrices are stored in contiguous blocks of memory (meaning row by row), we can treat this as if it is just a long vector of numbers to add. We are just adding two giant vectors element by element! By processing each row sequentially, we make the most of the memory layout, reducing cache misses and speeding things up. Fortunately, matrices usually *are* stored contiguously, because this is the best way to move data from host to device. Since we've already covered vector addition in *Chapter 4* we will not go through the code again.

One last comment regarding memory access is that we want to maximize memory accesses that are *coalesced*, meaning that they will maximize the efficiency of the GPU's memory system. An in-depth discussion of memory coalescing is beyond this book's scope, but can be found in the CUDA documentation at `https://docs.nvidia.com/cuda/cuda-c-best-practices-guide/index.html#coalesced-access-to-global-memory`.

Matrix multiplication, on the other hand, is a bit of a different beast. Suppose that A_{mn} and B_{np} are two matrices – and notice that the number of columns in A matches the number of rows in B. When multiplying matrices A_{mn} and B_{np}, the element at position $C[i][j]$ in the resulting matrix C_{mp} depends on the entire i-th row of A and the entire j-th column of B. This creates a 'many-to-many' dependency that is absent from matrix addition. For each element in C, we are calculating the sum of products across that row and column, which can be described as:

The k that indexes the summation of the elements allows us to access all the elements of row i from A while accessing all the elements of column j from B. For matrix A it runs across all the elements of a single row while for matrix B it traverses all the elements of a single column. This pattern causes more work for the processor, and it is harder on the memory system, leading to more cache misses.

In CUDA, matrix multiplication involves breaking the task down into many threads that each handle a portion of the computation, with each thread usually being responsible for a single element of the resulting matrix C. This means that each thread will use a row from A and a column from B. However, unlike matrix addition, we have to consider memory access patterns carefully to avoid performance drops. Accessing non-contiguous elements, as we do when reading across columns of matrix B, increases the chances of cache misses, which slows everything down. This happens because when we access the global memory for an element, the memory system brings a block that fits in the memory cache; if the next element that we need is not present in the cache, a new block will be copied from global memory to the cache. If after that we need the previous element again, a new copy will have to be made. This is a disastrous cycle that degrades performance.

Why is matrix multiplication important?

Matrix multiplication is important because it's at the heart of so much scientific computation – solving systems of equations, running simulations, analyzing data, or even training machine learning models. When you hear about AI models training on enormous datasets or weather models predicting hurricanes, there's a high chance they are performing matrix multiplication at massive scale. Scientists and engineers might spend years developing new ways to make these operations faster or more efficient, knowing that small improvements can have a big impact on the speed of these vitally important applications.

An image can help visualize the necessary memory access patterns and also shows how each element calculation is independent of the others.

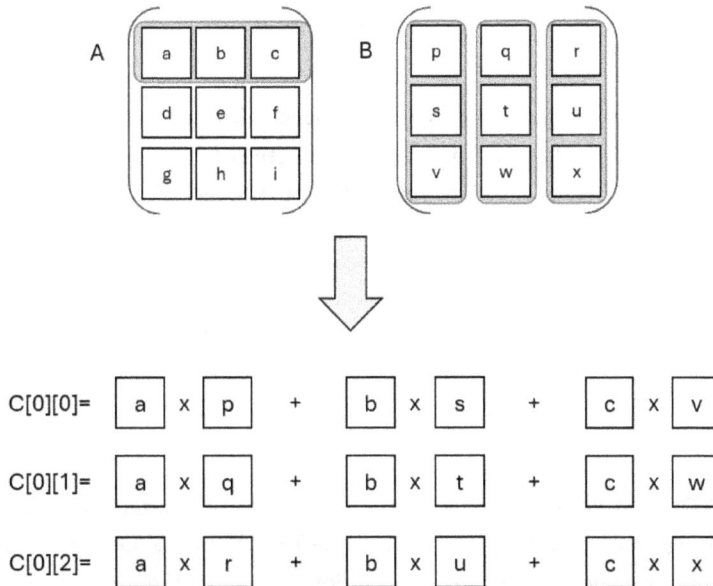

Figure 6.5: Independence of tasks in matrix multiplication

Here is a curious twist: even though matrix multiplication is more complex than matrix addition, it is still considered an embarrassingly parallel problem, since the core idea remains the same: each calculation of an element in *C* can be performed independently of the others. No thread needs to wait for another to finish before it can do its work, so there is no need for synchronization. This is a huge advantage, because we can assign multiple threads to work simultaneously without having to coordinate them very much.

Now it is time for our code. In this example we are considering *square matrices*, meaning that the number of rows equals the number of columns. Here is our kernel for the multiplication:

```
__global__ void matrixMulKernel(double *A, double *B,
    double *C, int width) {
    int row = threadIdx.y + blockIdx.y * blockDim.y;
    int col = threadIdx.x + blockIdx.x * blockDim.x;
    if (row < width && col < width) {
        double value = 0;
        for (int k = 0; k < width; k++) {
            value += A[row * width + k] * B[k * width + col];
        }
        C[row * width + col] = value;
    }
}
```

💡 **Quick tip:** Enhance your coding experience with the **AI Code Explainer** and **Quick Copy** features. Open this book in the next-gen Packt Reader. Click the **Copy** button (**1**) to quickly copy code into your coding environment, or click the **Explain** button (**2**) to get the AI assistant to explain a block of code to you.

```
                                                    Copy        Explain
function calculate(a, b) {                           1             2
  return {sum: a + b};
};
```

🔖 **The next-gen Packt Reader** is included for free with the purchase of this book. Scan the QR code OR go to packtpub.com/unlock, then use the search bar to find this book by name. Double-check the edition shown to make sure you get the right one.

It is worth noticing that now we are using two dimensions for the threadId, which makes it a little more comfortable to think about the indices.

Each thread will have a combination of row and col values that represent the indices of the element being calculated for the output matrix, but also represent the row from matrix *A* and column from matrix *B* that must be processed. Having a for loop allows us to access each corresponding element, multiply and store in a local variable.

Another important piece of code is the configuration to launch the kernel, as we can see below:

```
dim3 blockDim(16, 16);
dim3 gridDim( (N + blockDim.x - 1) / blockDim.x,
              (N + blockDim.y - 1) / blockDim.y );
matrixMulKernel<<<gridDim, blockDim>>>(d_A, d_B, d_C, N);
```

Here *N* represents the *order* of our matrices, or in other words it is the size of each dimension, meaning that we have *N* * *N* elements. What blockDim defines is the number of threads – we will have 256 threads being 16 rows and 16 columns at a time. Then we define the number of blocks, also using two dimensions on the gridDim, but we need to calculate the quantity based on the order of the matrices. If *N* = 1000 then we calculate as follows:

(1000 + 16 – 1) / 16 = 63.4375

However, since blockDim.x has an unsigned int type, the value will become 63, and this will be the same in both dimensions, meaning that we will have gridDim(63,63). This will create 3969 blocks and, remembering that each block will have 256 threads, we end up with 3969 x 256 = 1,016,064 individual threads for processing our data. Considering that we have 1000 × 1000 = 1,000,000 individual elements we are good to go, but we must take steps to ensure that the extra 16,064 threads that are off boundaries for our matrices will not compute anything. That is why the first lines of code in our kernels always include a test to check whether the threadId is within data limits.

Now would be a suitable time to experiment with the code downloaded from our repository, using different values for the size of the matrix in order to observe the effects on execution times.

In the next section will work with a different problem, but one that can also benefit from parallelism. We will be calculating integrals numerically, meaning that we're going to calculate many points and then sum them.

Calculating numerical integrals

To start with: what is an **integral**? Well, an integral is a concept in calculus that represents the area under a curve on a graph, between two points. Imagine you are tracking the path of a car moving along a road, and at fixed intervals you measure the car's speed. Now, if you plot that and calculate the area under the curve representing its speed over time, considering that distance = speed × time, you get the total distance the car traveled! In simple terms, an integral sums up tiny slices of area to find a total, making it a powerful way to measure quantities that accumulate over a range.

Why are integrals useful?

Integrals are everywhere in science, engineering, and beyond. They help us measure quantities that change continuously—like distance, energy, or growth— by calculating the total quantity over time or space. For example, engineers use integrals to determine forces on structures, economists use them to measure total income over time, and environmental scientists use them to model pollution spread. Integrals give us a way to understand the big picture from all the tiny parts.

Sometimes we want to know the area under a curve but don't have an easy formula to work with. That is where **numerical integration** comes in! It enables us to estimate the area when our math skills or formulae fall short. We need to make many small calculations and then sum them all – which sounds like something we could use a parallel algorithm for, right?

There are many numerical integration methods, but the simplest is called the **trapezoidal method**, because it uses many trapezoids inside the curve to calculate an approximation of the area of the curve.

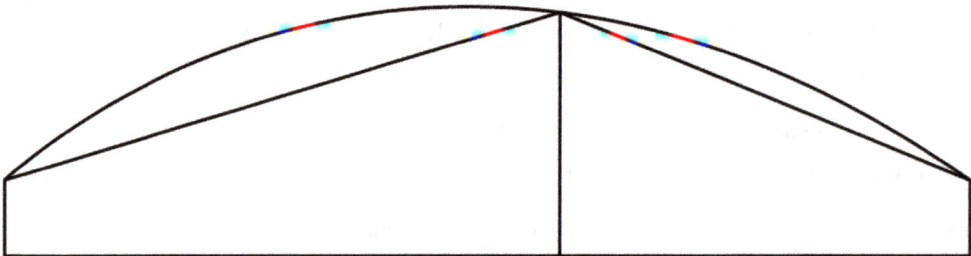

Figure 6.6: Two trapezoids inside a curve

In *Figure 6.6* we are using just two trapezoids to approximate the area under the curve, to make it easy to understand the concept, but in practice we usually add many more trapezoids. Of course, most of the times that we need this kind of approach the curve is not as well behaved as this one. What is interesting about using trapezoids is that as we decrease their width, the top line gets closer to the curve, and this enables them to provide a particularly good approximation considering that the math is quite simple to compute. So, as is always the case with numerical methods, there is a tradeoff of precision for computability.

Another interesting characteristic of the trapezoidal method is that we can use collected data directly in the computations. Using the road trip example mentioned at the beginning of this section, we might record the car's speed at 15-minute intervals (0.25 hours). Since we do not know where this trip is occurring, we will display speeds in both kilometers/hour as well as in miles/hour:

Id	Time (hours)	Speed (km/h)	Speed (mph)
0	0.00	60	37.28
1	0.25	65	40.39
2	0.50	70	43.50
3	0.75	72	44.74
4	1.00	68	42.25
5	1.25	65	40.39
6	1.50	62	38.53
7	1.75	60	37.28
8	2.00	58	36.04

To apply the trapezoidal method, we use the average of the heights at the two endpoints, multiplied by the width of the section. In this case the width of the section is 0.25, which is our interval, and the heights are the actual measured values.

Our first section is from 0 to 0.25; the height at 0 was 60 and at 0.25 was 65 so the average height is $(60 + 65)/2$ and multiplying by the section width of 0.25 we get a speed of 15.625 km/hour. Let's use a table for that:

id	kilometers	miles
1	(60+65)/2 x 0.25 = 15.63	(37.28+40.39)/2 x 0.25 = 9.42
2	(65+70)/2 x 0.25 = 16.88	(40.39+43.50)/2 x 0.25 = 10.11
3	(70+72)/2 x 0.25 = 17.75	(43.50+44.74)/2 x 0.25 = 10.56
4	(72+68)/2 x 0.25 = 17.50	(44.74+42.25)/2 x 0.25 = 10.25
5	(68+65)/2 x 0.25 = 16.63	(42.25+40.39)/2 x 0.25 = 10.16
6	(65+62)/2 x 0.25 = 15.88	(40.39+38.53)/2 x 0.25 = 9.73
7	(62+60)/2 x 0.25 = 15.25	(38.53+37.28)/2 x 0.25 = 9.45
8	(60+58)/2 x 0.25 = 14.75	(37.28+36.04)/2 x 0.25 = 9.33
Sum	130.25 km	79.01 miles

Of course, our example is so small that it could be calculated manually, and so would not amount to an effective use of our GPUs, but imagine that we had tens of thousands of data points: then it would start to make sense to use a GPU. The truth is that the more points we add, the better our approximation will be.

We should also notice that this is another type of problem that does not require synchronization between the executing threads.

This time our kernel is super simple:

```
#define N 10'000'000 // Number of speed measurements
#define T 0.25 //Interval between measurements (15 minutes)
__global__ void trapezoidalKernel(double *speeds, double *distances,
    int n) {
    int i = threadIdx.x + blockIdx.x * blockDim.x;
    if (i < n - 1) {
        distances[i] = 0.5 * (speeds[i] + speeds[i + 1]) * T;
    }
}
```

Remember that we must divide by 2 to calculate the average height of the trapezoids, so we multiply by 0.5 which is a little faster. Also, we must multiply by the section width; in this case we define *T* to be 0.25. All the values are calculated and stored in a different array. After executing this kernel, we copy the results back to the host and calculate the final distance by adding all the partial results. This is the code in the `main` function that performs that step:

```
cudaMemcpy(h_distances, d_distances,
          (N - 1) * sizeof(double),
          cudaMemcpyDeviceToHost);
double gpuResult = 0.0;
for (int i = 0; i < N - 1; i++) {
    gpuResult += h_distances[i];
}
```

One interesting aspect is that the GPU implementation has a performance close to that of the CPU. This is because we need to copy data, and because the reduction step is processed entirely on the CPU. The process of reduction is the topic of the next section, and we shall learn how to take advantage of parallelism to accelerate the process.

Reducing from many

In parallel computing, **reduction** is a key operation that allows us to take a collection of values and combine them into a single result. It might sound like a straightforward task — adding up a list of numbers or finding a maximum value, for instance — but in parallel contexts reductions can be trickier than you might suppose. This is because reductions require us to combine partial results from multiple threads, which introduces the need for synchronization. If we do not tackle this carefully, the performance gains from parallelism can quickly vanish, as we saw in the example from the last section.

The need for coordination comes from the fact that different threads are working together to reduce a dataset to a single result. Without synchronized timing and controlled data access, threads can get in each other's way, and this can potentially result in overwritten values or incorrect answers.

A classic example of a reduction is summing an array of numbers. When we perform this operation in parallel, each thread might handle a small portion of the array. But eventually, we need to combine these partial sums into a result, which requires threads to synchronize at certain points. This step distinguishes reductions from embarrassingly parallel tasks, where each thread completes its task without ever needing to check in with others.

To achieve an efficient reduction we can use a technique like **tree-based reduction**, where each thread processes a pair of numbers to compute a partial result. The partial results are then combined in pairs again at the next level, reducing the number of values by half each time until only one result remains. This method, inspired by the idea of a binary tree, can reduce the number of synchronization steps as each level of the 'tree' requires fewer interactions between threads.

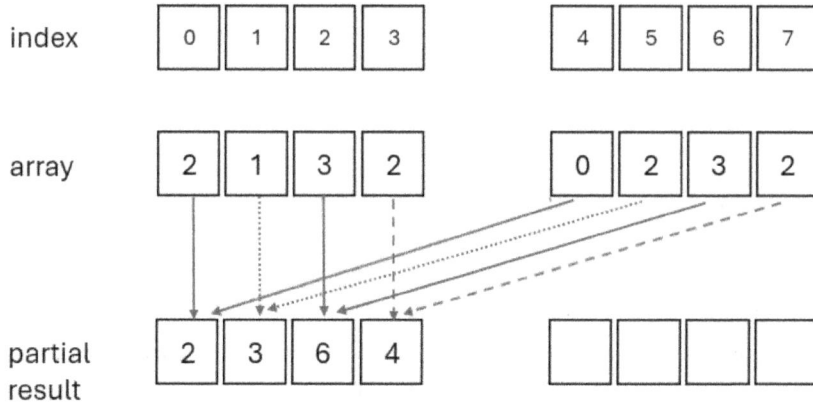

Figure 6.7: An example of a reduction to sum the array elements

One challenge with reduction is managing memory access. If multiple threads attempt to update the same variable simultaneously they can 'race' each other, leading to incorrect results or a slowdown in performance. To avoid this we employ atomic operations or other synchronization mechanisms that allow threads to safely access shared memory. This adds complexity, but without it reduction operations would become chaotic and unreliable.

Remember the previous section, where we calculated journey distance using the trapezoidal method for integration. When considering 1,000,000 data points, the execution times for CPU and GPU approaches were of the same order of magnitude. When we add a parallel reduction on the GPU, we can reduce the execution time by an order of magnitude. However, the code passes through many modifications, as we can see below.

```
#define N 10'000'000 //Number of speed measurements
#define T 0.25 //Interval between measurements (15 minutes)
__global__ void trapezoidalKernel(double *speeds, double *result, int n) {
    extern __shared__ double sharedData[];
    int tid = threadIdx.x;
    int i = threadIdx.x + blockIdx.x * blockDim.x;
    double localDistance = 0.0;
    if (i < n - 1) {
```

```
        localDistance = 0.5 * (speeds[i] + speeds[i + 1]) * T;
    }
    sharedData[tid] = localDistance;
    __syncthreads();
    for (int s = blockDim.x / 2; s > 0; s /= 2) {
        if (tid < s) {
            sharedData[tid] += sharedData[tid + s];
        }
        __syncthreads();
    }
    if (tid == 0) {
        result[blockIdx.x] = sharedData[0];
    }
}
```

Now we need to proceed step by step to understand the differences from the original kernel. Also, notice that in this example we are using shared memory to its best by keeping the partial results within this fast memory, which enables us to reduce among the thread blocks.

The first part of the code is remarkably similar, the only difference being the declaration of the sharedData array that is allocated externally by the kernel launch configuration. The use of the keyword extern on the shared memory declaration tells the compiler that the configuration is coming from the kernel launching configuration.

After calculating their own results, each thread saves their localDistance to their index in the sharedData array. Notice that this does not require any synchronization, because each thread uses the tid value, which is unique, to persist its results.

With partials in place we need to effectively reduce, and thus comes the first need to synchronize action. We use the __syncthreads() function to establish a checkpoint which all threads must reach before the kernel can continue.

After this point we loop with half the threads in the block to calculate the first round of partial sums. Notice that we use blockDim.x to get the number of threads in a block and divide by 2, to guarantee that variable s (for stride) will help us get half of the remaining set on each iteration.

Next all threads with an id less than the stride calculate their value plus the counterpart that's in the other half of the array. Again, for each step we must __syncthreads() and make sure that all the partials are correctly computed. This is a common source of computing errors; whenever we incur value errors in reduction the synchronization points are a great starting point to double-check.

Each step divides the stride by 2 and repeats the sums, until we reach a point where thread 0 adds sharedData[0] and sharedData[1] to produce the result for this block of threads.

Giving careful thought to this point again, in a large dataset we will have many blocks each with many threads. If we computed the partial results for each block, how would we reach the ultimate result? Well, we could have a second kernel call to compute this step, or we could move this small number of values to the host and compute it very quickly using the CPU. We will go with this last option, and will see some of the changes to the main code below.

```
int blockSize = 256;
int gridSize = (N + blockSize - 1) / blockSize;
double *d_speeds, *d_partialResults;
cudaMalloc(&d_speeds, N * sizeof(double));
cudaMalloc(&d_partialResults, gridSize * sizeof(double));
```

First we define the number of blocks necessary for our computation – this is our gridSize. This will also define the size of the partialResults array, because we need one slot for each block that completes the processing of speeds. And of course we need to allocate memory for that on the GPU.

Another important change is the way we call our kernel:

```
trapezoidalKernel<<<gridSize, blockSize, blockSize *
    sizeof(double)>>>(d_speeds, d_partialResults, N);
```

After gridSize and blockSize we pass in the size we want to allocate for the shared memory block to be used. This means the remaining space will be used as L1 cache.

With execution complete we need to copy the partial results to our host again and calculate the final reduction.

```
double *h_partialResults = (double*)malloc(gridSize * sizeof(double));

cudaMemcpy(h_partialResults, d_partialResults, gridSize * sizeof(double),
    cudaMemcpyDeviceToHost);
double gpuResult = 0.0;
```

```
for (int i = 0; i < gridSize; i++) {
    gpuResult += h_partialResults[i];
}
```

We allocate an array of `gridSize` on the host and perform the copy. Now a simple for loop will do the trick for us. Reducing on the CPU is not a big deal here because `gridSize` is many orders of magnitude smaller than the total number of elements, so this computation does not incur a heavy overhead. Performing this on the GPU, on the other hand, would leave many threads idle, which would not represent the most efficient use of energy.

In the next section we'll discuss how we can sort data in parallel with a simple algorithm, and that example will help us discuss the effects of synchronization.

Sorting data

When we think of **sorting**, the first image that comes to mind might be the orderly rearrangement of numbers into a sequence, from smallest to largest or vice versa. But in parallel programming, sorting turns out to be much more than simply lining things up. It is a problem that involves coordination, patience, and a hefty dose of synchronization. Sorting in parallel is not simply hard — it is a challenging puzzle, where each piece needs to know what the others are doing. In this exploration, we are going to dive into a parallel sorting method called **odd-even sort** and see what it tells us about the unique challenges of synchronization in parallel computation.

Odd-even sort gives us an elegant yet tricky solution to sorting with multiple processors. The basic idea is that rather than having each processor work on the entire array, we set processors up to work in pairs, comparing and swapping numbers in adjacent positions. In one round we compare the elements at odd indices with their immediate neighbors, and then in the next round we do the same for elements at even indices. By repeating these steps, or 'phases', we gradually move our unsorted numbers closer and closer to the correct order.

Sorting in parallel introduces a twist: we must figure out how to coordinate different threads so they do not get in each other's way. If they do not stay coordinated, they might end up undoing each other's work, leading to a jumble of data instead of the neatness we aim for.

Odd-even sort is one of those methods that we use specifically for learning, as there are more advanced sorting algorithms that lend themselves better to real-world applications. In parallel, however, odd-even sort shines a light on just how hard synchronization is. We'll see that just throwing more processors at a problem will not necessarily solve it faster — getting those processors to work together smoothly is where the magic happens.

Enough talk, let's see the code!

```
__global__ void oddEvenSortStepKernel(double *arr, int size,
    bool *swapped, bool isOddPhase) {
    int idx = threadIdx.x + blockIdx.x * blockDim.x;
    int i = isOddPhase ? 2 * idx + 1 : 2 * idx;
        if (i < size - 1) {
        if (arr[i] > arr[i + 1]) {
            double temp = arr[i];
            arr[i] = arr[i + 1];
            arr[i + 1] = temp;
            *swapped = true;
        }
    }
}
```

The actual kernel is amazingly simple. Given the phase, it determines whether it must compare and swap odd or even pairs of array elements. If we are in the odd phase then all the indices are multiplied by 2 and 1 is added, which guarantees an odd number. When in the even phase, on the other hand, all the indices are just multiplied by 2, guaranteeing an even number. After validating that the index is within our boundaries, we test to see if the values are out of order, and if they are, we swap them and update the swapped flag. Here is the first interesting part. Notice that we will have many threads working in parallel and, possibly, overwriting this variable. We spend time talking about the importance of synchronization and now we are simply letting chaos take place? Not exactly.

To understand this, we need to see another piece of code that executes on the host.

```
void oddEvenSortGpu(double *arr, int size) {
    double *d_arr;
    bool *d_swapped, h_swapped;
    int threads = 256;
    int blocks = (size + threads - 1) / threads;
    cudaMalloc((void **)&d_arr, size * sizeof(double));
    cudaMalloc((void **)&d_swapped, sizeof(bool));
    cudaMemcpy(d_arr, arr, size * sizeof(double), cudaMemcpyHostToDevice);
    do {
        h_swapped = false;
        cudaMemcpy(d_swapped, &h_swapped, sizeof(bool),
```

```
            cudaMemcpyHostToDevice);
        oddEvenSortStepKernel<<<blocks, threads>>>(d_arr, size, d_swapped,
            true);
        cudaDeviceSynchronize();
        oddEvenSortStepKernel<<<blocks, threads>>>(d_arr, size, d_swapped,
            false);
        cudaDeviceSynchronize();
        cudaMemcpy(&h_swapped, d_swapped, sizeof(bool),
            cudaMemcpyDeviceToHost);
    } while (h_swapped);
    cudaMemcpy(arr, d_arr, size * sizeof(double),
        cudaMemcpyDeviceToHost);
    cudaFree(d_arr);
    cudaFree(d_swapped);
}
```

Our main interest is with the do-while loop, but the rest of the code is the context in terms of declarations and preparation.

This algorithm alternates odd and even phases, but how do we reach termination? By monitoring to see if there were no swaps in the last iteration. And here is the cool part: we create the swapped control variable on the host and pass it to the kernel. The many threads operate and may even overwrite each others' results, but that is not a problem because no thread would set the value of the swapped variable to its original false value. Either one or more threads set the variable value to true, or they leave it as it is, regardless of the current value. This is also known as a benign data-race, something which is usually seen by NVIDIA as something to be avoided because it is considered as undefined behavior which might not compile correctly on future versions. However, our situation is very specific because, as mentioned above, no thread could set the shared variable to its original value.

The tricky part is that after execution of the two phases we need to copy the swapped variable back to the host to check its value and determine whether we need to keep going or not. After a certain number of iterations no more swaps occur, and we terminate the execution.

Although not sophisticated, this is the perfect algorithm to illustrate the complexity involved in creating sorting algorithms that execute efficiently in parallel.

Processing sensor data with a convolution

We've talked about calculating an integral which reduces from a lot of data to a single value, and we've also explored sorting that likewise operates on our input data. Now we'll explore an interesting but different concept called **convolution**.

A convolution is an operation that works like sliding a small window (called a filter) over our data and combining the data values with the weights on the filter to produce a transformed result. This kind of operation is very common in image and signal processing, and financial analysis as well. However, a simpler example is smoothing the values collected from sensors to filter out noise. That's exactly what we are going to work on now.

Let's suppose that in a factory there are machines bearing many sensors that measure the vibration of each piece of equipment. We can use a weighted moving average to process the last N measurements from each sensor and produce a smoothed value. After that, another function could check values against some threshold, but we'll ignore that detail for now. We will focus on sensor data processing.

Using a GPU to perform this type of computation is really effective, because we can process millions of data points independently – the ideal use case for GPUs.

Let's move to the code. First, our kernel:

```
__global__ void smoothSensorsKernel(float *buffers, int *indices,
    float *output, float *weights) {
    int idx = threadIdx.x + blockIdx.x * blockDim.x;
    if (idx >= NUM_SENSORS) return;
    float val = 0.0f;
    for (int i=0; i < NUM_READINGS; i++){
        val = weights[i] * buffers[indices[i] * NUM_READINGS + idx];
    }
    output[idx] = val;
}
```

This kernel receives four parameters: the data array, an array of buffer indices, an output array, and finally the array of weights – this is the filter itself.

In our code we have defined NUM_READINGS as a constant that represents how many sensor readings will be considered in weighted moving average operations; this means that buffers will have NUM_READINGS data points per sensor. And we will address the positions the same way we did for matrix rows. But now comes the challenging part: as new readings arrive from sensors, we have to discard the oldest set of readings and overwrite them with the new values. To achieve this, we use an auxiliary structure that holds the references to the access orders, and we rotate these indices at each step. This allows us to write to memory addresses that are already allocated in the GPU memory.

Let's look at the function that makes this rotation possible:

```
void rotateIndices(int *indices) {
    int newData = indices[0];
    indices[0] = indices[1];
    indices[1] = indices[2];
    indices[2] = newData;
}
```

The indices array starts with values 0, 1, and 2 to indicate the order in which the data arrays were filled. After the first processing cycle we need to move position 1 to be considered the oldest, and we overwrite the values corresponding to position 0 on the buffers array. The result of this is that we can control where the oldest and the newest values are at any point in time.

Our main function is very similar to our previous programs in terms of allocating memory on the GPU and copying data, although there is one difference between the first execution and the next data to arrive: the first time, we need to load a larger buffer containing the data corresponding to the NUM_READINGS datasets, but after that we will only update one set. Check out this code:

```
int newDataIdx = h_indices[0];
if (i == 0) {
    for(int j = 0; j < NUM_READINGS; j++) {
        initializeBuffer(h_buffers, j);
    }
} else {
    newDataIdx = h_indices[0];
    rotateIndices(h_indices);
    initializeBuffer(h_buffers, newDataIdx); //one new reading for all
sensors
}
```

Here we can see that we are initializing many times for the first execution, but after that we initialize only one buffer. Of course our initialization is generating random numbers, but this is the code that would receive data from somewhere, maybe from the network. Notice that we save the value of h_indices[0], which holds the oldest buffer, and after that we call rotateIndices().

Later, when it is time to copy the new indices and buffers to the GPU memory, we do the following:

```
cudaMemcpy(d_indices, h_indices, NUM_READINGS * sizeof(int),
    cudaMemcpyHostToDevice);
if (i == 0) {
    cudaMemcpy(d_buffers, h_buffers, NUM_READINGS * bufferSize,
        cudaMemcpyHostToDevice);
} else {
    cudaMemcpy(&d_buffers[newDataIdx], &h_buffers[newDataIdx], bufferSize,
        cudaMemcpyHostToDevice);
}
```

The first thing to note here is that we need to copy the indices because we have rotated them. If we are on the first execution we copy the full h_buffers array, but for other executions we index h_buffers with the newDataIdx variable representing the offset of the oldest portion of the array.

After that we proceed to call the kernel and copy the results back to the host, as can be seen in the full code in the GitHub repository.

Summary

In this chapter we learned what makes a parallel algorithm really parallel, and how to look for those special parts that can be used to reduce the execution time. We also discussed the idea that we are looking for a specific type of parallelism that will fit in well with the way GPUs execute programs.

We discussed synchronization, now with more context, and saw it in practice with our example programs. Those addressed real-world problems like matrix multiplication, numerical integration, and parallel reductions, we tackled the hard challenge of sorting in parallel, and finally we saw how to process millions of data points from sensors using a weighted moving average.

In the next chapter we will discuss performance strategies to improve application efficiency, using techniques that are more advanced in order to make the most of our hardware.

Unlock this book's exclusive benefits now

UNLOCK NOW

Scan this QR code or go to packtpub.com/unlock, then search this book by name.

Note: Keep your purchase invoice ready before you start.

7

Performance Strategies

We have learned many concepts and techniques for creating CUDA programs, and we have already seen some performance improvements in our small examples. However, simply converting a program to run on the GPU may not yield the desired speed-up, and indeed it may incur costs that are at odds with expectations. One example is the time needed to load data to the GPU memory. Use the right strategies, however, and you can overcome these problems.

In this chapter we revisit our old friend matrix multiplication, and discuss some ways to improve its performance. But most importantly, we'll investigate *why* the changes we make help to improve performance. Along the way we shall cover the following topics:

- Introducing optimization
- Profiling with NVIDIA Nsight Compute

Technical requirements

We will use the environment configured during *Chapter 3* with VS Code and our development container. If you have chosen to install the CUDA Toolkit on your machine, you can simply run the build commands on a terminal. We will also use a new tool called NVIDIA Nsight Compute to profile our code, which is a GUI-based tool available both in our container as well as on the local installation. The official documentation can be found at `https://docs.nvidia.com/nsight-compute/index.html`. All the code for this chapter is provided in the GitHub repository `https://github.com/PacktPublishing/GPU-Programming-with-CPP-and-CUDA/tree/main/ch7`.

Introducing optimization

When we go through official documentation it is easy to feel lost or overwhelmed by the information about different hardware architectures. Every new GPU release brings hardware innovations that affect the way we need to write our code, and knowing our hardware is of paramount importance if we are to squeeze out every last drop of performance. Furthermore, knowing the details of our hardware brings to light any limitations we may have in terms of memory bandwidth, available memory, and clock speed.

It is also our responsibility to gauge the effort needed to achieve greater performance, and that is when using a **profiler** is a great advantage, for it enables us to figure out what the best items are to optimize. **Code optimization** may lead to code that is harder to read, because we need to deal with many more hardware details, but that does not mean that the code will be impossible to maintain. We just need to be careful and follow some software engineering best practices to compensate for the added complexity.

In *Chapter 6* we learned about a simple matrix multiplication kernel which already performed better than a single-thread CPU version, but the time needed to load data impacted total execution time. We are now going to revisit our matrix multiplication kernel and apply some optimizations. This is the perfect example in which to study their effects because while it is one of those embarrassingly parallel problems, the techniques we are about to discuss will also apply to other scenarios.

> **Debug versus Release compilation flags**
>
> The instructions we pass to our compiler are fundamental to the type of code that will be generated for us. In CMake we can define different configurations that determine how the configuration generator prepares our environment. We are using **Makefile**, which is a single configuration generator, and this means that to change from Debug to Release, and back again if necessary, we have to execute the CMake configuration step again. We will see this command in detail in the section *Optimizing to speed up our code*, where we will be applying the optimizations.

Nevertheless, before jumping into the optimizations, it will be of immense value to learn how to measure what is going on with our code. That way we can compare what we have with what we may achieve by applying changes to the code. In *Chapter 4* we used NVIDIA Nsight Compute from the command line, which does not allow interactive sessions, but now we will use its graphical interface to learn more about our code. So let's get to know our new tool, the NVIDIA Nsight Compute Graphical Interface.

Profiling with NVIDIA Nsight Compute

We are currently working in a lab-like environment where all our programs for the book are small, and most of the time they have a single kernel that relates to the technique we are learning about. However, in real-world programs we will face situations in which many distinct functions interact with each other, passing their results forward to achieve results for our users. In such scenarios, the use of profiling tools becomes fundamental to identifying the hot spots where we should concentrate our time-saving efforts.

Optimizing code without proper information can make us spend too much time on a piece of code that is rarely executed. Such blind optimization can unfold in many ways, but one possible result is that after applying various optimizations we find no improvement at all. It is important to use tools that help us identify where the bottlenecks really are.

Configuring access to GPU performance counters

We need to make sure that we will be able to access the performance parameters. To do this we need to add a file `nvidia.conf` in `/etc/modprobe.d`, with the following content:

```
options nvidia NVreg_RestrictProfilingToAdminUsers=0
```

The actual name of the file does not affect the behavior. After adding the file it is recommended to restart the system.

A more detailed discussion about this configuration for other systems can be found here: https://developer.nvidia.com/nvidia-development-tools-solutions-err_nvgpuctrperm-permission-issue-performance-counters.

Running the profiler

To execute the tool we use the following command on the terminal of our VS Code session (which is connected to our development container):

```
ncu-ui
```

This will open a separate window, as seen in *Figure 7.1*.

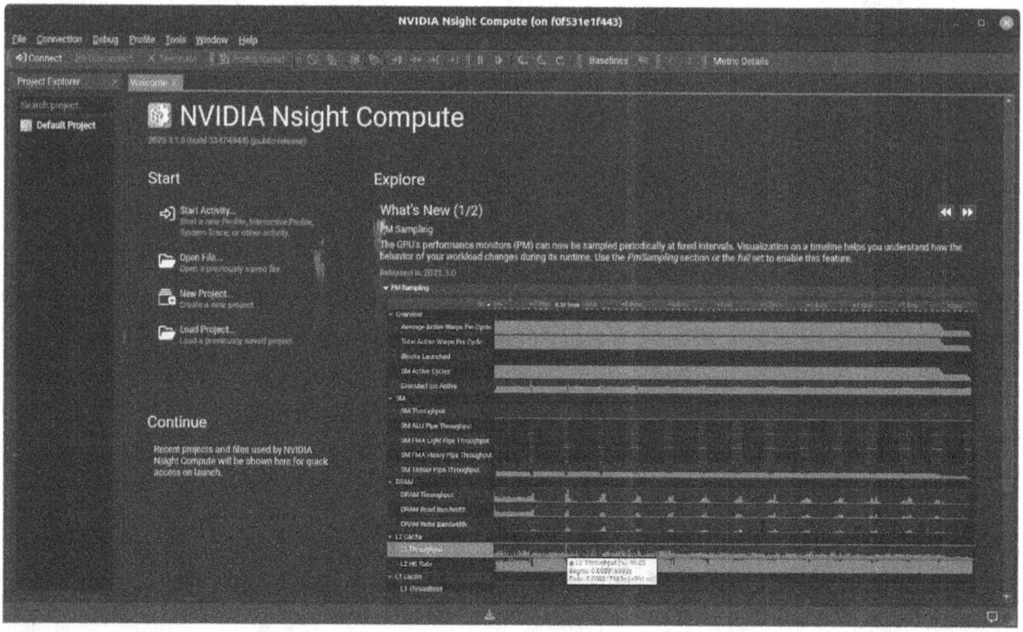

Figure 7.1: The Welcome screen

🔍 **Quick tip**: Need to see a high-resolution version of this image? Open this book in the next-gen Packt Reader or view it in the PDF/ePub copy.

🔒 The **next-gen Packt Reader** and a **free PDF/ePub copy** of this book are included with your purchase. Scan the QR code OR visit packtpub.com/unlock, then use the search bar to find this book by name. Double-check the edition shown to make sure you get the right one.

Here we can create a **New Project** to analyze our code, as we can see in *Figure 7.2*.

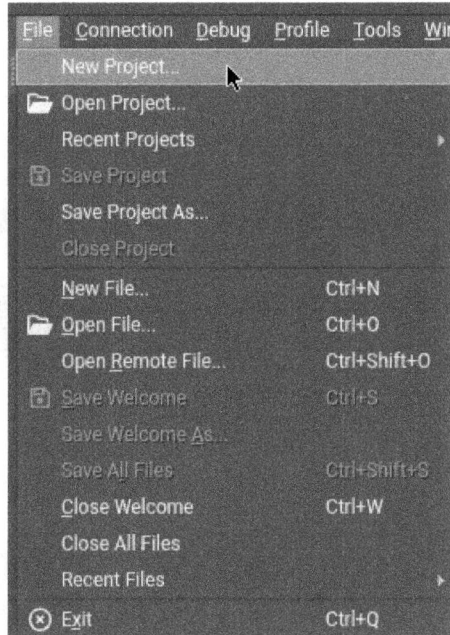

Figure 7.2: New Project option

After clicking **New Project** we will be presented with a dialog, shown in *Figure 7.3*, in which to enter the name of the project and select the folder in which it will be created.

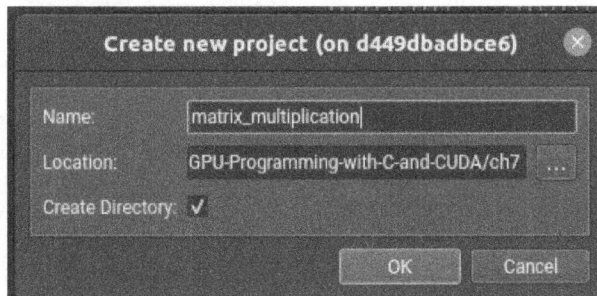

Figure 7.3: Creating the project folder

Here we have selected to create this inside our ch7 folder from the book repository, but we may choose any location we see fit. After clicking the **OK** button we will be prompted to configure the project, as shown in *Figure 7.4*.

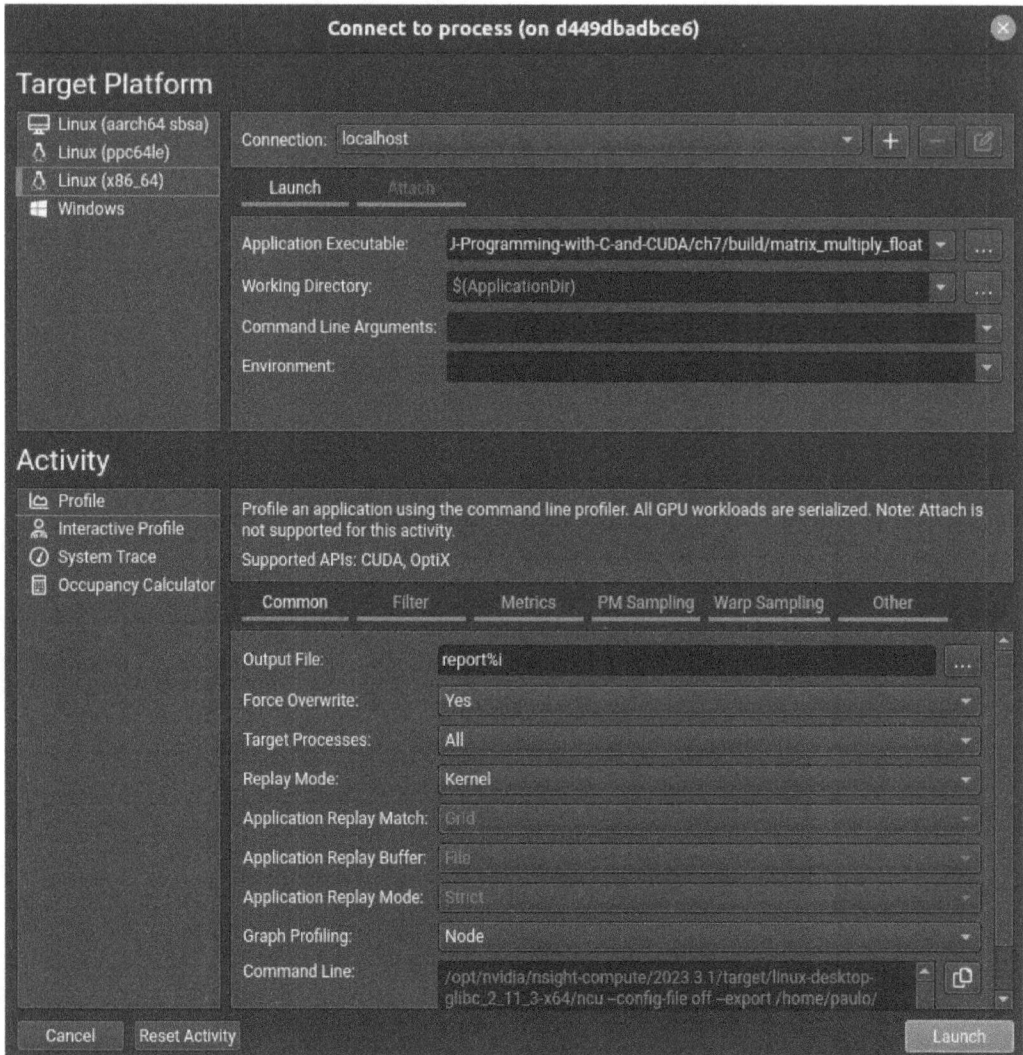

Figure 7.4: Application executable and report name

Here we must pay attention to several points. First, we have to select the platform in which we are working; our selection is **Linux x86_64**. The connection is selected as **localhost**, but in advanced scenarios we might connect to a remote host executing our application.

The next item to select is the **Application Executable**, and note that we are using the build folder where our projects create the executables. The last item to edit on this screen is the report name (**Output File**), and here we use report%i so that each profiling session generates a new report file, with %i being substituted by the number of the execution. Notice that the report name is configured on the **Profile** tab of the **Activity** panel, but before we run a specific profiling session we will change to the **System Trace** tab on the **Activity** panel as shown in *Figure 7.5*. This option allows us to run the application and have the tool trace the application. We do not need to change any other options for now; simply click the **Launch** button.

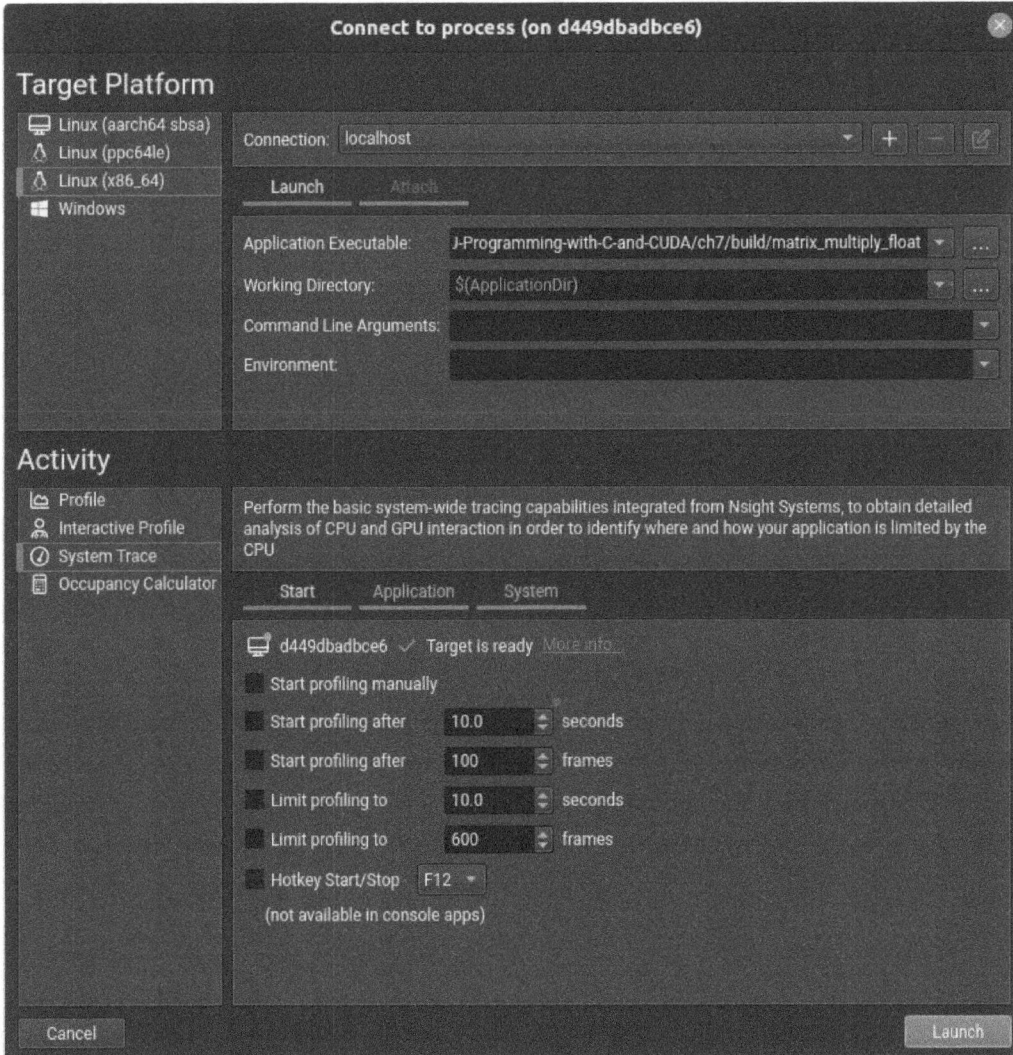

Figure 7.5: The system trace

After the trace execution we will see the analysis shown in *Figure 7.6* (the image was split in the middle to fit it onto the page).

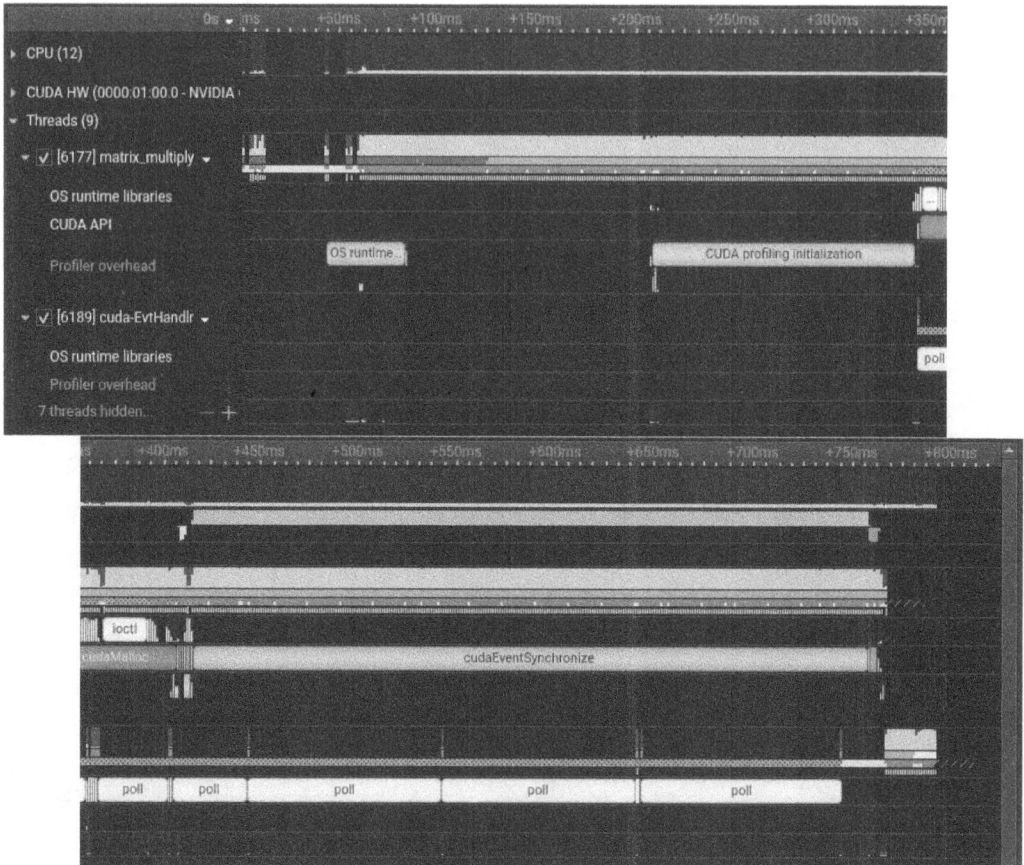

Figure 7.6: System trace timeline (broke down for visualization)

Here we have a lot of information, but the main items of interest are under the **CUDA HW** block on the left-hand side of the window. When we expand this item we see a section for kernel execution and another for memory operations. Our code first copies the matrices from the host system to the device, so we will see two **Memcpy** operations with **HtoD** marked, as shown in *Figure 7.7*.

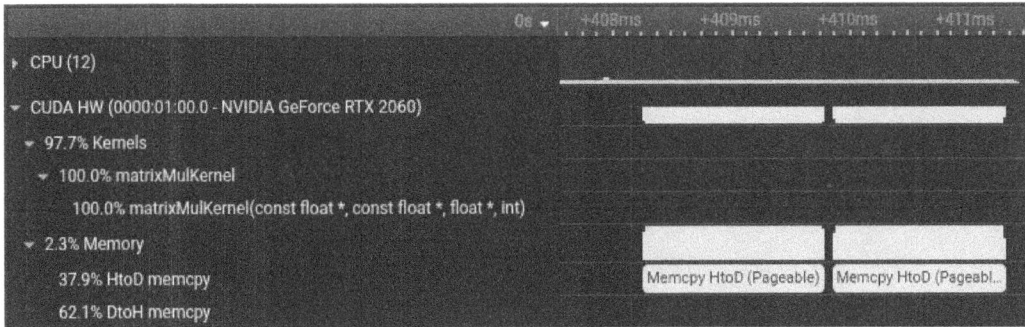

Figure 7.7: Zoom on memory copy – Host to Device

After that we see a large block with our kernel's name, representing execution of the kernel as shown in *Figure 7.8*.

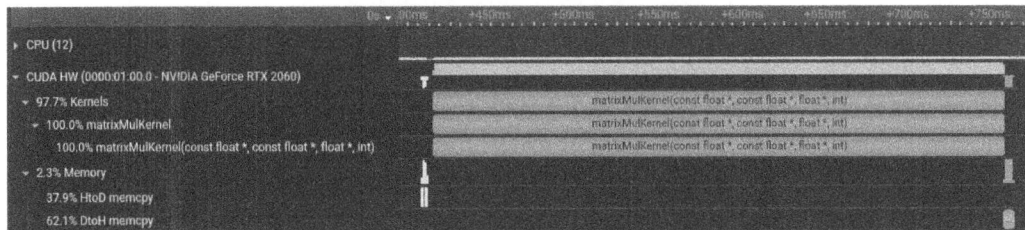

Figure 7.8: Zoom on kernel execution

After that, our application executes a new **Memcpy** operation marked as **DtoH** to copy the result matrix from the device to the host (*Figure 7.9*).

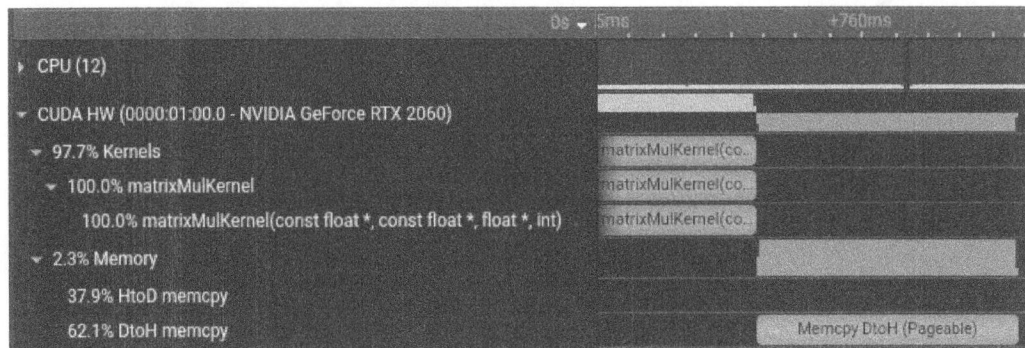

Figure 7.9: Zoom on memory copy – Device to Host

One interesting feature is that we can right-click on any kernel that was executed and select the **Profile Kernel** option as shown in *Figure 7.10*.

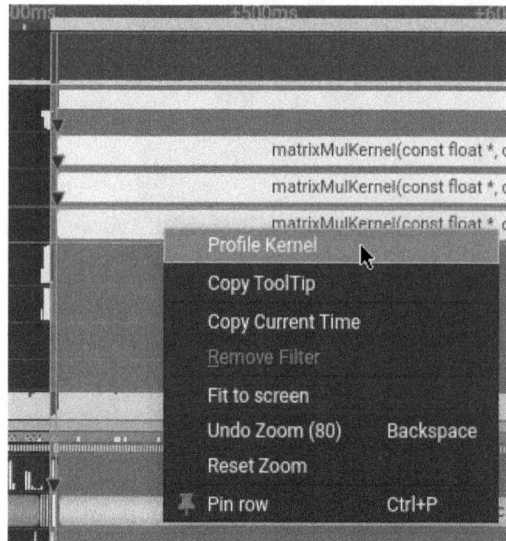

Figure 7.10: Selecting a kernel to profile

This will bring back the initial configuration screen. Since we are about to execute the profile of a specific kernel we need to change some details. The first item is already filled for us since we came from a System Trace, while the name of the kernel to profile is defined on the second tab as shown in *Figure 7.11*.

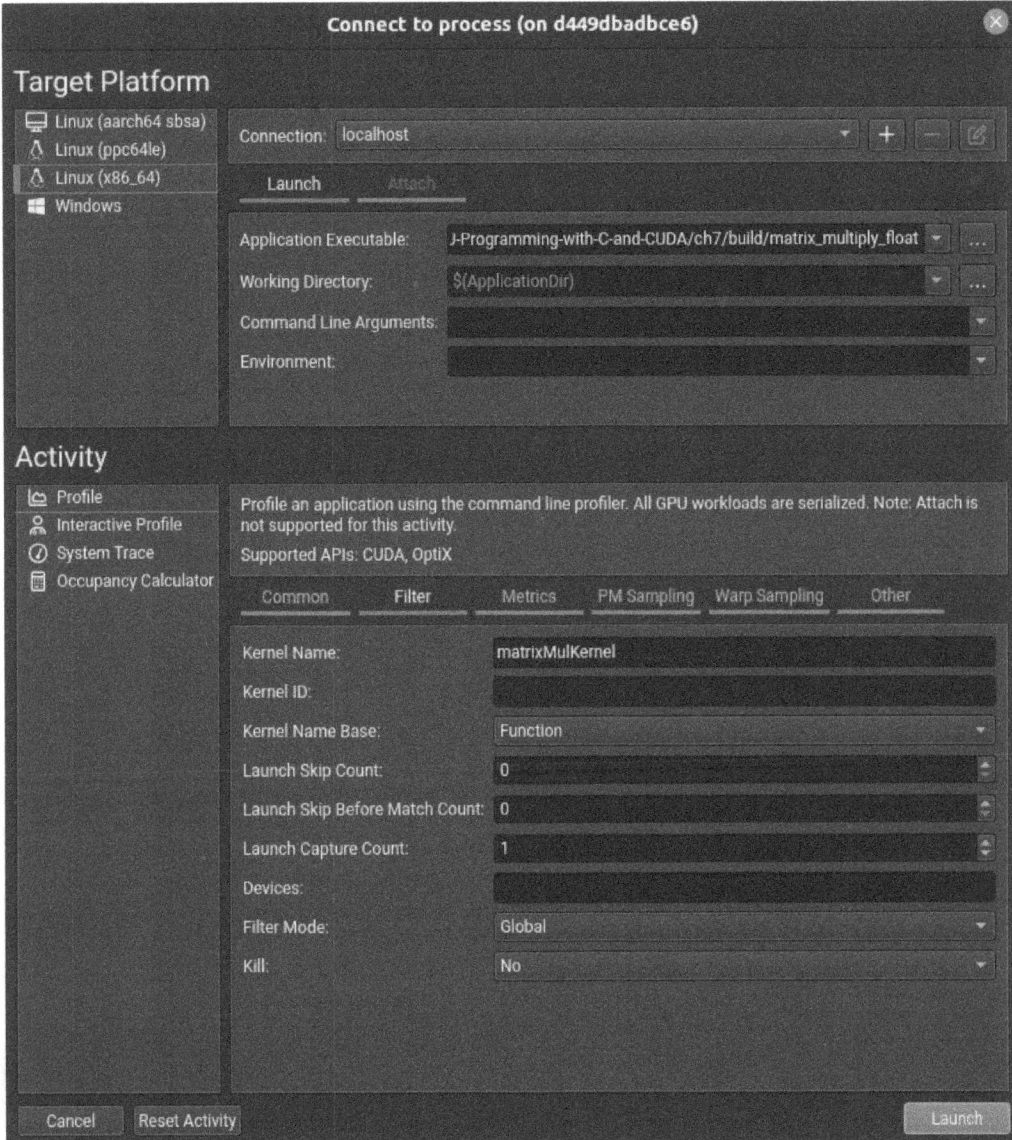

Figure 7.11: The selected kernel name

Selecting the name of the kernel informs the profiler about which item to analyze in detail, and with the help of the System Trace we can figure out which kernels we are spending more time on and focus our efforts on optimizing those first. Our example has only one kernel, so this decision is obvious, but in a larger application we would have to pay attention to this to avoid spending time in the wrong places.

We then select which metrics we want to track, on the **Metrics** tab where we select the full analysis as shown in *Figure 7.12*. This option generates data for all available metrics.

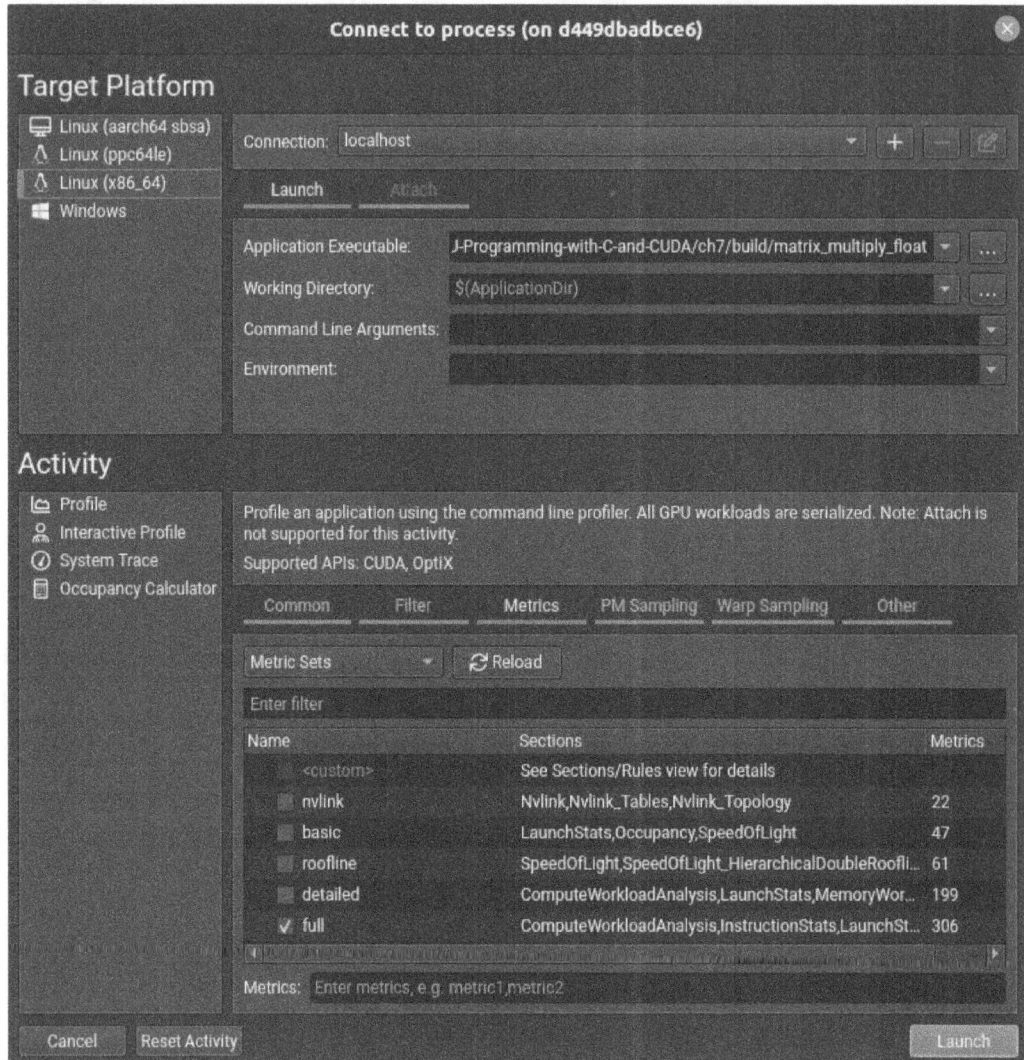

Figure 7.12: Selecting the metrics set to profile the kernel

As we can see in *Figure 7.12*, five predefined categories of metric are listed, with numbers of metrics shown in ascending order. Those categories cover the following:

- **nvlink** – this is related to peer-to-peer communication in multi-GPU systems.
- **basic** – provides the essential metrics for us to start understanding what is happening with our kernel.
- **roofline** – gathers data that helps to compare the performance achieved by our kernel and the theoretical hardware limits.
- **detailed** – provides an in-depth look at the metrics, with a good balance between information and profiling overhead (can slow down execution).
- **full** – retrieves all the performance counters available, which incurs the greatest overhead of all but provides the highest level of information.

After clicking the **Launch** button we will see the **Progress Log** as shown in *Figure 7.13*. We have to wait for processing to complete in order to get the report.

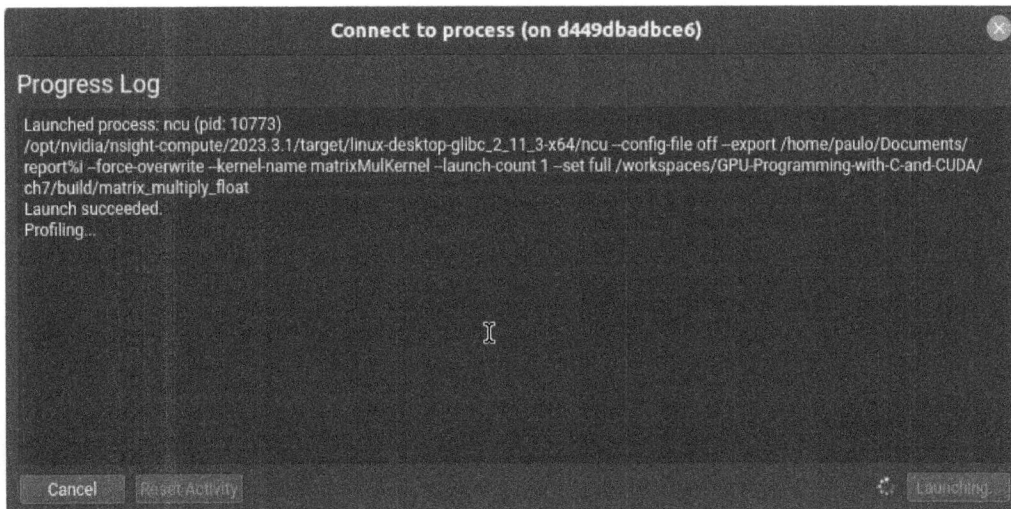

Figure 7.13: Running the profiler

After the profiling process completes we get a new screen with the report. The default screen is the summary, and in the next section we follow a step-by-step approach to understanding what the tool is telling us and how to use the techniques we've already learned for optimizing our code so as to extract the most from our hardware.

Optimizing to speed up our code

Now that we've profiled our kernel we have our first report, which provides the information we need to optimize our code. In *Figure 7.14* we see the basic information resulting from the execution we specified. We see the time it took to execute the kernel of the current session, and we can also see the launch configuration that was used: (125,125,1) blocks of (16,16,1) threads.

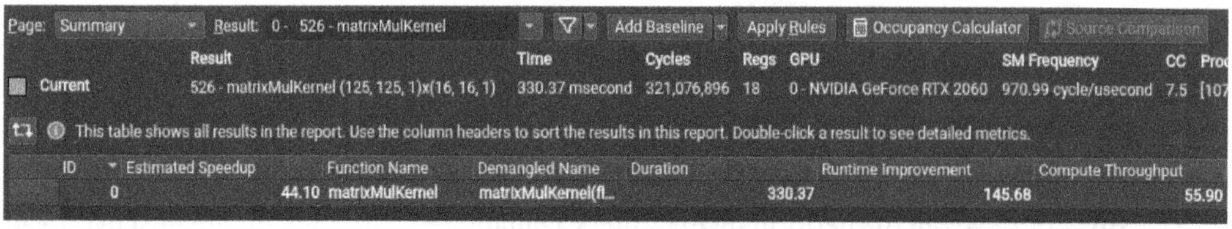

Figure 7.14: The summary of profiling the kernel

We also find, on the **Summary** page, a list of recommendations based on what the tool found out about our code that could be improved, as shown in *Figure 7.15*. However, we need to look at the details page to understand the recommendations in depth.

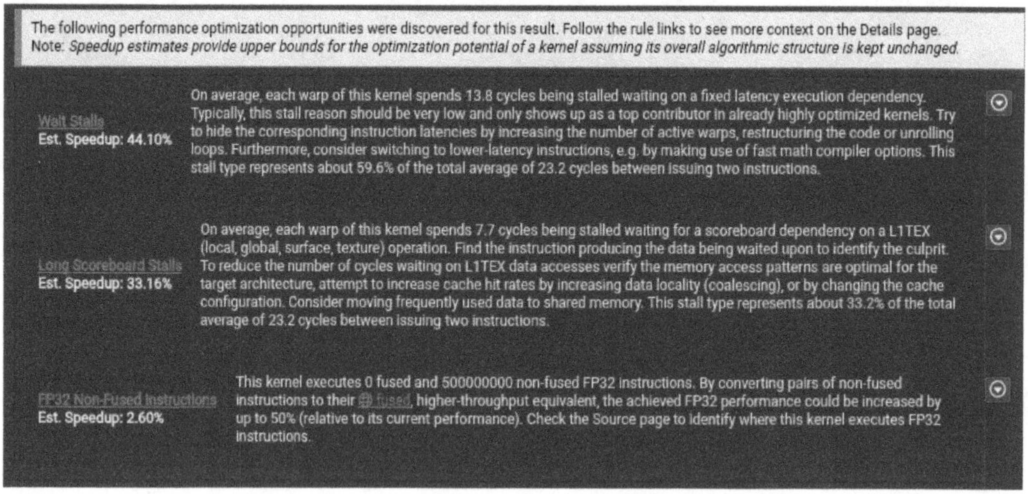

Figure 7.15: The recommendations for the kernel

We do this by selecting the **Details** page on the top left corner of the report, as shown in *Figure 7.16*.

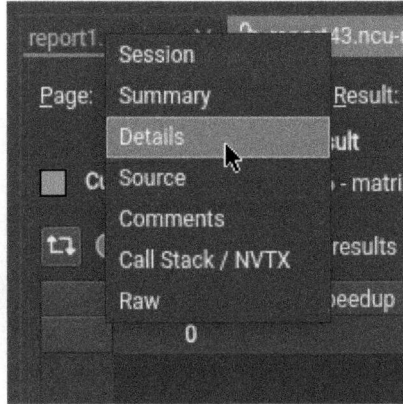

Figure 7.16: Selecting the Details page

We then reach the **Details** page, where we have sections that organize the collected metrics, as shown in *Figure 7.17*.

The first section is **GPU Speed of Light Throughput**, where we can see a dropdown in the top right side of the screen. Initially it is disabled, as can be seen in *Figure 7.17*. We have to open the section to be able to select from the available information.

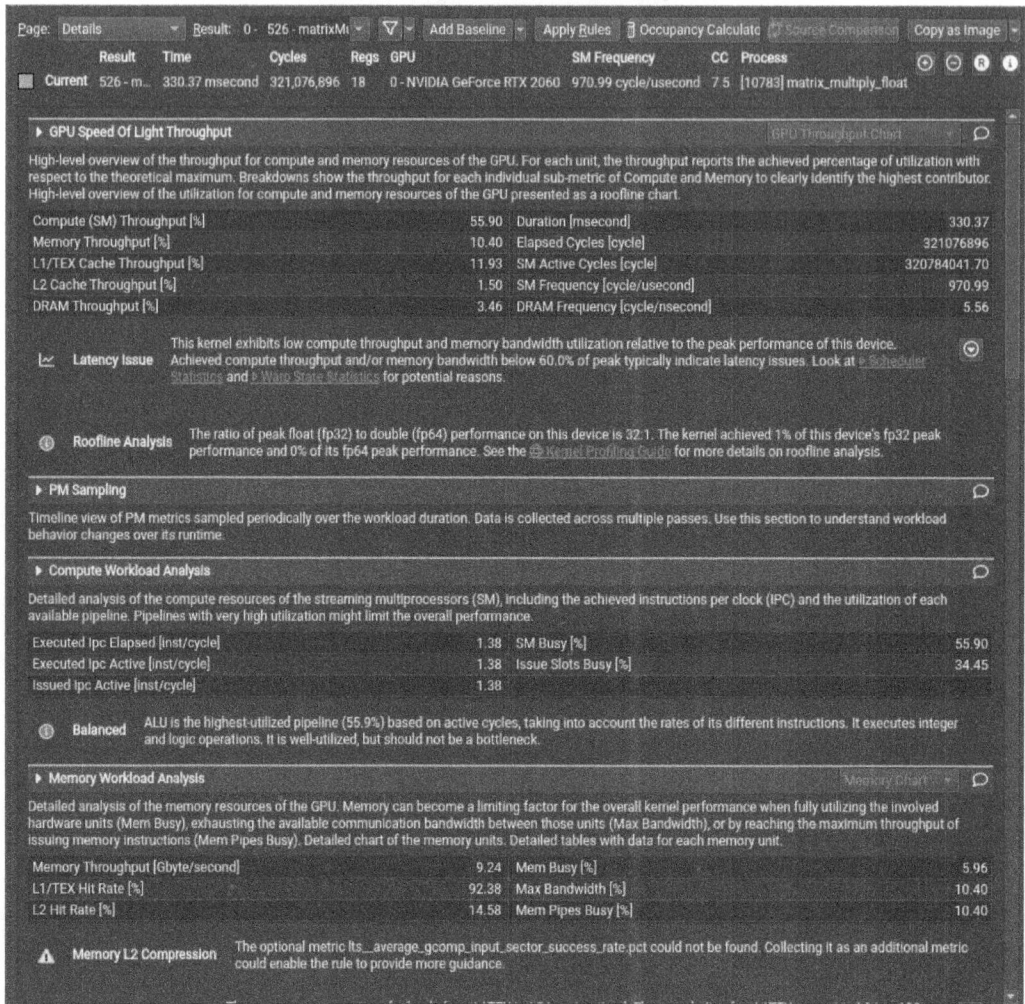

Page: Details ⌄ Result: 0 - 526 - matrixM ⌄ ▽ ⌄ Add Baseline ⌄ Apply Rules 🗐 Occupancy Calculato Source Comparison Copy as Image ⌄ ⊕ ⊖ Ⓡ ❶

	Result	Time	Cycles	Regs	GPU	SM Frequency	CC	Process
☐ Current	526 - m...	330.37 msecond	321,076,896	18	0 - NVIDIA GeForce RTX 2060	970.99 cycle/usecond	7.5	[10783] matrix_multiply_float

▶ GPU Speed Of Light Throughput   GPU Throughput Chart ⌄ 🔎

High-level overview of the throughput for compute and memory resources of the GPU. For each unit, the throughput reports the achieved percentage of utilization with respect to the theoretical maximum. Breakdowns show the throughput for each individual sub-metric of Compute and Memory to clearly identify the highest contributor. High-level overview of the utilization for compute and memory resources of the GPU presented as a roofline chart.

Compute (SM) Throughput [%]	55.90	Duration [msecond]	330.37
Memory Throughput [%]	10.40	Elapsed Cycles [cycle]	321076896
L1/TEX Cache Throughput [%]	11.93	SM Active Cycles [cycle]	320784041.70
L2 Cache Throughput [%]	1.50	SM Frequency [cycle/usecond]	970.99
DRAM Throughput [%]	3.46	DRAM Frequency [cycle/nsecond]	5.56

〰 **Latency Issue**   This kernel exhibits low compute throughput and memory bandwidth utilization relative to the peak performance of this device. Achieved compute throughput and/or memory bandwidth below 60.0% of peak typically indicate latency issues. Look at ▷ Scheduler Statistics and ▷ Warp State Statistics for potential reasons.   ⊙

ⓘ **Roofline Analysis**   The ratio of peak float (fp32) to double (fp64) performance on this device is 32:1. The kernel achieved 1% of this device's fp32 peak performance and 0% of its fp64 peak performance. See the ⊕ Kernel Profiling Guide for more details on roofline analysis.

▶ PM Sampling   🔎

Timeline view of PM metrics sampled periodically over the workload duration. Data is collected across multiple passes. Use this section to understand workload behavior changes over its runtime.

▶ Compute Workload Analysis   🔎

Detailed analysis of the compute resources of the streaming multiprocessors (SM), including the achieved instructions per clock (IPC) and the utilization of each available pipeline. Pipelines with very high utilization might limit the overall performance.

Executed Ipc Elapsed [inst/cycle]	1.38	SM Busy [%]	55.90
Executed Ipc Active [inst/cycle]	1.38	Issue Slots Busy [%]	34.45
Issued Ipc Active [inst/cycle]	1.38		

ⓘ **Balanced**   ALU is the highest-utilized pipeline (55.9%) based on active cycles, taking into account the rates of its different instructions. It executes integer and logic operations. It is well-utilized, but should not be a bottleneck.

▶ Memory Workload Analysis   Memory Chart ⌄ 🔎

Detailed analysis of the memory resources of the GPU. Memory can become a limiting factor for the overall kernel performance when fully utilizing the involved hardware units (Mem Busy), exhausting the available communication bandwidth between those units (Max Bandwidth), or by reaching the maximum throughput of issuing memory instructions (Mem Pipes Busy). Detailed chart of the memory units. Detailed tables with data for each memory unit.

Memory Throughput [Gbyte/second]	9.24	Mem Busy [%]	5.96
L1/TEX Hit Rate [%]	92.38	Max Bandwidth [%]	10.40
L2 Hit Rate [%]	14.58	Mem Pipes Busy [%]	10.40

⚠ **Memory L2 Compression**   The optional metric lts__average_gcomp_input_sector_success_rate.pct could not be found. Collecting it as an additional metric could enable the rule to provide more guidance.

Figure 7.17: Details page for the current profiling session

The chart that we want to access is the Roofline, which shows the performance our code has achieved so far. As we can see in *Figure 7.18*, a circle indicates current performance.

This chart presents three important lines, two of which are horizontal. The lower line is the limit for double-precision floating point operations, while the higher is the limit of the single-precision floating point operations. The diagonal line represents the memory limit, and indicates that if our circle has bumped more on the left-hand side of the chart it is probably being limited by the memory access patterns, while if it is bumping more on the right-hand side of the chart it is being limited by the computation being performed. Remember that we have hardware to process integer operations, as well as single-precision and double-precision floating point operations. If we use a mix of these our arithmetic intensity will increase.

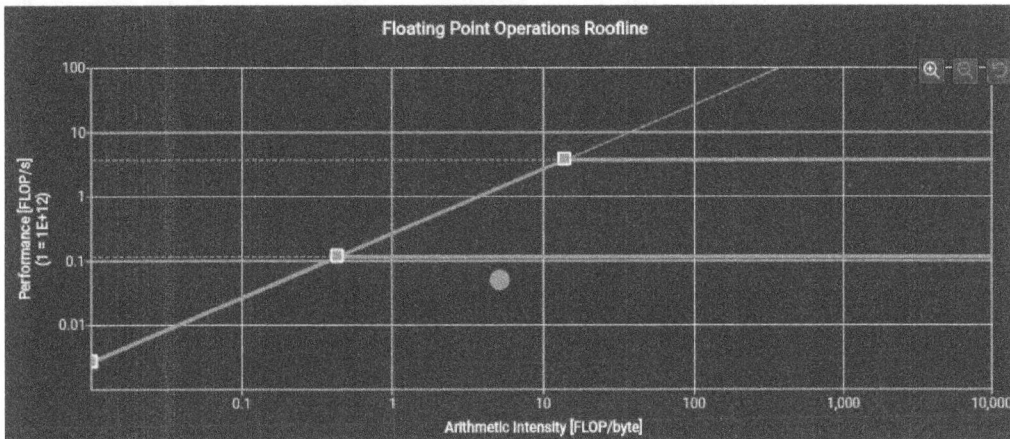

Figure 7.18: Roofline for the kernel

Our first execution was the basic matrix multiplication algorithm compiled with **Debug configuration** – meaning no optimizations at all! As we can see in the *Figure 7.18*, the circle representing the arithmetic intensity of our code is in the middle of the chart, so we can improve on both memory and computations.

The next chart that we are going to look at is the **Memory Chart**, which is found in the **Memory Workload Analysis** section. This chart is important because it shows us how memory is used by our application.

As we see in *Figure 7.19*, our kernel only accesses global memory, which is the slowest type of memory in the GPU memory hierarchy. Let's keep in mind that GPU global memory is off-chip, meaning that it is connected to executing cores via a bus, which causes big delays when we need to access many times. That is why our recommendations mentioned **Long Scoreboard Stalls** back in *Figure 7.15*; it mentions that our kernel is waiting on L1 cache, which actually depends on the rest of the memory hierarchy.

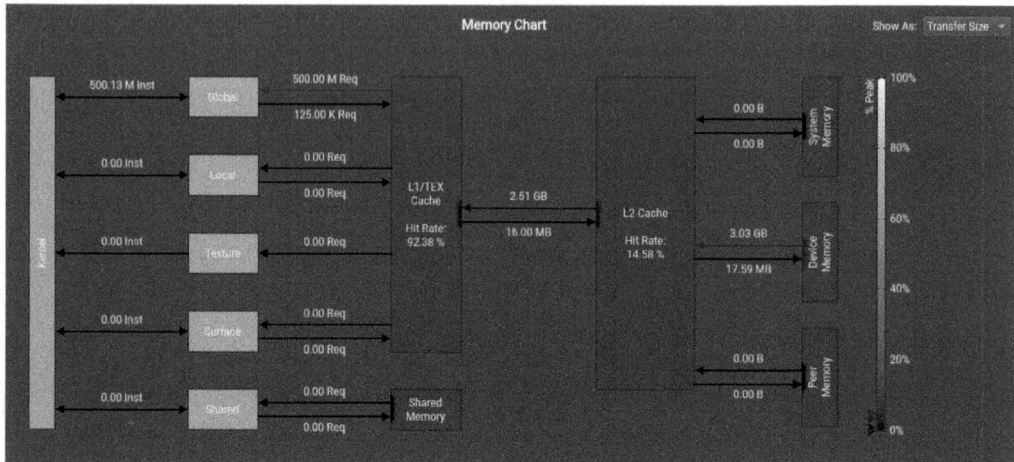

Figure 7.19: Memory Chart for the kernel

The next important section is Occupancy, which shows how our GPU resources are being used. As shown in *Figure 7.20*, we can learn what the impact would be of varying the number of threads per block, the number of registers (which are very fast for data access), and the amount of shared memory used by the threads.

In this version of our code we are not using any shared memory, so this is a hint that we should consider making changes that would help us accelerate our calculations by not going back to global memory so often.

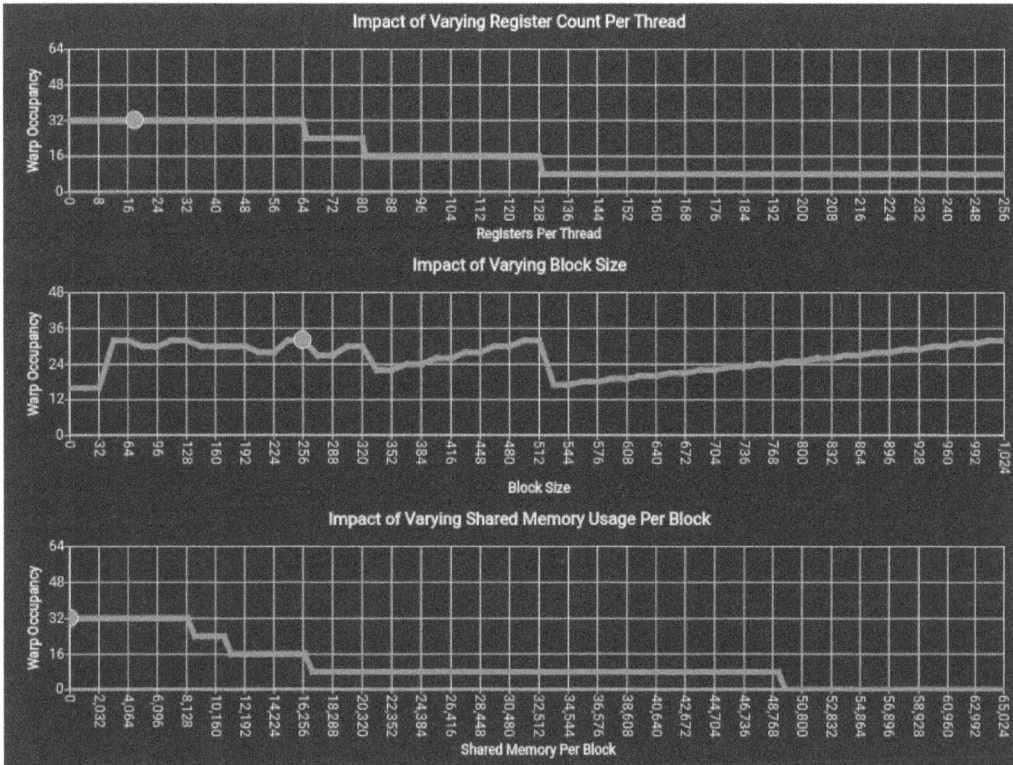

Figure 7.20: Occupancy for the kernel

The next section that we will explore is **Source Counters**, where the **Most Instructions Executed** panel enables us to click on a link to go to the **Source** page. In *Figure 7.21* we can see the line of the source code file that was most executed.

Most Instructions Executed

Location	Value
matrix_multiply_float.cu:15 (0x7f...	250,125,000
matrix_multiply_float.cu:15 (0x7f...	250,125,000
matrix_multiply_float.cu:15 (0x7f...	250,125,000
matrix_multiply_float.cu:15 (0x7f...	250,125,000
matrix_multiply_float.cu:15 (0x7f...	250,125,000

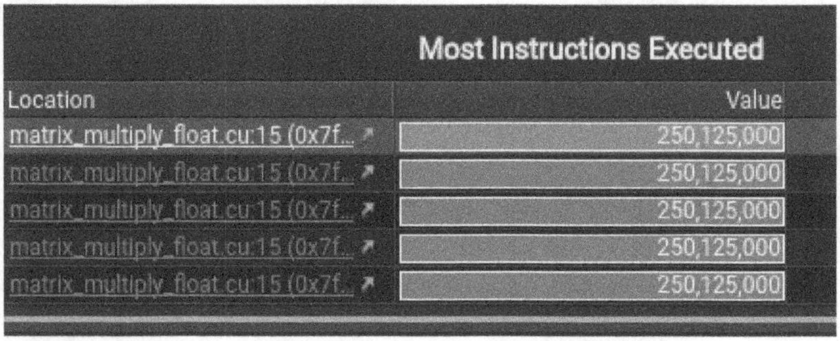

Figure 7.21: Source Counters – Most instructions Executed

Since it was compiled with Debug information we can click on this to get to the relevant line, as shown in *Figure 7.22*. An important note here is that the first time we load this page it may have problems finding our program's source file, because our executable is under the build folder whereas our source file is one folder up. So we need to click the **Resolve** button and select the correct source folder. The **Resolve** button appears the first time we load the screen, and then once the source file location is configured it becomes a **Redo Resolve** button as we can see in *Figure 7.22*.

Now, getting back to the source, we can see that line 15 is the for loop, which of course is the most executed instruction. However, our real problem is on line 16.

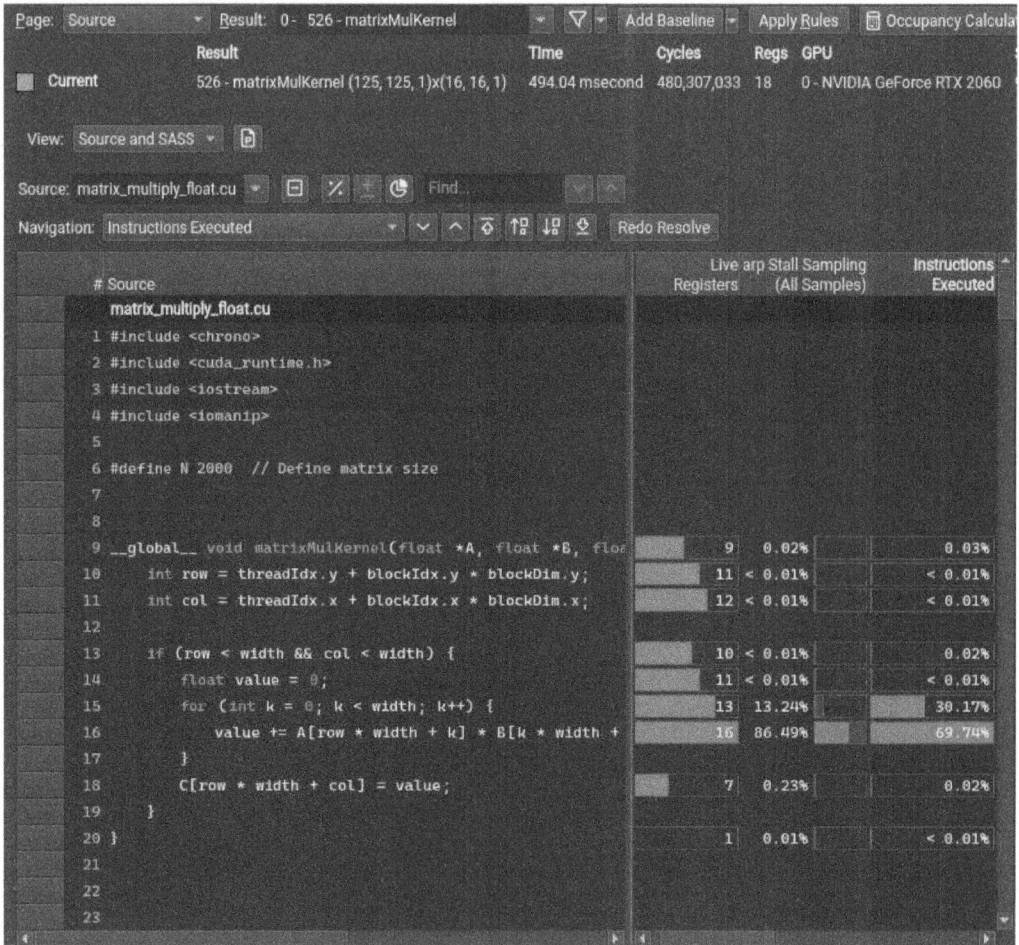

Figure 7.22: The line of code that was most executed

Line 16 is responsible for two global memory accesses and will be the focus of our optimizations in the section *Using shared memory*. However, for now let's continue exploring the tool a bit more. *Figure 7.23* presents the assembly code panel that relates to the source code we saw in *Figure 7.22*. On the screen both C++ code and assembly code are presented side by side so that we can check whether the generated code is what we expect. (We are not going to dive into assembly code for GPUs in this book, but it is important to know how to access this information if you would like to see the result of compiling our code.)

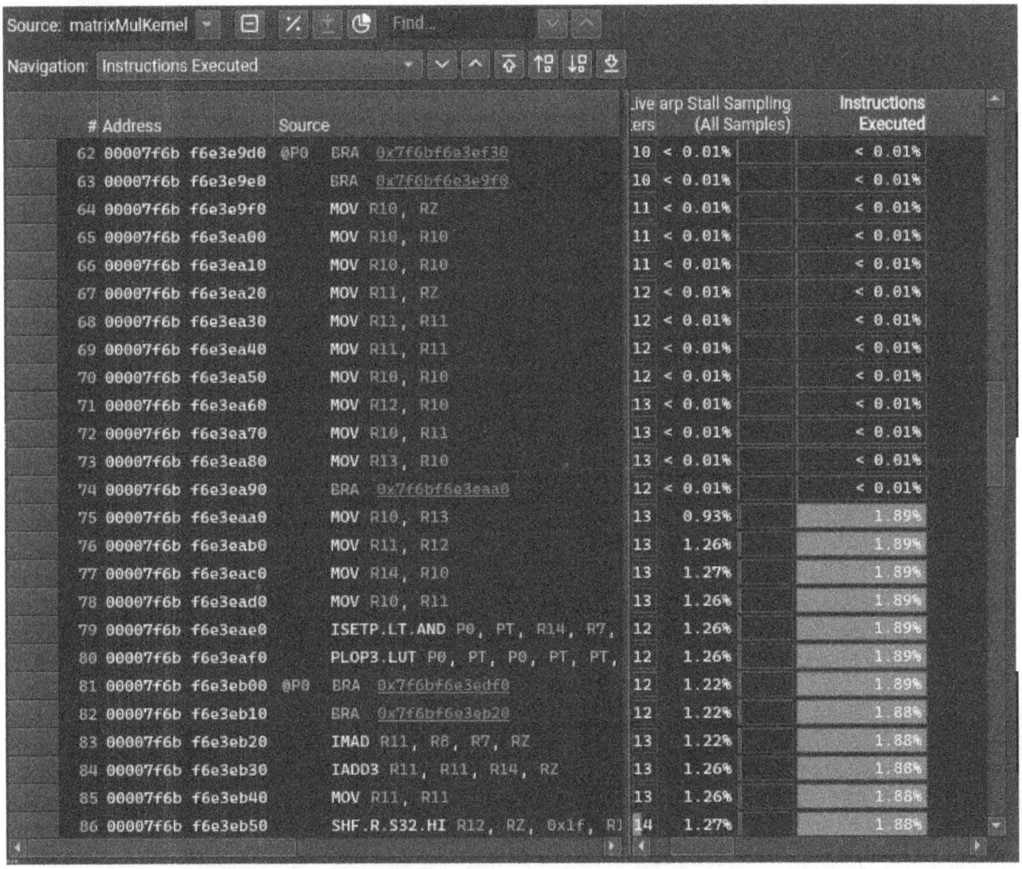

Figure 7.23: The assembly code for the selected line of code

Before we continue, let's check out another interesting tool. We can click on **Add Baseline** to retain the current value for comparison with other profiling sessions. After clicking the button we get the result seen in *Figure 7.24*.

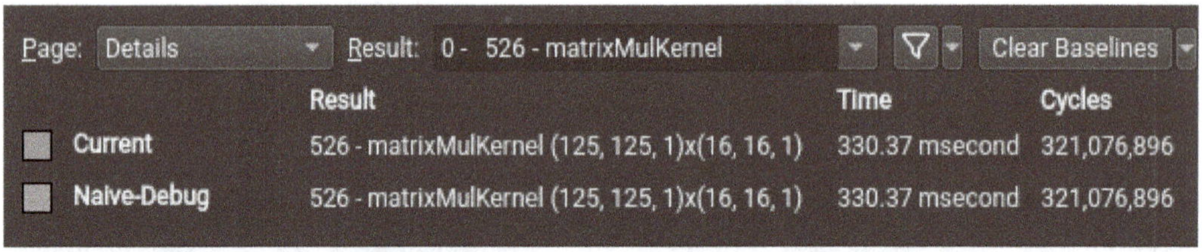

Page: Details ▼	Result: 0 - 526 - matrixMulKernel	▼	▽ ▼	Clear Baselines ▼
	Result		**Time**	**Cycles**
☐ Current	526 - matrixMulKernel (125, 125, 1)x(16, 16, 1)		330.37 msecond	321,076,896
☐ Naive-Debug	526 - matrixMulKernel (125, 125, 1)x(16, 16, 1)		330.37 msecond	321,076,896

Figure 7.24: The current execution added as a baseline

Now that we understand what to look for on the **Details** page, and we have our first baseline to compare against, let's see in the next section how to use the simplest of all possible approaches to optimizing our code: using the **Release configuration** with compiler optimization flags.

Using the Release configuration

In the previous section we profiled the basic version of our matrix multiplication kernel, which uses what we call a *naive* approach to the problem in which there are no code optimizations. The simplest approach to optimizing the code is to use the compilation flags that configure the compiler to perform optimizations.

As we are using CMake we need to configure the project to compile differently, and we do that with the following command in our VS Code terminal:

```
cmake -DCMAKE_BUILD_TYPE=Release ..
```

This changes our Makefiles so that they compile using the -O3 optimization level and do not include Debug information in the generated code. This way the compiler will try to analyze our code as much as possible, to apply small changes like unrolling loops (more about this in the forthcoming section *Using loop unroll for further improvements*) and using more registers if possible.

After the new configuration we need to run make again:

```
make
```

And after compilation, we need to run the profiler once more with this new executable, which we do by clicking on the project again and clicking the **Launch** button.

We see the result of profiling the code again with the new version in *Figure 7.25*.

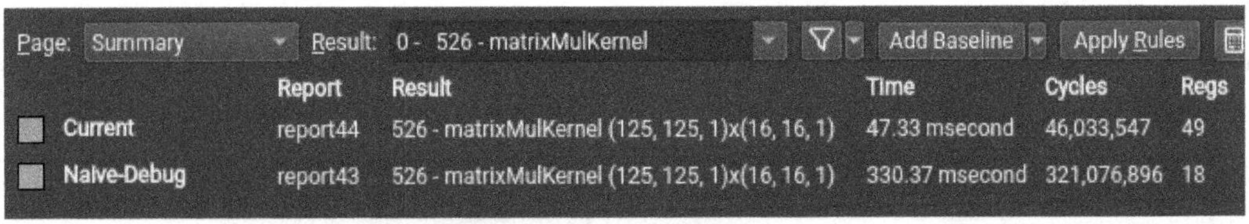

Figure 7.25: Summary for the release compilation of the same kernel

Note that the number of registers has increased and the time has dropped dramatically. Given that we only changed a simple configuration this is a pretty good start!

In *Figure 7.26* we can see that the new version has improved on performance, as reflected in the Roofline chart.

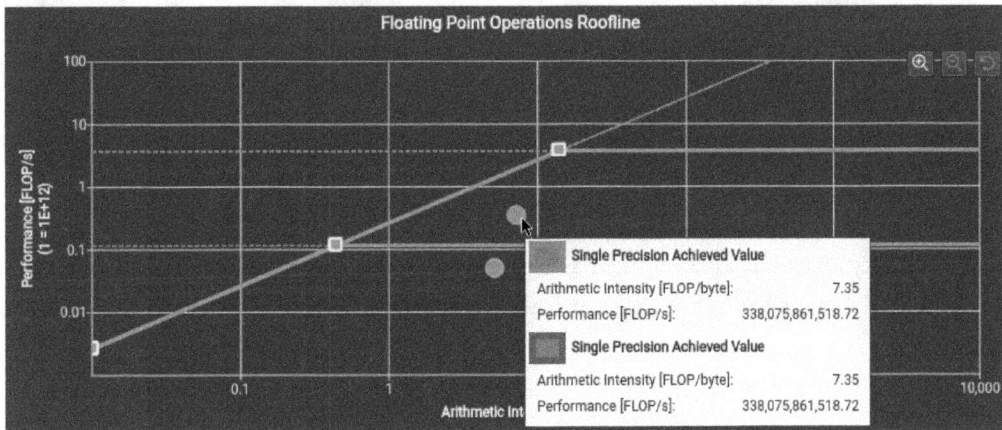

Figure 7.26: Roofline for the release kernel

Another thing that we notice, in *Figure 7.27*, is that the cache hit rate, for both L1 as well as L2, has improved, which is also responsible for the decreased execution time. But again there was no use of shared memory, because this cannot be directed by the compiler alone but instead demands a different algorithm.

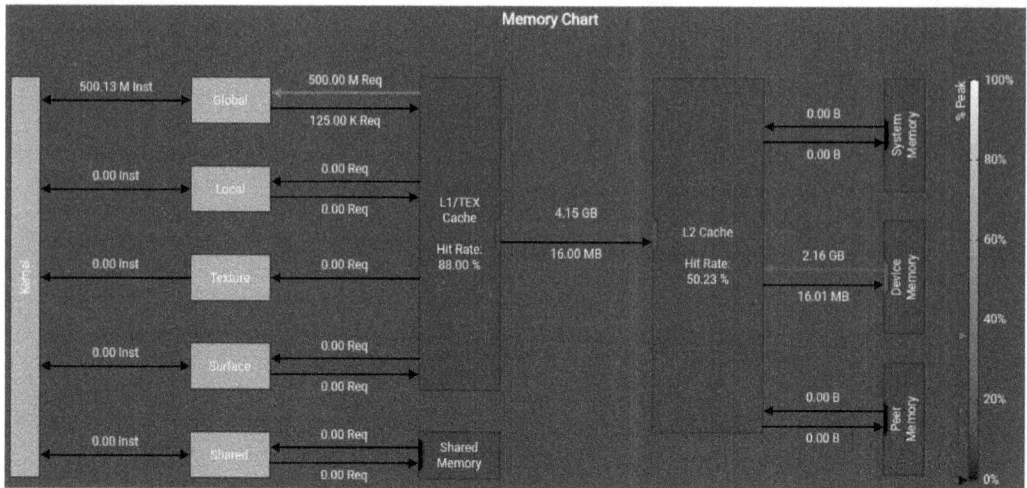

Figure 7.27: Memory Chart for release kernel

Our Occupancy chart has also changed as we now have more registers being used, but again the number of threads has not changed and nor has the use of shared memory, as we can see in *Figure 7.28*.

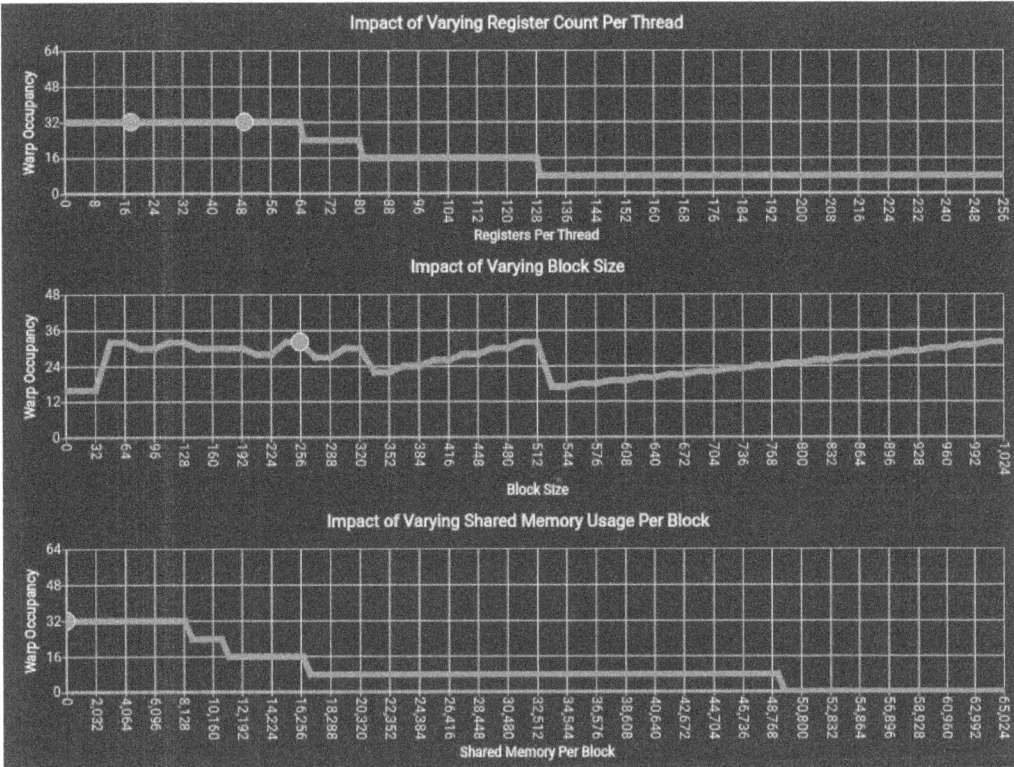

Figure 7.28: Occupancy for release kernel

Now if we take a closer look at *Figure 7.29* we see the tool tip indicating that no source information is available. The reason for this is that we did not include debug information during code generation.

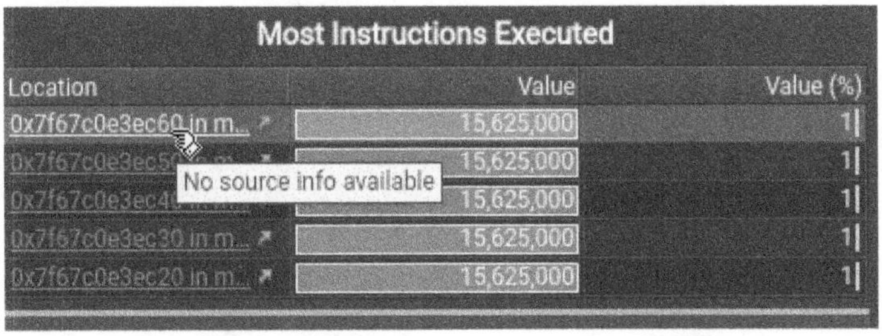

Figure 7.29: Source counters for the release kernel

One immediate effect of using the Release configuration is that we lose debug information from the source code, making it much harder to understand what the next steps of optimization could be. However, it is important for our study to compare the impacts of using compiler flags before proceeding with code changes. We can see that by simply changing the configuration an incredible optimization was achieved.

Now, in the next section, let's apply our first real code optimization: changing the code to use shared memory.

Using shared memory to improve time

The first real optimization that we'll apply will be to use shared memory to improve the execution time. This will change our kernel drastically, so let's check the code first. This code uses the same approach that we can find in the CUDA Toolkit Samples at `https://github.com/NVIDIA/cuda-samples/blob/master/Samples/0_Introduction/matrixMul/matrixMul.cu`. This is based on a research paper presented in 2008 [1], so the strategy is not something new.

```
#define TILE 16
__global__ void matrixMulKernel_shared
        (const float* A, const float* B, float* C, int n){
    __shared__ float Asub[TILE][TILE];
    __shared__ float Bsub[TILE][TILE];
    int tx = threadIdx.x;
    int ty = threadIdx.y;
    int row = ty + blockIdx.y * blockDim.y;
    int col = tx + blockIdx.x * blockDim.x;
    float sum = 0.0f;

    for(int i=0; i < (n + blockDim.x - 1) / blockDim.x; i++)
    {
        if (row < n && (i * blockDim.x + tx) < n)
            Asub[ty][tx] = A[row * n + i * blockDim.x + tx];
        else
            Asub[ty][tx] = 0.0f;


        if (col < n && (i * blockDim.y + ty) < n)
            Bsub[ty][tx] = B[(i * blockDim.y + ty) * n + col];
        else
```

```
            Bsub[ty][tx] = 0.0f;


        __syncthreads();

        for (int k = 0; k < blockDim.x; k++) {
            sum += Asub[ty][k] * Bsub[k][tx];
        }


        __syncthreads();
    }

    if (row < n && col < n)
        C[row * n + col] = sum;
}
```

The first thing to mention about this code is that our launch configuration is setting a 2D block with a 2D grid; that is why we use tx and ty to identify our threads. Also, we use block dimensions to calculate which row and column a thread is working with. Each thread will handle one element of the resulting *C* matrix, but to calculate that it will need to load many elements from global memory into the block-local shared memory.

To do that we have created two local submatrices that can hold up to 256 elements of the corresponding original matrix. We have 256 elements since TILE is our constant defined as 16 and TILE x TILE = 256.

Our main for loop has its limits calculated by dividing the width of the matrix by the block dimension. In addition note that resource allocation within the GPU may not match the size of our data structures. That is why we need to keep track of boundaries and fill padding positions with zeros.

We now do something that we talked about in *Chapter 5*: prefetch data into shared memory for reuse. Let's walk through how this is done.

Our local shared memory is limited, so we have to select a few elements from global memory. Also, we have to remember that in global memory, our matrices are stored as contiguous arrays so we have to calculate what the actual index is for a given element. We can calculate the position based on the start of each row, given by row * n, and once we find the starting position we have to find the current element that we want to copy with i * blockDim.x + tx. Remember that tx is our index for this thread and i is incremented until we reach the limit n/blockDim.x of the matrix. (Here we simplified the limit just for sake of clarity, but the actual code divides it in a way that is already familiar to us, so that the resulting value is equal to or greater than a multiple of the width).

But what does this mean? All this calculation allows the threads to access different positions in the global memory (remember that tx is different!), and since we multiply i by blockDim.x to find the tile we are loading it is as if we were moving a camera over a really long drawing and taking snapshots. Pretty clever right?

We use the same approach to fill our local sub-matrix *B*, so we do not need to discuss the calculations again.

After loading our first set of tiles we need to make sure that all threads have completed their work, so we issue a __syncthreads() command to make them all get together. After this, we know we can perform calculations because our shared memory is filled.

Next we use another for loop that processes, for each thread, a piece of the calculation. We do not have to worry because the sum variable is local to each thread, so we will have multiple variables in play, each one storing the partial sum for a given element of the resulting matrix. On each iteration of the main loop, the sum variable will be incremented by one more partial sum, until we reach the final result.

Once all the tiles have been processed our threads will save their results to global memory, as long as the values for row and col are within the boundaries of the matrix width n.

After all these changes we need to compile our code again, but first we need to go back to our Debug configuration by using:

```
cmake -DCMAKE_BUILD_TYPE=Debug ..
```

And again build the application with:

```
make
```

This is a necessary step because using a Debug configuration allows us to get much more information from the code. Now let's analyze this version of the code with our profiler, by clicking on the project inside NVIDIA Nsight Compute and clicking the **Launch** button again. We can see the current session in *Figure 7.30*.

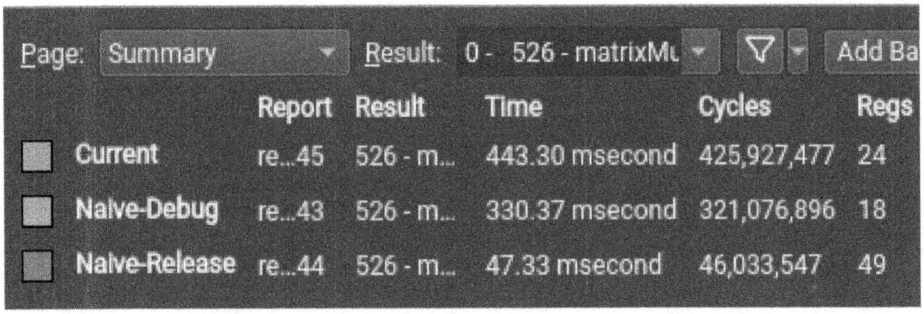

Figure 7.30: Summary for shared memory kernel

Notice that it took longer to execute this version than the naive one. This might seem odd, but it is due to us compiling in Debug mode. However, we can see that the number of registers has increased, so optimizations are on their way!

Next let's take a look at our Roofline chart, in *Figure 7.31*.

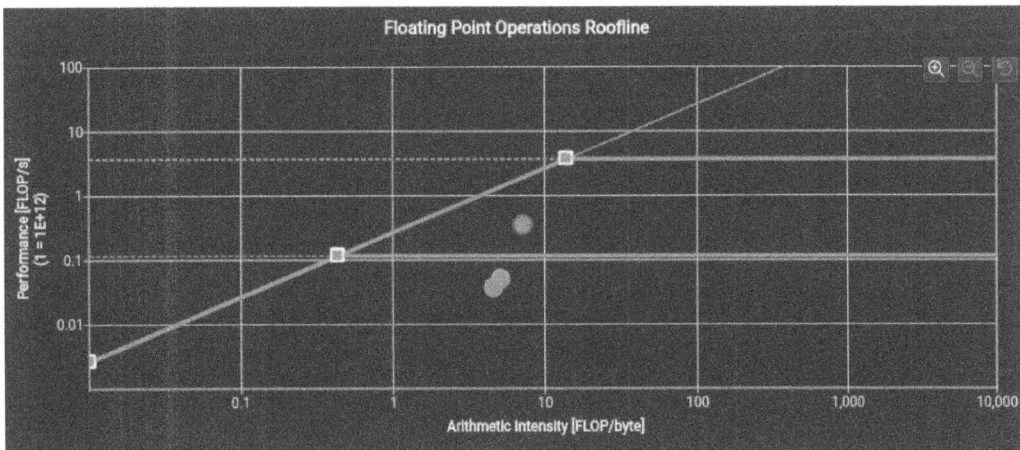

Figure 7.31: Roofline for the shared memory kernel

The Roofline chart gives us another surprise, as the new version performs below the original naive implementation. The higher circle is the release version, the slightly lower one is our current version in debug mode and in between is the naive implementation. However, we notice a drastic change in our Memory Chart, shown in *Figure 7.32*.

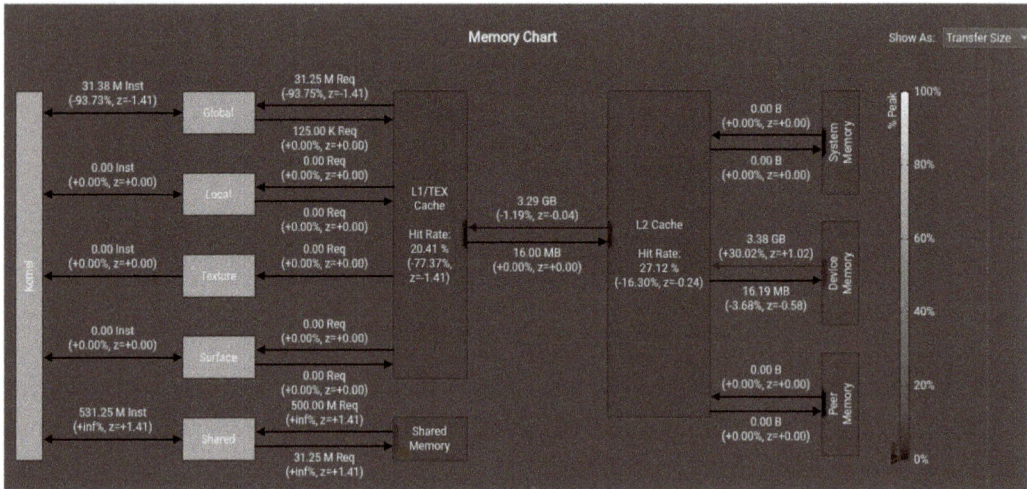

Figure 7.32: Memory chart for shared memory kernel

What we notice is that the many accesses that were being made directly to global memory are now focused on shared memory, which is much faster. Here it is worth pausing for consideration. While we are prefetching data from global memory, it may seem that it is not worth the trouble of dealing with shared memory, since we have to access global memory anyway. However, there is a catch here. Since we are loading data to shared memory, we need to make a load from global memory first for each element of the matrix, but for subsequent computations – remember that for each row we compute against *all* columns – data is already present in shared memory, and this boosts our access dramatically. Notice that the majority of the accesses were redirected to this block in our Memory Chart.

If we take a look at our Occupancy we will notice that the changes were more registers as well as use of shared memory, as we can see in *Figure 7.33*.

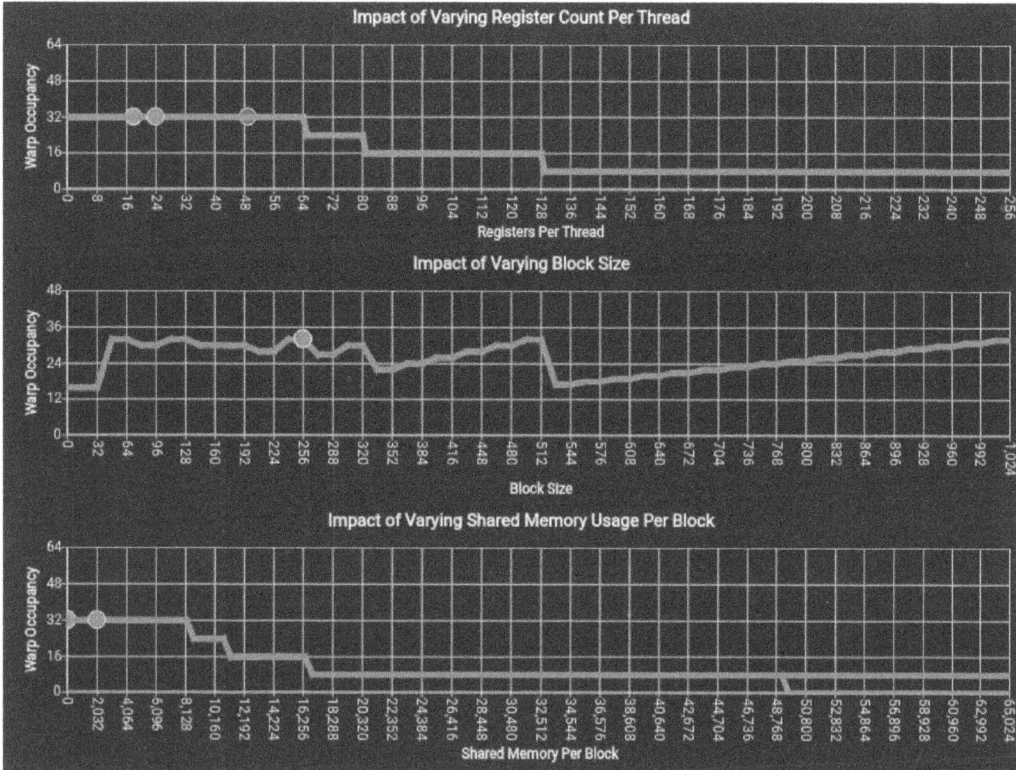

Figure 7.33: Occupancy for shared memory kernel

By using the Debug configuration it seems that we are not improving when considering the execution time, but we have to consider all the dimensions on which we are applying optimizations to understand the details.

Next let's unroll our partial sum calculation loop to improve things a little bit further.

Using loop unroll for further improvements

Loop unrolling is a technique for expanding the calculations performed within a loop so that the application benefits from better use of registers and parallelization of more instructions. However, doing this manually can be confusing, so we will rely on **compiler directives** so that the compiler performs this for us. Let's take a look at the code.

```
#pragma unroll
for (int k = 0; k < blockDim.x; k++) {
    sum += Asub[ty][k] * Bsub[k][tx];
}
```

New here is the use of #pragma unroll, which asks the compiler to unroll this for us.

Now we do not need to perform the CMake configuration again, but we do need to build the application by using the make command as before.

In *Figure 7.34* we see a summary comparison of our different versions, all of them now in Debug configuration.

	Report	Result	Time	Cycles	Regs
Current	report46	526 - matrixMulKernel (125, 125, 1)x(16, 16, 1)	443.31 msecond	425,932,166	24
Naïve-Debug	report43	526 - matrixMulKernel (125, 125, 1)x(16, 16, 1)	330.37 msecond	321,076,896	18
SharedMem-Debug	report45	526 - matrixMulKernel (125, 125, 1)x(16, 16, 1)	443.30 msecond	425,927,477	24

Figure 7.34: Summary for loop unroll kernel

Following our flow, we will take a look at the Roofline chart (*Figure 7.35*).

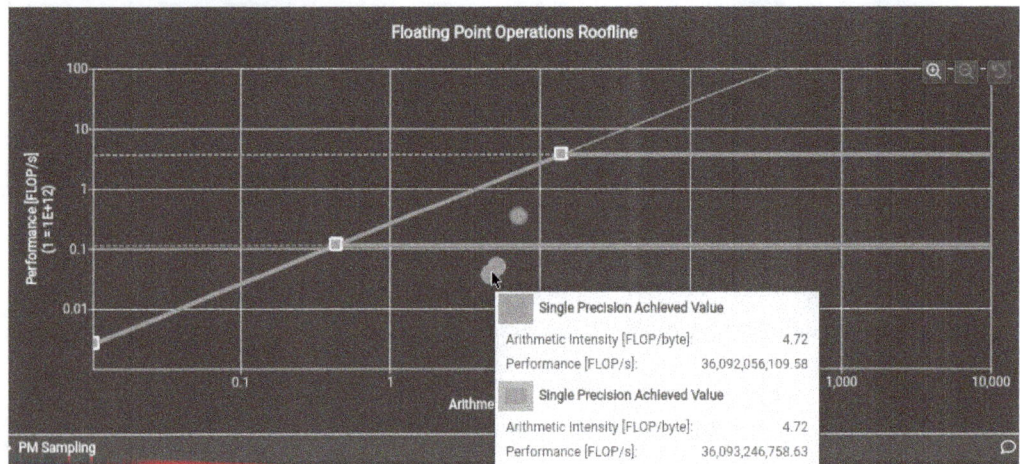

Figure 7.35: Roofline for loop unroll kernel

The current session matches the previous one in terms of performance, but remember that we are in a Debug configuration which limits the effectiveness of optimizations.

Next stop is the Memory Chart, seen in *Figure 7.36*, where we also notice that there is not much difference from *Figure 7.32*.

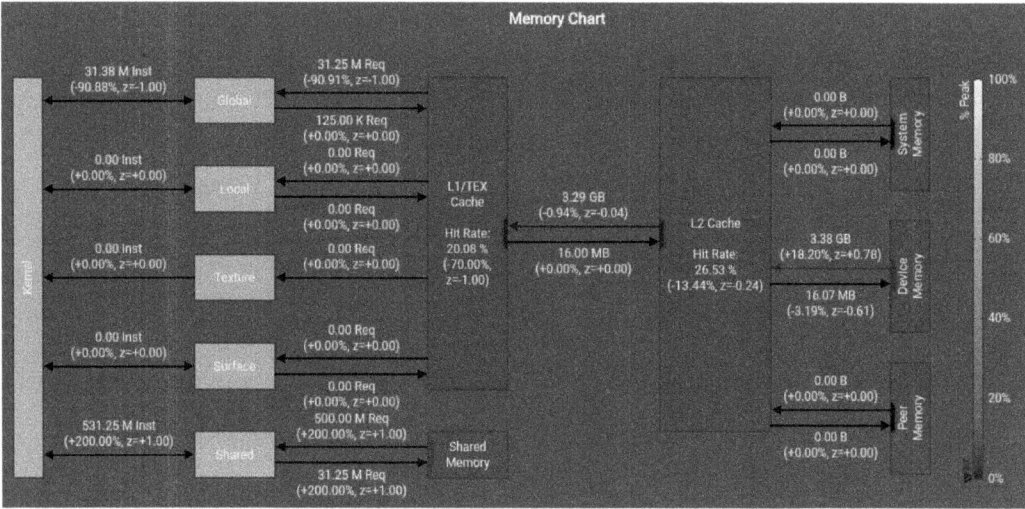

Figure 7.36: Memory Chart for loop unroll kernel

Moving on to Occupancy, we find that (as expected) it is the same as before, because we did not change the amount of shared memory or the number of registers.

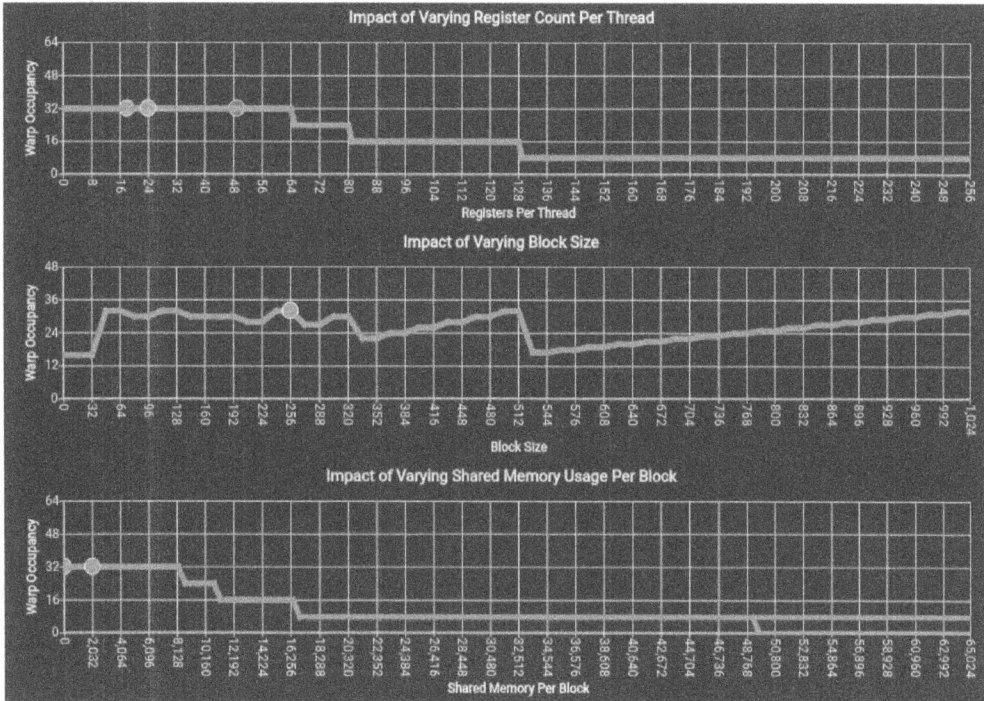

Figure 7.37: Occupancy for loop unroll kernel

Every optimization cycle will lead us through the same steps, and we have to take note of the hints and recommendations provided by the tool. Now that we are using shared memory and have unrolled our loop we could pay attention to one further recommendation. Under **Instruction Statistics**, the tool mentions that we are not making use of fused instructions (see *Figure 7.38*).

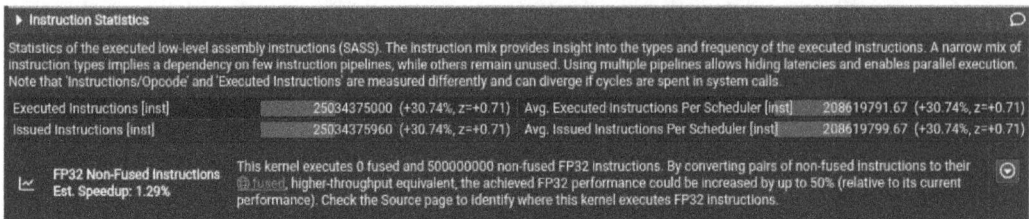

Figure 7.38: A new recommendation for loop unroll kernel

Fused instructions are a special type of instruction that together perform a multiplication and an addition. This improves the overall performance, and we discuss it in the next section.

Using fused instructions as the next step

One common example is the fused multiply-add (FMA) instruction. This operation performs a multiplication and an addition in one step. The key advantage of FMA is that it avoids intermediate rounding between multiplication and addition steps. This means the operation is not only faster (since it uses a single instruction) but also more precise, as it reduces the accumulation of rounding errors. In essence, FMA allows the GPU to maximize its computational efficiency and accuracy, making it a critical tool for high-performance tasks.

Our code change is simple this time.

```
#pragma unroll
for (int k = 0; k < blockDim.x; k++) {
    sum = fmaf(Asub[ty][k], Bsub[k][tx], sum);
}
```

Again we don't need to perform the CMake configuration, but we need to build the application by using the make command as before.

In *Figure 7.39* we can see the summary comparison of our versions, all of them now in Debug configuration.

	Report	Result	Time	Cycles	Regs
Current	report47	526 - matrixMulKernel (125, 125, 1)x(16, 16, 1)	495.03 msecond	475,384,968	33
SharedMem-Debug	report45	526 - matrixMulKernel (125, 125, 1)x(16, 16, 1)	443.30 msecond	425,927,477	24
Unroll-Debug	report46	526 - matrixMulKernel (125, 125, 1)x(16, 16, 1)	443.31 msecond	425,932,166	24

Figure 7.39: Summary for fused instructions kernel

We notice that the number of registers used has increased and the time has also increased, which was not expected – but again we are in Debug mode.

Figure 7.40 shows the Roofline chart.

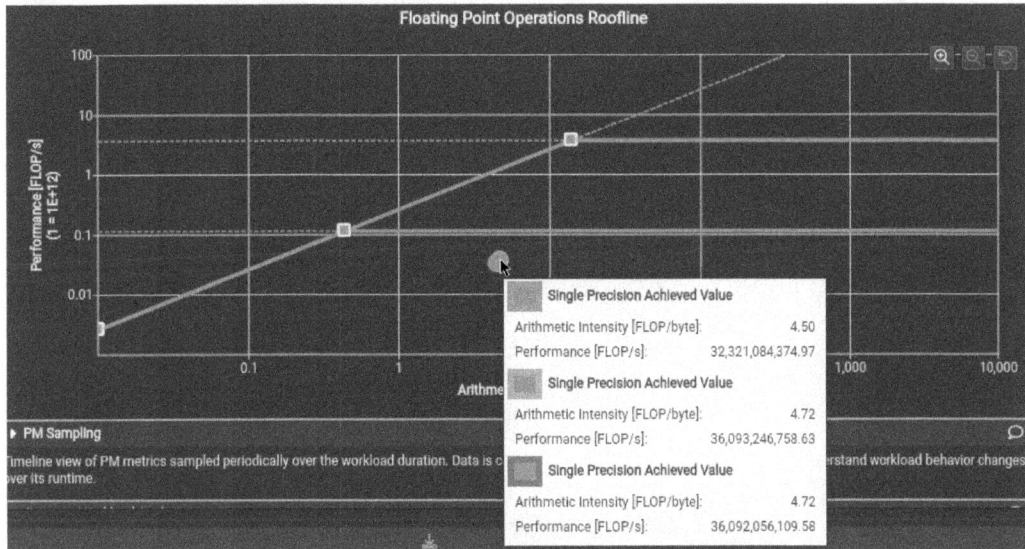

Figure 7.40: Roofline for fused instructions kernel

The current session is slightly below the previous ones, but again this is related to use the Debug configuration.

Next, we analyse our Memory Chart (*Figure 7.41*).

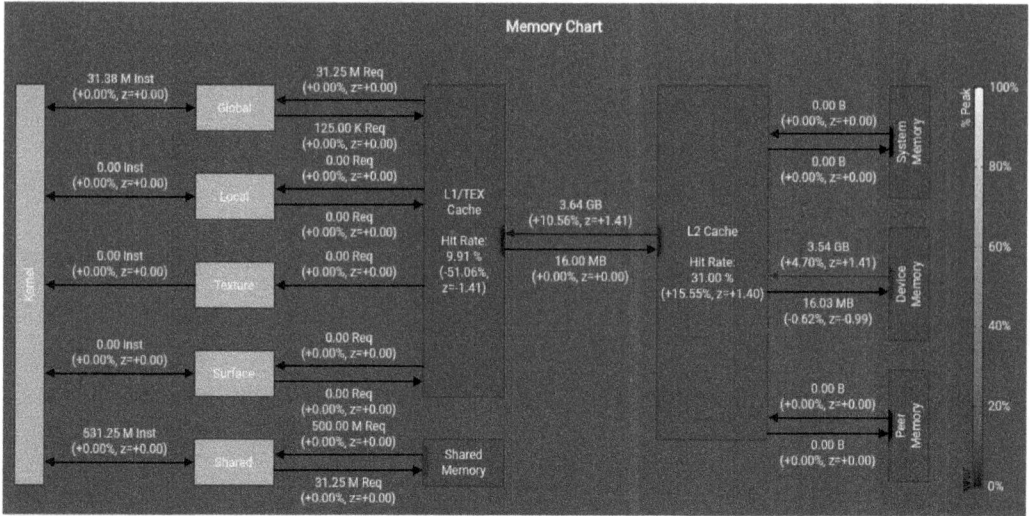

Figure 7.41: Memory Chart for fused instructions kernel

Our change did not result in any specific improvements in memory usage, but it did not worsen things either.

Now let's check the Occupancy, in *Figure 7.42*.

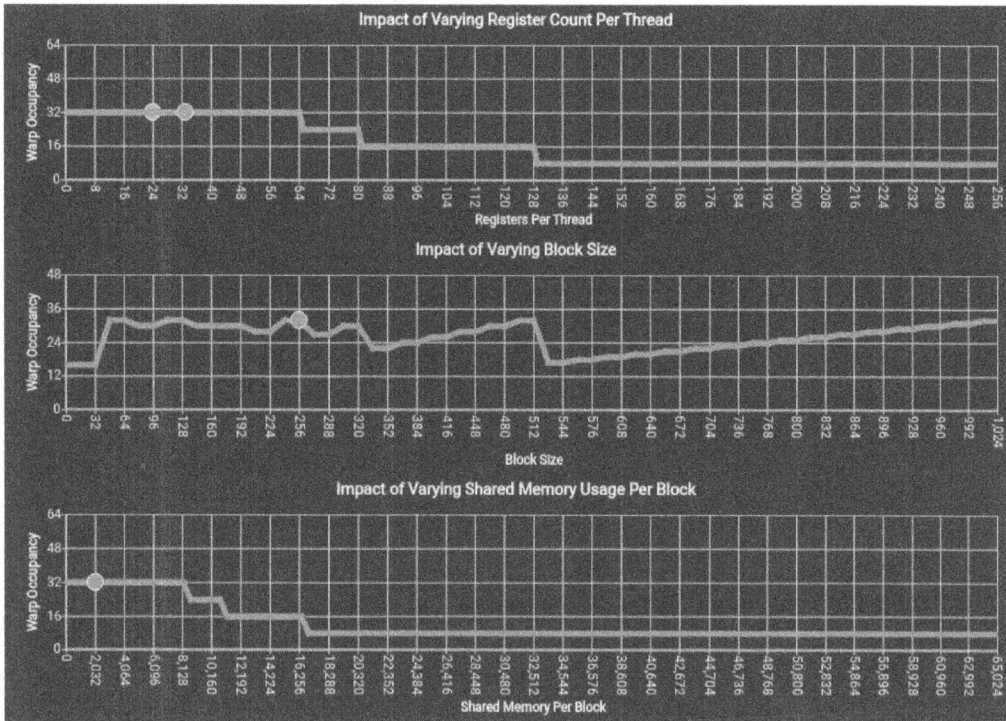

Figure 7.42: Occupancy for fused instructions kernel

What we notice is that the number of registers has increased because the fused instruction makes better use of them.

Now that we have used all our strategies, let's put everything together and use the Release configuration.

Putting it all together with Release configuration

Now we do not need to change any code, but we need to reconfigure our project with the following command:

```
cmake -DCMAKE_BUILD_TYPE=Release ..
```

After that we run `make` and execute the profiler again. The results can be seen in *Figure 7.43*. Notice that the time has decreased from 47.33 milliseconds to 33.37 milliseconds, which is approximately a 42% improvement, by using the correct strategies. It shows why we needed to compare with the naive version using the Release configuration as well: it validates the idea that simply using compiler optimizations is not enough to maximize the use of our hardware resources.

Page: Summary | Result: 0 - 526 - matrixMulKernel | Clear Baselines

	Report	Result	Time	Cycles	Regs
Current	re...48	526 - matrixMulKernel (12...	33.37 msecond	32,630,266	25
Naive-Release	re...44	526 - matrixMulKernel (12...	47.33 msecond	46,033,547	49
SharedUnroll-Release	re...48	526 - matrixMulKernel (12...	33.37 msecond	32,630,266	25

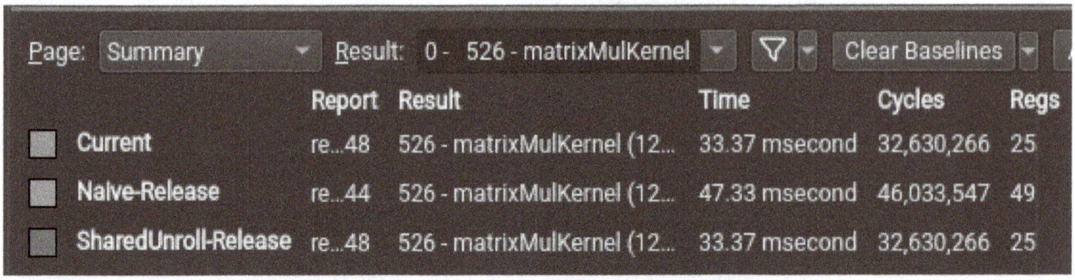

Figure 7.43: Summary for the kernel in Release version with all optimizations

Our Roofline Chart (*Figure 7.44*) shows that our current session has a greater throughput than the previous one.

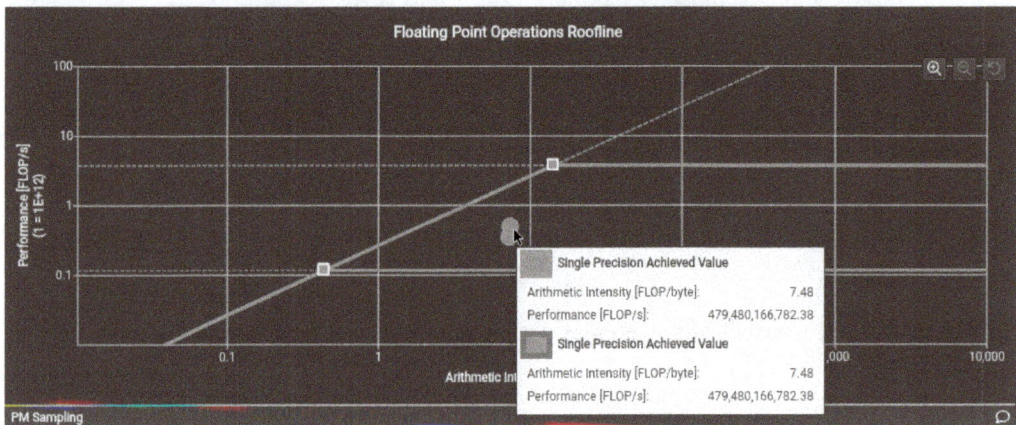

Figure 7.44: Roofline for the kernel in Release version with all optimizations

Let's check the Memory Chart too (*Figure 7.45*).

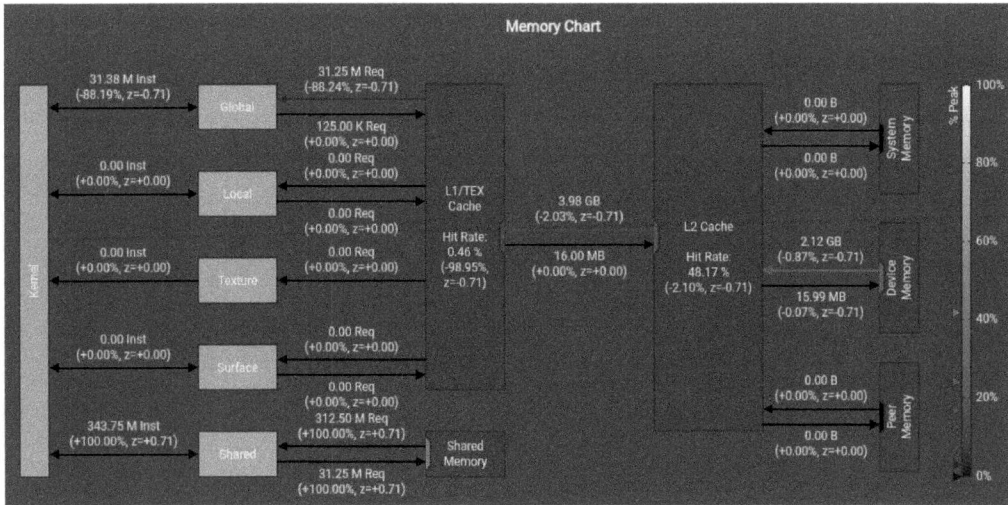

Figure 7.45: Memory Chart for the kernel in Release version with all optimizations

When we compare with the previous version we can see the use of shared memory as expected. Next let's analyse our Occupancy (*Figure 7.46*).

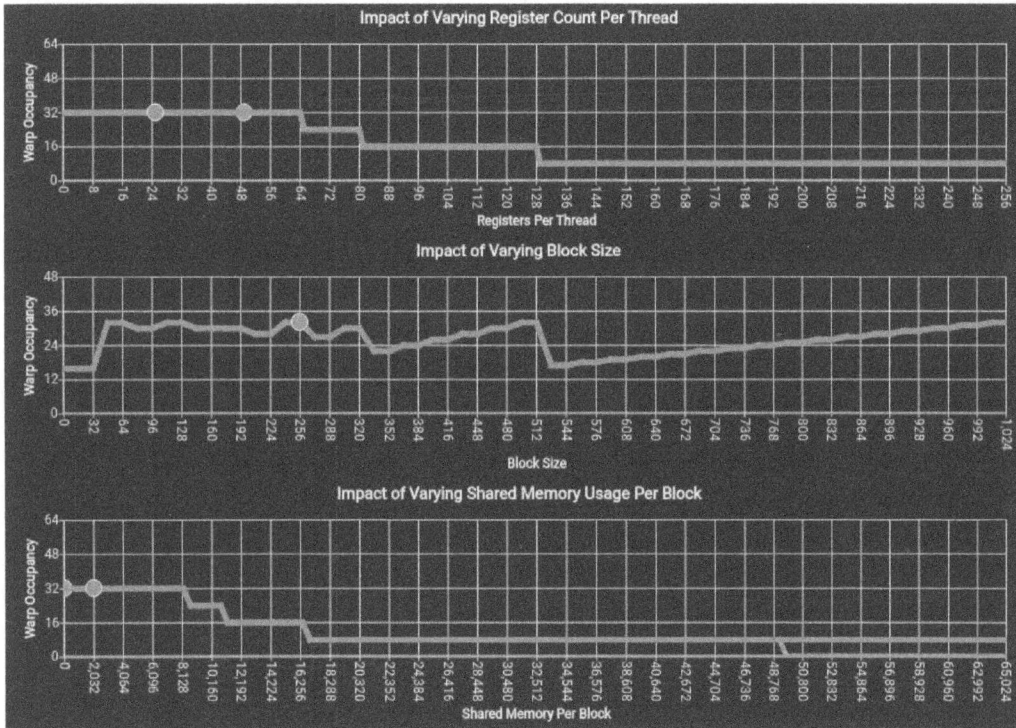

Figure 7.46: Occupancy for the kernel in Release version with all optimizations

Our current version is using 25 registers and the same shared memory that was already in place from the Debug version.

Just for comparison, let's have all our versions together on the same Roofline Chart (*Figure 7.47*).

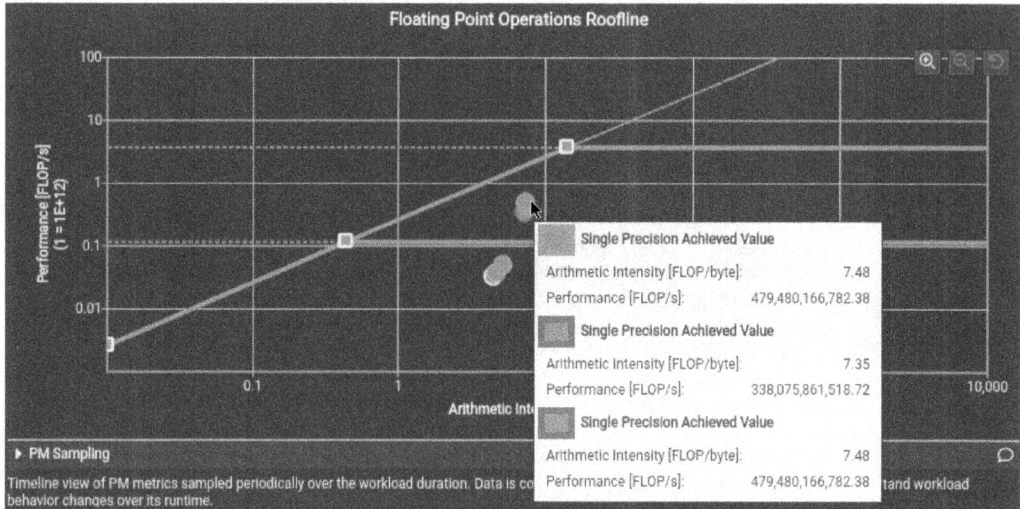

Figure 7.47: Roofline for all versions together

We can see the significance of using compiler flags, together with specific algorithms and code structures, for getting the most from our hardware.

Considering other algorithms

Before we close this chapter, we are going to look at some interesting results from other algorithms, which might seem to represent better alternatives to our first, naive implementation. Remembering the discussion about coalesced memory access from *Chapter 6*, it may seem natural to suppose that we would obtain higher performance if we changed our kernel so that each CUDA thread could process an entire row of our matrix. On the other hand, we might think that having each CUDA thread calculate an entire column would yield the worst performance possible. Let's see the code for both kernels.

```
__global__ void matrixMulKernel_row(float *A, float *B, float *C,
    int width) {
    int row = threadIdx.x + blockIdx.x * blockDim.x;
    if (row < width) {
        for (int col = 0; col < width; col++) {
            float sum = 0.0f;
```

```
        for (int i = 0; i < width; i++) {
            sum += A[row * width + i] * B[i * N + col];
        }
        C[row * N + col] = sum;
    }
  }
}
```

This is similar to the original code, but as you can see, we are accessing the matrix in a 1D pattern, with each thread responsible for a single row. Now, let's see the column-oriented version.

```
__global__ void matrixMulKernel_col(float *A, float *B, float *C,
    int width) {
    int col = threadIdx.x + blockIdx.x * blockDim.x;
    if (col < width) {
        for (int row = 0; row < width; row++) {
            float sum = 0.0f;
            for (int i = 0; i < width; i++) {
                sum += A[row * width + i] * B[i * N + col];
            }
            C[row * N + col] = sum;
        }
    }
}
```

It is also similar to our original code, but now we fix on a column for calculation and access the elements of each row.

As counterintuitive as it may sound, the column-oriented version performs better than the row-oriented version!

This deserves some commentary. First, both versions yield performance that is much worse than our original naive version, even without any optimizations. This is because both versions launch far fewer CUDA threads than our naive version, which operates with 2D indexing. Remember that CUDA will create millions of threads to process each element, and as soon as any thread gets blocked waiting for data, other threads enter for processing, which allows the processing to move forward as a whole.

Despite that, the other interesting effect is that the row-oriented version incurs more cache misses, because for each row it tries to access many different positions at each column. However, the column-oriented version incurs cache misses at each column access, but then when accessing the rows there is some opportunity for reuse of accessed values in cache.

Even if we try to apply the techniques that we studied in this chapter, these versions still will not improve things much, because they limit the number of possible threads to be allocated. Let's keep that in mind.

Summary

In this chapter we have worked our way through a variety of optimization strategies, as well as the use of the graphical profiler that is available in the CUDA toolkit. This is an essential tool to help attack the hot spots in our kernels so that we use our time as effectively and efficiently as possible.

In the next chapter we will learn another strategy to accelerate our code: overlaying memory transfers with kernel execution.

Reference

[1] Volkov, V. and Demmel, J.W. (2008) Benchmarking GPUs to tune dense linear algebra. *SC '08: Proceedings of the 2008 ACM/IEEE conference on Supercomputing*, Article No. 31, pp. 1-11. (https://dl.acm.org/doi/10.5555/1413370.1413402)

Part 3

Moving Forward

In this last part we learn about more advanced levels of optimization and about how to use multiple GPUs on the same machine. Then we explore how to create and expose code as a library to Python, before concluding with an overview of the CUDA ecosystem of existing libraries that can help accelerate our development activities.

This part of the book includes the following chapters:

- *Chapter 8, Overlaying Multiple Operations*
- *Chapter 9, Exposing Your Code to Python*
- *Chapter 10, Exploring Existing GPU Models*

8

Overlaying Multiple Operations

An interesting possibility with GPUs is to execute multiple operations at the same time. Remember that NVIDIA GPUs have special hardware dedicated to performing memory transfers separate from the execution cores. By using CUDA streams, it is possible to execute memory transfers to and from the GPU at the same time as we execute a kernel, thereby overlaying the operations. This means we can have three things happening in an interleaved way.

Another possibility is to have more than one GPU on the same machine, although its higher cost means this is a less common setup. We will touch on this interesting alternative in a brief overview; it requires careful thinking about the algorithm to ensure we make the most of our devices.

But before we jump into those interesting topics, we will start this chapter by exploring how to use VS Code to debug our code. This is a useful skill, especially when we have multiple operations happening at the same time.

Over the course of the chapter we're going to cover the following main topics:

- Debugging CUDA code with VS Code
- Using CUDA streams to copy memory and execute code
- Using multiple GPUs together

Technical requirements

We will use the environment we configured during *Chapter 3* with VS Code and our development container. If you have chosen to install the CUDA Toolkit on your machine, you can simply run the build commands on a terminal. We will also learn how to use VS Code to debug GPU code. The code is provided on the GitHub repository `https://github.com/PacktPublishing/GPU-Programming-with-CPP-and-CUDA/tree/main/ch8`.

Debugging CUDA code with VS Code

Debugging CUDA applications can sometimes feel like untangling a knot in the dark, but with the right tools the process becomes much more manageable. The official documentation for **cuda-gdb**, NVIDIA's debugger for CUDA applications, can be found at `https://docs.nvidia.com/cuda/cuda-gdb`. However, a powerful combination for CUDA debugging is to use cuda-gdb with VS Code. This setup offers an intuitive interface and seamless experience for tracking down issues in GPU code.

Our setup already has everything we need to debug our code. We just need to add launch configurations for the programs we would like to debug. First, we click on the **Run and Debug** icon on the sidebar.

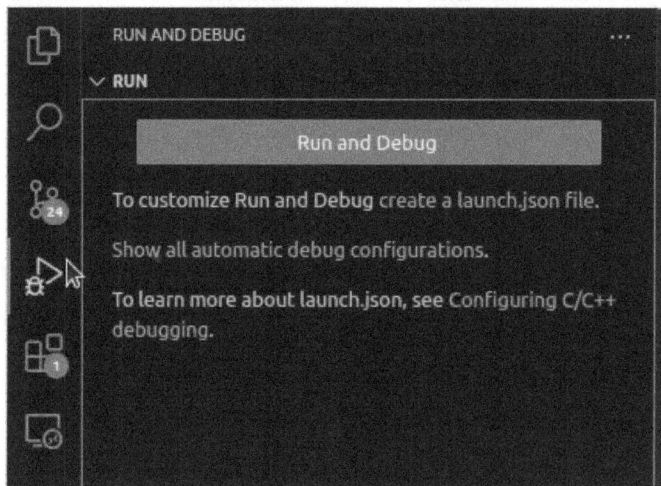

Figure 8.1: Accessing Debug configuration

As we can see in *Figure 8.1*, we need to create a `launch.json` file. This file is needed because it's where we can configure some actions for VS Code to perform for us. To create the file click on the **create a launch.json file** link, and VS Code will guide us through the process.

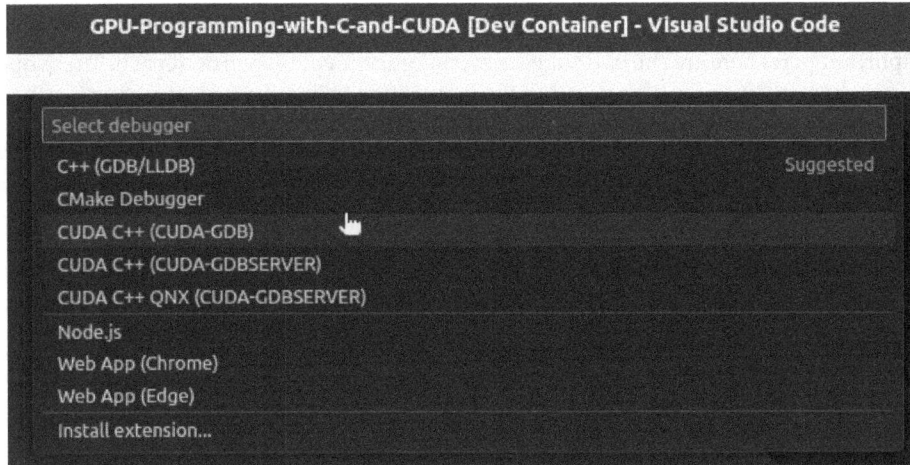

GPU-Programming-with-C-and-CUDA [Dev Container] - Visual Studio Code

Select debugger

C++ (GDB/LLDB)   Suggested
CMake Debugger
CUDA C++ (CUDA-GDB)
CUDA C++ (CUDA-GDBSERVER)
CUDA C++ QNX (CUDA-GDBSERVER)
Node.js
Web App (Chrome)
Web App (Edge)
Install extension...

Figure 8.2: Selecting the debugger

We can see in *Figure 8.2* that VS Code asks which debugger we will be using. This is because VS Code will just be the interface: the heavy lifting work will be carried out by the selected debugger. We will go with cuda-gdb. Once the `launch.json` file is created for us (in the `.vscode` folder) the interface is updated, and the file appears open to us. We still need to add some information about the program we want to debug. The initial code in the file looks like this:

```
{
    // There are some comments about IntelliSense
    "version": "0.2.0",
    "configurations": [
        {
            "name": "CUDA C++: Launch",
            "type": "cuda-gdb",
            "request": "launch",
            "program": ""
        },
        {
            "name": "CUDA C++: Attach",
            "type": "cuda-gdb",
            "request": "attach"
```

```
        }
    ]
}
```

The file has some comments right at the beginning that we have removed for the sake of space. The important parts here are the two suggested configurations: launch or attach. These options represent different situations that not everybody may be familiar with. When we select the launch option the debugger will start the program on its own, which is a good option when our program starts processing independently. When we select attach, however, the debugger will attach to a running operating system process and start the debugging session. This is useful in situations when we have, for example, a server application that will need some kind of interaction or connection to start the processing. We will use launch for now, and change the configuration file as follows:

```
{
    "version": "0.2.0",
    "configurations": [
        {
            "name": "Vector Addition",
            "type": "cuda-gdb",
            "request": "launch",
            "program": "${workspaceFolder}/ch8/1_vector_add/build/vector_add",
            "stopAtEntry": true,
            "cwd": "${workspaceFolder}/ch8/1_vector_add/build"
        }

    ]
}
```

The name attribute is anything that we would like to appear in the dropdown menu to enable us to identify the configuration. The attributes type and request are the same as before. The program attribute is key: we must pass in the path to the executable we will be using during our session. We also have stopAtEntry, which is straightforward: it stops the debug session at the program's entry point; and finally cwd which stands for current working directory, where dependencies will be looked for.

We also must remember that our CMakeLists has to be set to our Debug profile and we must compile our code again using the make command:

```
cmake -DCMAKE_BUILD_TYPE=Debug ..
make
```

Now we have everything in place to set **breakpoints** directly in the CUDA C/C++ code within VS Code! Let's use a broken program to go through the process of debugging. We will be using a simplified version of our vector addition program from *Chapter 4*, but we have removed all time measurements and have introduced an obvious bug. Here's the code for our kernel:

```
__global__ void vectorAddKernel (int *a, int *b, int *c, int N){
    int idx = threadIdx.x + blockIdx.x * blockDim.x;
    if (idx < N) {
        c[idx] = a[idx] * b[idx];
    }
}
```

Instead of adding the two values we are multiplying them, and with such a small kernel we can spot that immediately, but the point here is to use this as an example as we walk through the tool. Now we will click the play button on the left of the **Add Vectors** dropdown.

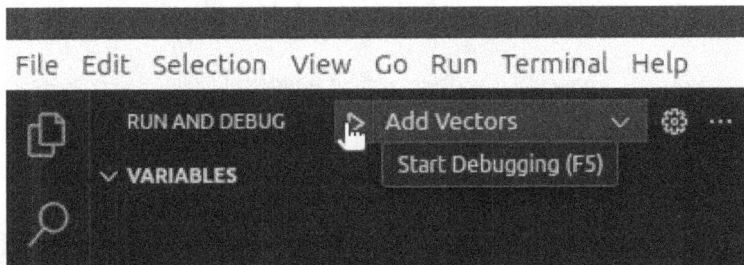

Figure 8.3: Start Debugging the Add Vectors configuration

After it starts, since we configured `"stopAtEntry"`: `true`, we will see that the code stops at the main function and waits for our command.

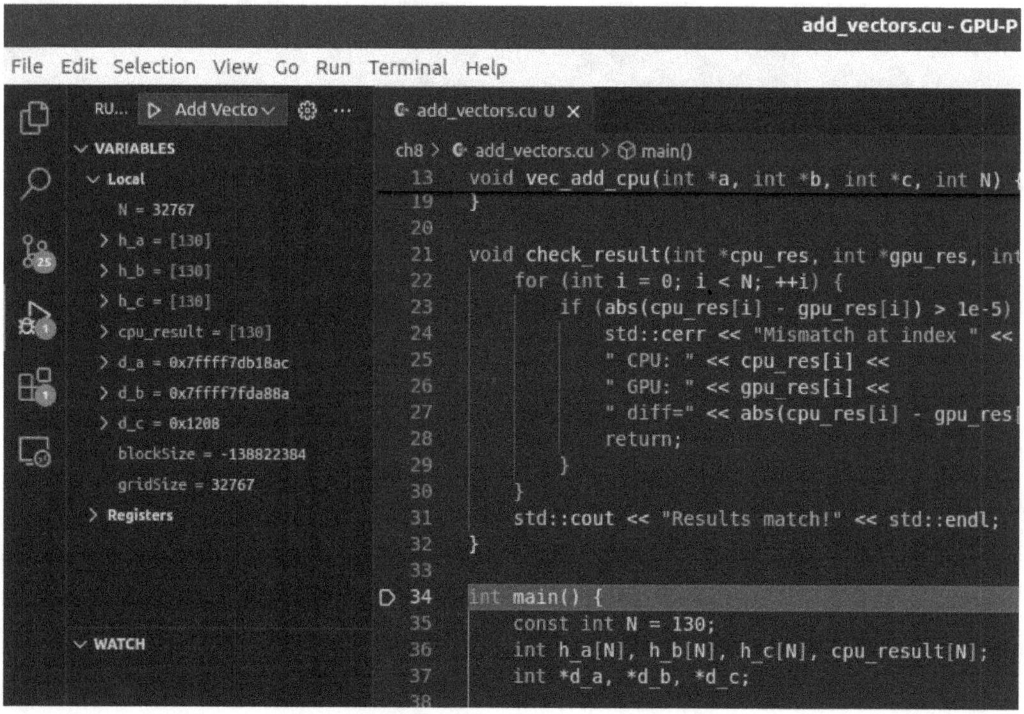

Figure 8.4: The debug session stopped at line 34

To add breakpoints, we can click on the left side of the line numbers (*Figure 8.5*).

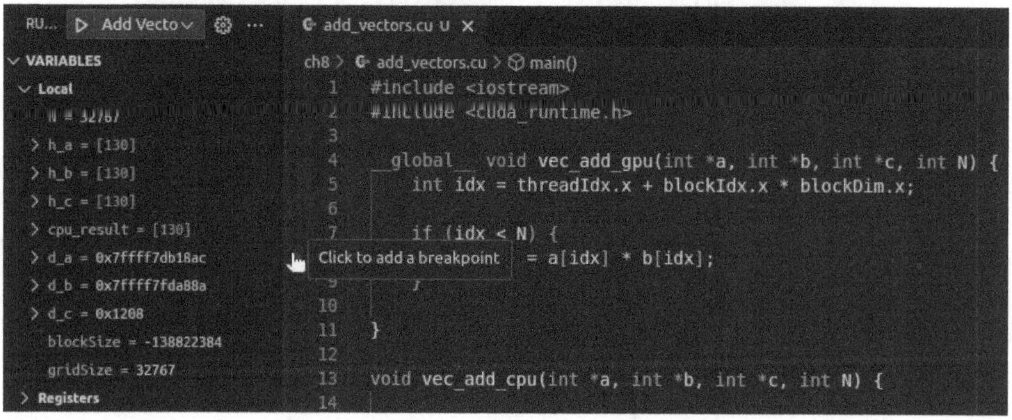

Figure 8.5: Adding a breakpoint

We also have a toolbar that allows us to control execution flow. The options are:

- **Continue** – to run the code until the next breakpoint
- **Step Into** – to enter a function call
- **Step Over** – to run the next command without entering the code in case of a function
- **Step Out** – if we entered a function call and want to continue on the next line after the function call that we entered

We also have the **Restart** and **Stop** commands. This toolbar can be moved on the screen if needed.

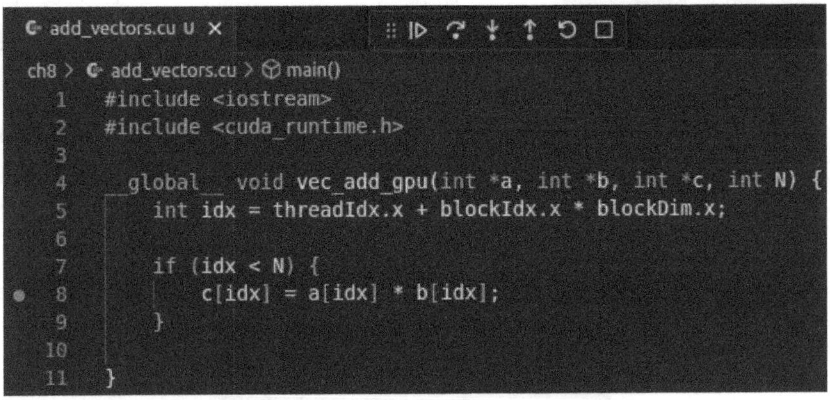

Figure 8.6: The Debug toolbar and our breakpoint at line 8

We can now use the debugger to figure out what the problem is with our code by inspecting the values at runtime. When execution hits a breakpoint we can inspect variables, step through code, and even evaluate expressions. Since we have a breakpoint set inside our kernel, we can click on the **Continue** button of the Debug Toolbar and our code will run until that point.

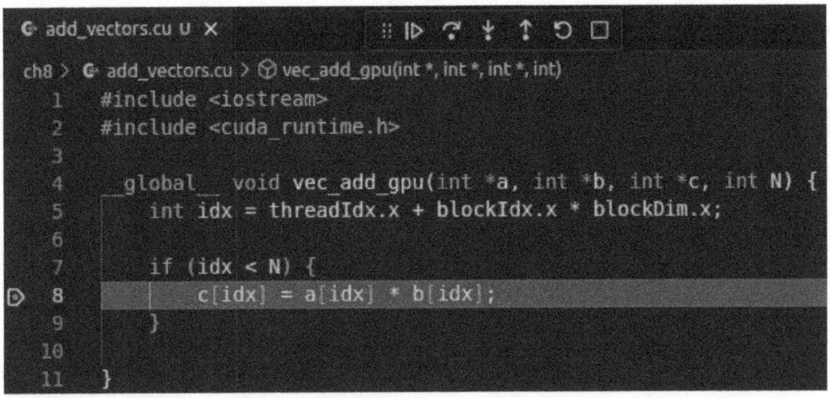

Figure 8.7: Hitting the breakpoint

Using VS Code, we can inspect the values of our variables and the results of processing. We can even add watches to certain variables of interest. Unlike breakpoints, which trigger on specific code lines, **watchpoints** activate when the value of a variable changes. To add a watchpoint, we select the variable or expression and right-click on it and select the **Add to Watch** option from the menu.

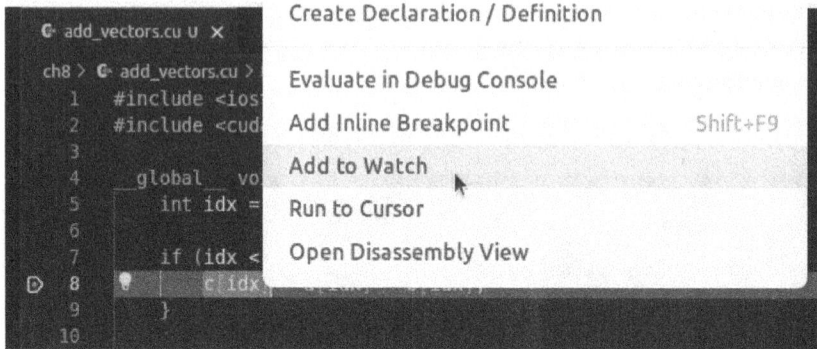

Figure 8.8: Adding a variable to watch

After that we have the **Watch** panel on the left-hand side of VS Code, like the following.

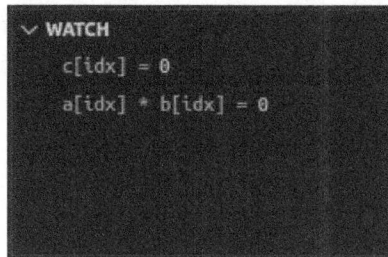

Figure 8.9: The Watch panel with two expressions

Conditional breakpoints are another great resource. They allow us to pause the code only when specific conditions are met, minimizing noise and helping us to focus more effectively. Even within the current Debug session we can edit a breakpoint to turn it into a conditional breakpoint.

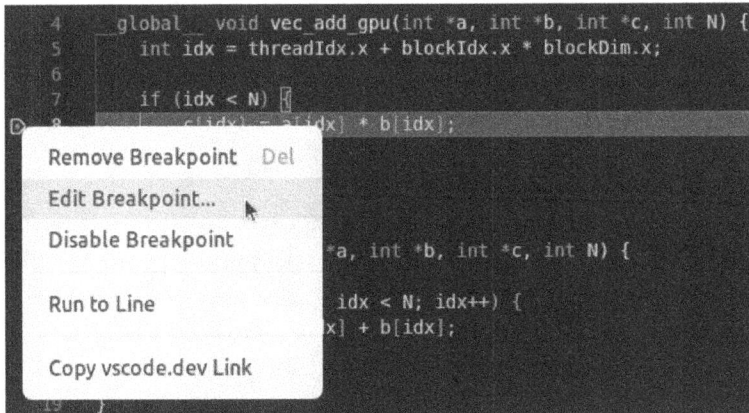

Figure 8.10: Editing the breakpoint

After that we can enter our conditional expression for the breakpoint and hit enter to accept it.

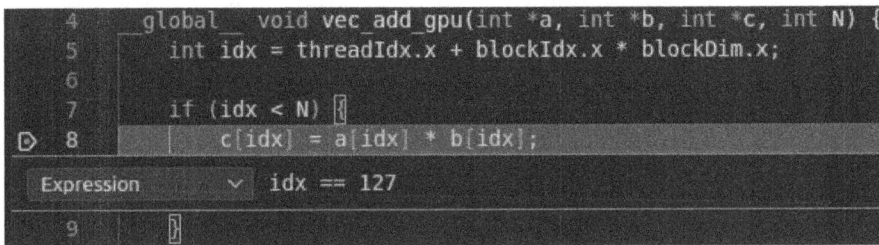

Figure 8.11: The breakpoint expression

Now when we start a Debug session it will run until the variable idx reaches the value 127. It is very unlikely that we will be able to add a conditional breakpoint for a current Debug session, because once it has started, idx will reach 127 faster than we can intervene to add the conditional breakpoint.

Another powerful debugging technique involves inspecting the **call stack**. When a breakpoint is hit, cuda-gdb provides a call stack showing how the code arrived at the current execution point (*Figure 8.12*).

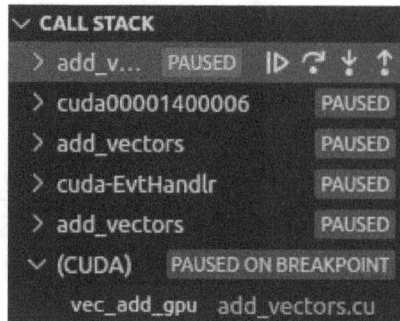

Figure 8.12: The call stack paused on the breakpoint

Another practical aspect of this debugging configuration is the ability to visualize variables in different scopes. The variables pane in VS Code can show local variables, global memory contents, and even shared memory if our code makes use of it.

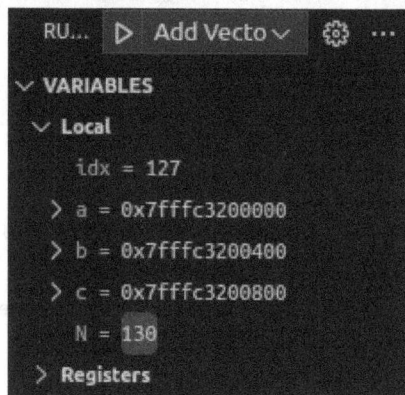

Figure 8.13: The variables pane

One last resource that is worth mentioning is the **Debug console**.

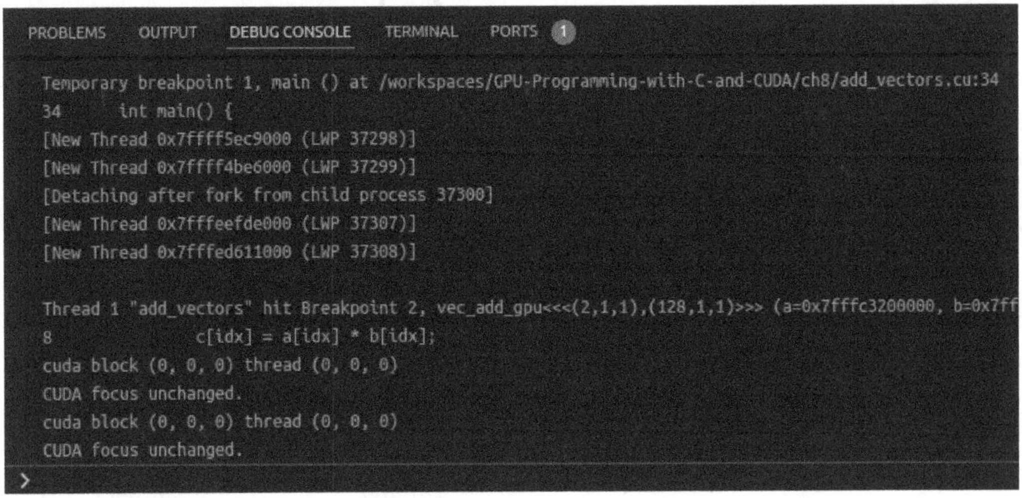

Figure 8.14: The Debug console

As we can see in *Figure 8.14*, the Debug console shows information relevant to program execution. However, for the majority of our cases the use of breakpoints and flow control is enough to make our lives considerably easier.

Overall, using VS Code with cuda-gdb for CUDA debugging offers a rich, user-friendly, and powerful environment. It combines the low-level control and insights of cuda-gdb with the modern, intuitive interface of VS Code. Whether we are tracking down memory issues, examining thread behavior, or stepping through complex kernels, this setup provides all the tools we need to make CUDA debugging highly effective.

In the next section we will see a remarkably interesting and powerful way to use our GPUs. We have already explained the concept of CUDA Streams, but now we'll use them to really accelerate a real program.

Using CUDA streams to overlay operations

In *Chapter 5* we had an introduction to CUDA streams, but now it's time to learn how to use them in practice. CUDA streams are a powerful feature in NVIDIA's CUDA programming model that allow us to execute multiple operations concurrently, increasing the throughput of GPU workloads. And this sounds confusing because we know that GPUs have a large number of processing cores and that is why they execute instructions concurrently, right? Well, that is a part of the story, but we also have another level of parallelism to explore. By properly leveraging streams, we can overlap memory transfers and kernel executions to maximize the efficiency of the hardware. This is possible because most consumer-grade GPUs have three asynchronous engines: one for kernel execution and two for memory transfers (one for host-to-device and one for device-to-host). We will discuss how to best utilize these resources given memory bandwidth limitations.

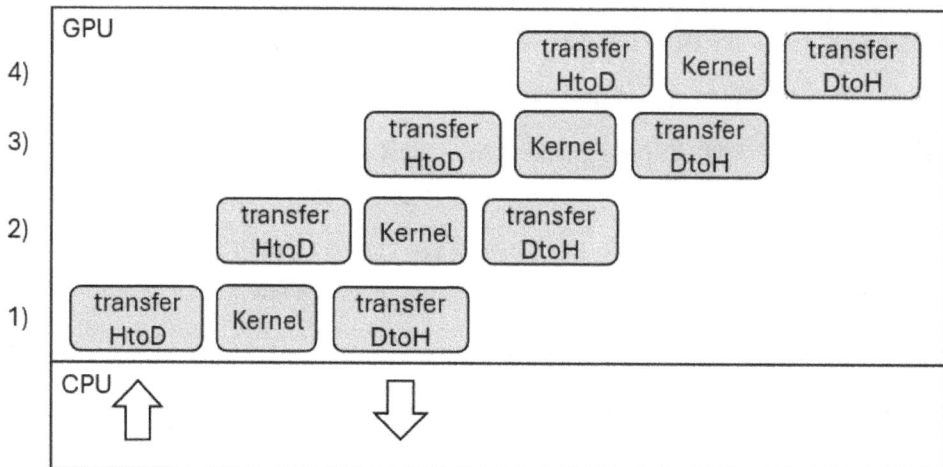

Figure 8.15: Multiple cycles of overlapping memory transfers and kernel execution

Figure 8.15 shows a cycle of calls to memory transfers overlapping with kernel execution. This is possible thanks to the asynchronous engines present in the NVIDIA GPUs being able to handle two transfers simultaneously, one from host to device and the other from device to host. Moreover, during memory transfer a kernel execution is also possible, as long as it operates on a different memory address, which is already available inside the GPU memory.

The key strength of CUDA streams is their ability to enable concurrent execution. Without streams, operations are typically executed sequentially—first, data is copied from the host (CPU) to the device (GPU), then the kernel is launched, and finally, the results are copied back from the device to the host. This **serial execution** leads to idle time where resources remain underutilized. By using multiple streams, we can overlap these tasks so that while one data transfer is happening, a kernel can be executing, and another data transfer (in the opposite direction) can take place. This approach makes full use of the three available engines, increasing throughput.

To visualize this, imagine preparing a large meal in a busy kitchen. If only one person were cooking and they had to first chop vegetables, then boil water, then cook the pasta, and finally make the sauce—one step at a time—the meal would take much longer to prepare. However, if three people worked together—one chopping ingredients, another boiling water, and another preparing the sauce—everything would come together much faster. CUDA streams function in an analogous way, ensuring that different tasks, like memory transfers and kernel execution, happen simultaneously rather than sequentially, keeping the hardware fully utilized and minimizing idle time.

However, there are hardware constraints that define the limits of concurrency. Most consumer GPUs, as mentioned earlier, have three asynchronous engines, meaning that only two memory transfers (one in each direction) and one kernel execution can happen at the same time. If we try to enqueue more operations than the hardware can support, they will be scheduled but will not be truly parallel, leading to performance bottlenecks. Thus, the correct use of CUDA streams involves carefully structuring workloads so that the available engines are always kept busy without overloading them.

Another critical factor in optimizing CUDA streams is understanding **PCIe bus** bandwidth limitations. The PCIe bus serves as the primary connection between the CPU and the GPU, and while it provides high-speed data transfer, it is still significantly slower than the internal memory bandwidth of the GPU. For example, a PCIe 3.0 x16 connection has a theoretical maximum bandwidth of about 16 GB/s, but it may be lower if we are not using an x16 slot. Meanwhile, the internal memory bandwidth of modern GPUs can exceed hundreds of gigabytes per second (GB/s), depending on the model. This vast difference means that data transfers over PCIe must be carefully managed to prevent the bus from becoming a bottleneck in GPU workloads.

Bearing that in mind, now is a suitable time for our first code discussion. Let's measure our memory transfer bandwidth!

Measuring our limits

First, we will use a simple program to understand our GPU's memory bandwidth in practice.

```cpp
#include <cuda_runtime.h>
#include <iostream>
int main() {
    cudaDeviceProp prop;
    cudaGetDeviceProperties(&prop, 0);
    int memClockMHz = prop.memoryClockRate / 1000;// to MHz
    int busWidth = prop.memoryBusWidth;   // In bits
    float bandwidthInBytes = memClockMHz * busWidth / 8;
    float bandwidthInGB = bandwidthInBytes / 1024;
    float bandwidthGBs = 2.0 * bandwidthInGB;
    std::cout << "Mem Clock Speed: " << memClockMHz << " MHz\n";
    std::cout << "Mem Bus Width: " << busWidth << " bits\n";
    std::cout << "Estimated Mem Bandwidth: " << bandwidthGBs << " GB/s\n";
    return 0;
}
```

This CUDA code retrieves GPU properties using `cudaGetDeviceProperties()` and calculates the theoretical peak memory bandwidth. The `memoryClockRate` property, initially given in kHz, is converted to MHz by dividing by 1000. The `memoryBusWidth` property represents the total width of the memory interface in bits. We calculate the `bandwidthInBytes` by multiplying the `memClockMHz` by the `busWidth` in bits and dividing by 8 to get the result in bytes. Right after that we divide by 1024 to get `bandwidthInGB`. Since modern GPUs use **GDDR (Graphics Double Data Rate)** memory, the formula multiplies the memory clock by 2.0 to account for this doubling effect. The resulting `bandwidthGBs` value is the GPU's theoretical peak memory bandwidth in gigabytes per second (GB/s).

This measurement helps evaluate the GPU's memory subsystem, which is crucial for program performance. The calculated value represents the maximum achievable bandwidth under ideal conditions *inside the GPU memory bus*, assuming fully efficient memory access patterns. However, actual performance may be lower due to factors such as memory latency, access patterns, and contention between threads.

But let's see some execution numbers. Here are the results when running this code on my machine:

```
Memory Clock Speed: 5501 MHz
Memory Bus Width: 192 bits
Estimated Memory Bandwidth: 257.859 GB/s
```

Although the theoretical memory bandwidth on the specification says 336 GB/s for RTX2060, in real conditions it is a little lower. But wait a minute: we mentioned that PCIe x16 has a theoretical limit of 16 GB/s – so we would not be able to keep up with the GPU bandwidth in any case.

Let's use another program to measure the real transfer rate that we are able to achieve in practice. There is nothing special about this program, which uses CUDA events to measure the time taken to complete a cudaMemcpyAsync with increasing data transfer sizes. (The full code is available in our repository.) Here are the results:

```
Size:    1 MB, Time:  0.0915 ms, Bandwidth: 10.667 GB/s
Size:   10 MB, Time:  0.8858 ms, Bandwidth: 11.024 GB/s
Size:   30 MB, Time:  2.6194 ms, Bandwidth: 11.185 GB/s
Size:   50 MB, Time:  4.2118 ms, Bandwidth: 11.593 GB/s
Size:  100 MB, Time:  8.2360 ms, Bandwidth: 11.857 GB/s
Size:  300 MB, Time: 24.5889 ms, Bandwidth: 11.915 GB/s
Size:  500 MB, Time: 40.8161 ms, Bandwidth: 11.963 GB/s
Size: 1024 MB, Time: 83.3972 ms, Bandwidth: 11.991 GB/s
```

As we can see, we are below the theoretical 16 GB/s bandwidth, and if we look at the last row, to transfer 1 GB we must wait 83 ms. During that time the GPU is idle, processing nothing, and here comes our strategy: split our data into chunks, copy a little bit, start processing that while copying the next chunk to a different memory buffer, and then when the new buffer is ready start processing that. This is what we are going to do, and then we will use these results to also help us determine the best transfer size to process.

Multiplying matrices with CUDA streams

In *Chapter 7* we used the traditional matrix multiplication problem to learn about the optimization techniques available to us. We'll now use a similar problem, but for the sake of comprehensibility one which is a little simpler. We will use vector-matrix multiplication – think of it as the first step in a matrix multiplication problem. Since we will be having multiple things occurring at the same time it might be wise to simplify the problem a little, so that we can follow everything that is going on.

In our repository we also have a version of the program that does not use streams, so that we can compare the results. A curious thing to note is that, typically, the kernel that works in our multi-streams program is the same as that in the no-streams version. The difference is really in the main program, which needs to track multiple memory copies and data chunks – as we are about to see.

In fact the kernel is amazingly simple, and so as not to mix the concepts of using streams and the optimizations we looked at in *Chapter 7* it does not use any advanced optimization strategy. However, everything that was discussed in *Chapter 7* could also be applied here. We will launch our kernel with a one-dimensional configuration, each thread accessing a single row from the matrix and performing the multiplication against the vector:

```
__global__ void vectorMatrixMulKernel(float* d_vec, float* d_mat,
    float* d_res, int rows, int cols) {
    int row = threadIdx.x + blockIdx.x * blockDim.x;
    if (row < rows) {
        float sum = 0.0f;
        for (int col = 0; col < cols; ++col) {
            sum += d_mat[row * cols + col] * d_vec[col];
        }
        d_res[row] = sum;
    }
}
```

We use the received vector and matrix to calculate the inner product, accessing global memory directly. So, let's focus on the main function where the magic happens.

We start by declaring the size of our matrix to be 16,380 × 16,380 elements, to make sure that we have around 1 GB of data (since 16,380 × 16,380 × 4 bytes for each float gives us 1,073,217,600 bytes, which translates to 0.9995 GB). This is enough for testing purposes.

The next step is to define the chunk size. We are using a multiple of our matrix order to simplify flow control, so we choose a chunk size of 1638. And we have 268,304,400 elements (16,380 × 16,380), which when divided by the chunk size gives us 163,800 chunks (268,304,400 / 1638 = 163,800). Each chunk has (1638 × 16,380 × 4) bytes / 1024 / 1024, which is approximately 100 MB. Breaking that down: we are using 1638 as the chunk size times the number of columns, which is 16,380, times the number of bytes per float number, and after that we divide by 1024 twice to express that value in megabytes.

According to our previous measurements 100 MB is already at peak transfer rate for this machine, and although larger sizes are also at peak transfer rates, we can observe that after 100 MB the performance starts to drop. This is related to how PCIe handles the breakdown of data packages that will be transferred. However, we will return to this after we've seen all the code.

```
int main() {
    int rows = 16380;
    int cols = 16380;
    int chunkSize = 1638;
    float *h_vec = (float*)malloc(rows * sizeof(float));
    float *h_res_cpu = (float*)malloc(rows * sizeof(float));
    float *h_mat_pinned, *h_res_gpu;
    cudaMallocHost(&h_mat_pinned, rows*cols * sizeof(float));
    cudaMallocHost(&h_res_gpu, rows * sizeof(float));
```

We should also note that, to work with **asynchronous memory transfers**, we need to use pinned memory, and for that we use cudaMallocHost instead of the traditional malloc. Since the vector is going to be copied only once we may use traditional memory allocation and a synchronous memory transfer. We will also use a local function to initialize the matrix and vector with random data.

Now, when it comes to memory allocation on the device we have our first modification. Instead of simply allocating buffers large enough to hold the matrix and the resulting vector, we will allocate two buffers for matrix chunks of size (chunk size * cols) – we will keep 1638 matrix rows – and two buffers of size 1638 for vector results which will receive parts of the result:

```
    float *d_vec, *d_mat1, *d_mat2, *d_res1, *d_res2;
    cudaMalloc(&d_vec, rows * sizeof(float));
    cudaMalloc(&d_mat1, chunkSize * cols * sizeof(float));
    cudaMalloc(&d_mat2, chunkSize * cols * sizeof(float));
    cudaMalloc(&d_res1, chunkSize * sizeof(float));
    cudaMalloc(&d_res2, chunkSize * sizeof(float));
```

After this we will do something we are already familiar with: create CUDA events to measure the execution time, and copy the input vector like we did before. What is new is the creation of the CUDA Streams:

```
    cudaStream_t stream1, stream2;
    cudaStreamCreate(&stream1);
    cudaStreamCreate(&stream2);
```

As we saw in *Chapter 5*, the default stream is synchronous, so to achieve what we wish here in terms of parallelization we must create two streams *and not* use stream number 0 (which is the default). So here we have created two streams, to be passed as parameters on our function calls to identify where the transfer or code should happen.

Now we have reached the crucial part of our program: the point where we break our data into chunks and process it in parallel. We will go into more detail here.

First let's understand how we are going to break our data into chunks.

```
int blocks = (chunkSize + BLOCK_SIZE - 1) / BLOCK_SIZE;
for (int i = 0; i < rows; i += chunkSize * 2) {
```

Our block dimension is defined in terms of the chunk size, our for loop starts at 0 and iterates until the number of rows is reached – nothing special there. But our step increment is twice the chunk size (1638), so at the start the index i has a value of 0, but on the second iteration it will be 3276. The reason we are multiplying the chunkSize by 2 is that we are using two streams, so at each step we need to move accordingly.

We now unroll our loop to process two chunks of the matrix on different destination buffers:

```
        cudaMemcpyAsync(d_mat1, h_mat_pinned + i * cols, chunkSize  * cols *
            sizeof(float), cudaMemcpyHostToDevice, stream1);
        vectorMatrixMulKernel<<<blocks, BLOCK_SIZE, 0, stream1>>>(d_vec,
            d_mat1, d_res1, chunkSize, cols);
        cudaMemcpyAsync(h_res_gpu + i, d_res1, chunkSize * sizeof(float),
            cudaMemcpyDeviceToHost, stream1);

        cudaMemcpyAsync(d_mat2, h_mat_pinned + (i + chunkSize) * cols,
            chunkSize * cols * sizeof(float), cudaMemcpyHostToDevice,
                stream2);
        vectorMatrixMulKernel<<<blocks, BLOCK_SIZE, 0, stream2>>>(d_vec,
            d_mat2, d_res2, chunkSize, cols);
        cudaMemcpyAsync(h_res_gpu + i + chunkSize, d_res2, chunkSize *
            sizeof(float), cudaMemcpyDeviceToHost, stream2);
    }
    cudaStreamSynchronize(stream1);
    cudaStreamSynchronize(stream2);
```

We will go through the code first and then explain some of the simplifications. Here we have two similar blocks of code that start an asynchronous memory transfer, then they schedule a kernel execution, and finally perform a memory transfer from the device to the host to collect the partial results for that chunk. So, what are the differences here? First, the two blocks operate on different streams and with different sets of variables. Also, the second code block is always operating on i + chunkSize, to guarantee that we are processing two chunks of data per iteration.

Another important detail to notice is that executions on streams other than the default *may* be asynchronous. What this means is that we must use cudaMemcpyAsync to schedule an asynchronous memory transfer; using cudaMemcpy instead would yield a synchronous transfer. On the other hand, kernel scheduling is always asynchronous to request but will synchronize if executed on the same stream as a memory transfer. Finally, the secondary memory transfer for the partial results is also synchronized with the kernel execution within its stream.

Putting it all together, we have a transfer + execution + transfer on stream 1 and another transfer + execution + transfer on stream 2. This ensures that once the execution step starts on stream 1, the transfer on stream 2 starts. Also, once the first execution is complete on stream 1 it starts the results transfer which will occur *at the same time* as the transfer on stream 2 that has just started.

After the for loop we have two requests for stream synchronization. This is just for safety, to guarantee that we will only use the host buffer after we've made sure that the partial results have been computed and copied.

One important thing regarding the partial results: we are writing to distinct positions of the same buffer in the host memory, and that is why we do not overwrite our parallel computed results. Cool, isn't it?

When we loop for the next iteration, remember that i has jumped the size of two chunks, allowing us to get two more chunks, and this will continue until we reach the end of the matrix.

Let's remember too that we are using a simplified version – all the numbers were carefully selected so that we don't need to carry out boundary verifications here. However, even if we were performing those checks they would not affect the final performance.

Remember that the chunk size we are using not only provides approximately 100 MB of data but it is also a divisor for our total matrix size, and hence we know that when iterating two chunks at a time as we are doing, we can perform the unroll of the loop using two streams and that everything will match the sizes. If we were using a matrix derived from a real-world problem our numbers would not be so nice, and we would have to check whether for the last iteration there would be enough rows left to copy or whether we would need to adapt the last chunk to a smaller size.

This is the part that really changed from our version that uses no streams. We will now compare some numbers for execution performance.

We have compiled data for ten executions of each program version and calculated simple averages of their execution times. To calculate the size of data to use we calculated the number of matrix elements times four bytes per float number divided by 1024 two times to express the number in megabytes. We have collected data for two execution sets, the first for a total data size of 1020 MB (16,380 × 16,380 × 4 / 1024 / 1024) when our matrix is 16,380 × 16,380, exactly as per our code listed here. Then we also collected data for execution of a matrix of size 32,760 × 32,760, which gives a total data size of 4092 MB (32,760 × 32,760 × 4 / 1024 / 1024). *Table 8.1* shows the compiled results.

total data size	chunk size	data size	data partitions	average time	gain
1020	273	16	60	128.427	-7.65%
	546	32	30	89.1392	25.28%
	819	48	20	88.0554	26.19%
	1638	100	10	87.0306	27.05%
	4095	252	4	88.8127	25.55%
	8190	508	2	92.5483	22.42%
4092	273	32	120	445.549	11.00%
	546	68	60	356.581	28.77%
	819	100	40	347.283	30.63%
	1638	204	20	343.555	31.37%
	4095	508	8	344.598	31.17%
	8190	1020	4	351.386	29.81%
	16,380	2044	2	363.88	27.31%

Table 8.1: Execution times for different chunk and data sizes

It is interesting to notice that in both cases, with a data size of 100 MB for the transfer we achieve the greatest performance; the second case has an improvement of only 0.74% when using 204 MB for the transfer size. Also, notice that after the peak performance the execution time starts to rise again.

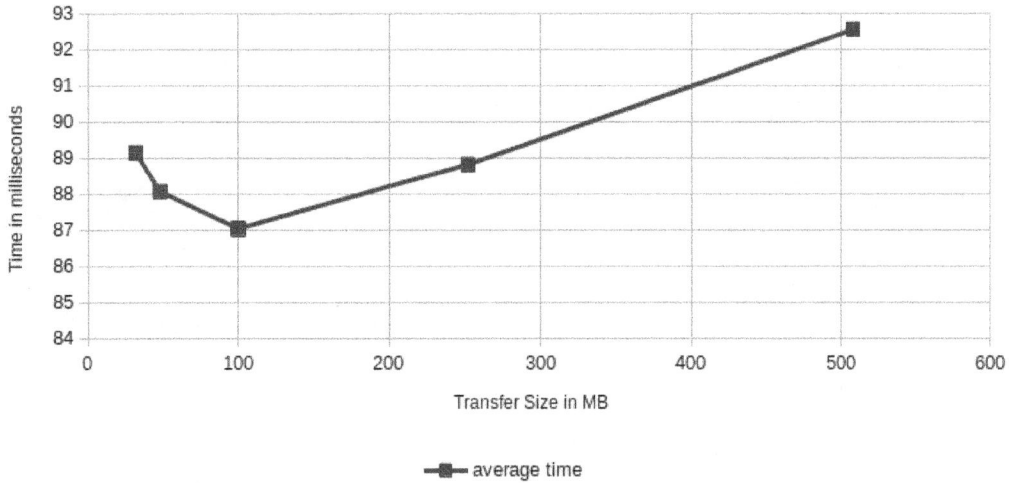

Figure 8.16: Effect of transfer size on execution time for 1020 MB

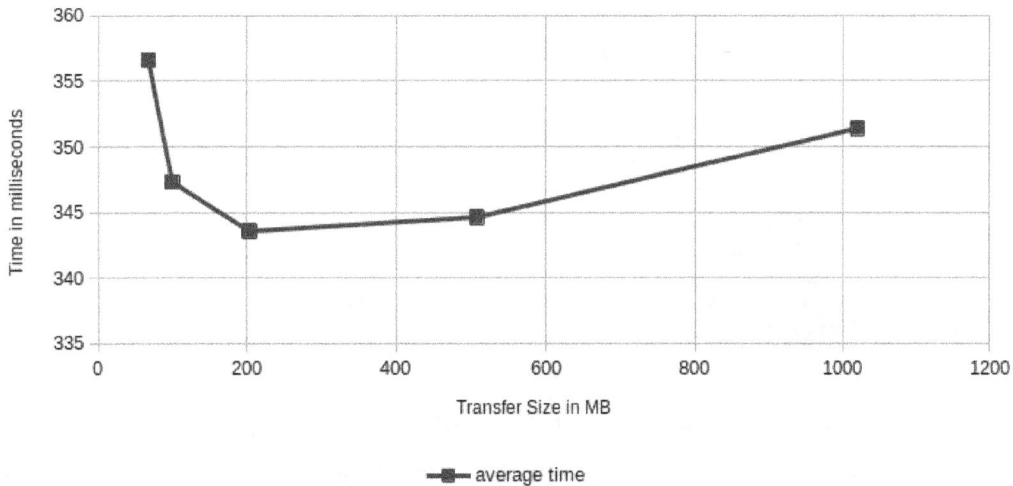

Figure 8.17: Effect of transfer size on execution time for 4092 MB

As we can see in *Figures 8.16* and *8.17*, as we increase the size of the transfer, we achieve better execution times, but beyond a certain point (at transfer size 200 MB) further size increases degrade the execution time. It would be super-useful if we could visualize why this happens, and thanks to the visual profiler that we learned about in *Chapter 7* we can! Let's compare the system trace for some of the executions and understand those effects.

First, we will look at the behavior of the program that does not use streams:

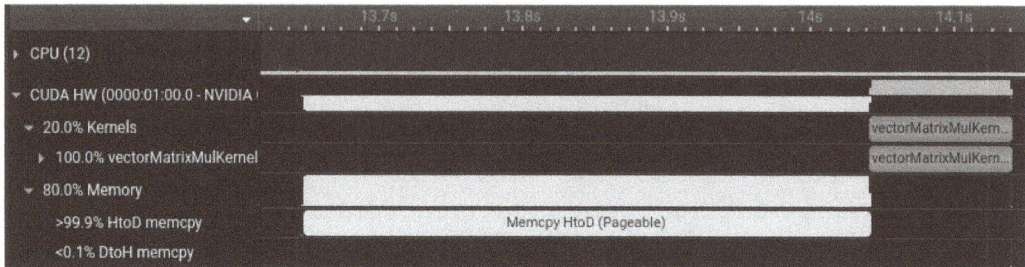

Figure 8.18: Transfer the whole data set and then compute

🔍 **Quick tip**: Need to see a high-resolution version of this image? Open this book in the next-gen Packt Reader or view it in the PDF/ePub copy.

📖 **The next-gen Packt Reader** and a **free PDF/ePub copy** of this book are included with your purchase. Scan the QR code OR visit packtpub.com/unlock, then use the search bar to find this book by name. Double-check the edition shown to make sure you get the right one.

We can see in *Figure 8.18* that we must wait for the whole data transfer to complete before we can compute our results. This is a key concept here: we have a transfer time and a computing time that we want to better use.

Now, we'll compare the traces for three scenarios where total data size is 1020 MB.

Figure 8.19: Overlap data transfer with computation, too many partitions

We can see in *Figure 8.19* the system trace for a chunk size of 273, and as we can see in the first part of our table, it is actually *slower* than the no-streams version. This comes as no surprise, since the data transfer is too small and compute time ends up dominating program execution. It's so bad that we even kept it out of the charts in *Figures 8.16* and *8.17*.

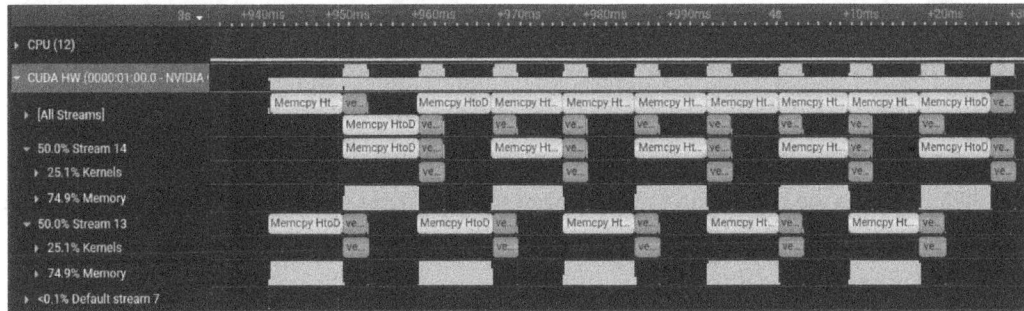

Figure 8.20: Computation time is totally absorbed by transfer time

Figure 8.20 shows the system trace for a chunk size of 1638, and as we can see in the first part of *Table 8.1*, it delivers the best performance. This is due to the good balance of execution time being overlapped by memory transfers and those transfers being able to fully use the PCIe bus. In this case, every time the transfer of a new chunk completes, processing starts, and a new memory transfer occurs at the same time.

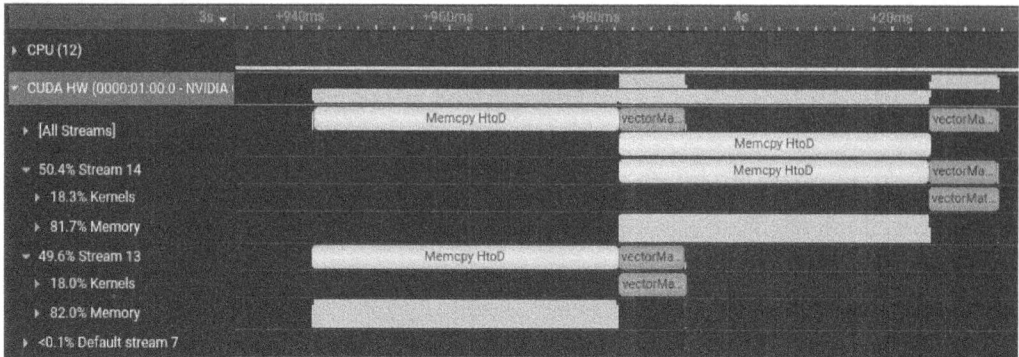

Figure 8.21: Transfer time is too big, like the no-streams version

In *Figure 8.21* we see the system trace for a chunk size of 8190, which gives a total transfer size of 508 MB. This is too big, making the GPU wait too long before it can start to process anything. The effect is that execution time rises again, as we can see both in our table and in the charts shown in *Figures 8.16 and 8.17*.

Finally, we'll compare the traces for three scenarios where the total data size is 4092 MB.

Figure 8.22: Overlap data transfer with computation, too many partitions

We can see in *Figure 8.22* the system trace for a chunk size of 273, and as we can see in the second part of Table 8.1 this can achieve some benefit since it uses just 32 MB, but computation time is larger than the memory transfer times.

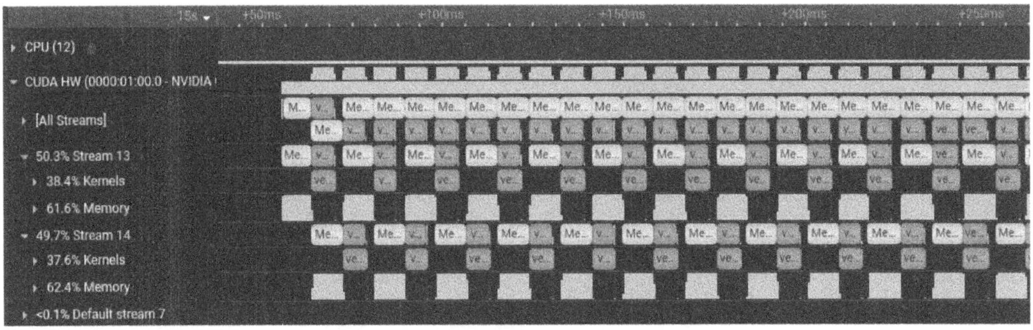

Figure 8.23: Computation time is totally absorbed by transfer time

In *Figure 8.23* we see the system trace for a chunk size of 819, and as we can see in the second part of our table this is almost the best performance for total data 4092 MB, but we selected this based on the 100 MB size to be able to compare with the scenario of *Figure 8.20*. Here, the time to compute and copy results back is almost the same as the time to copy another chunk.

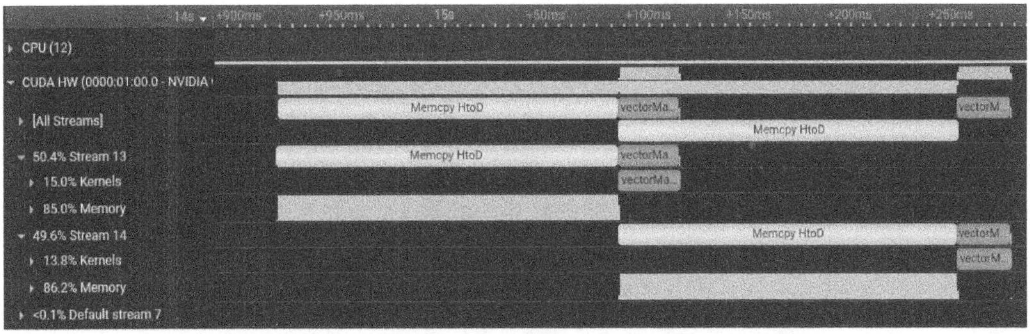

Figure 8.24: Transfer time is too big, like the no-streams version

Finally, *Figure 8.24* shows the system trace for a chunk size of 16,380, which gives a total of 2044 MB of transfer size. This is too big, and again the GPU sits idly waiting to process the data, with the result that execution time rises.

We did not use the advanced optimization techniques we saw in *Chapter 7*, yet we were still able to achieve a 25 to 31% improvement on execution time. This is a remarkable achievement! Of course, we have simplified our code to make it easier to understand how to use this powerful feature, but nevertheless, it can be adapted to real-world situations.

By using `ncu-ui` we were able to visualize how the overlap happened, making it possible to gain a concrete understanding of why this works.

However, this is not the only way to overlap multiple executions, and we have one more ride to take. So let us now see how to use more than one GPU at the same time on the same program!

Running multiple GPUs together

As we mentioned in the chapter introduction, having multiple GPUs on the same machine is not a very common setup, due to the great cost. Nevertheless, it is still a form of overlapping computation that we can use to our advantage. We will look in this section at an adaptation of the previous vector matrix multiplication program, in which the problem is divided into two parts and each part is submitted to a different GPU.

We will not be using streams in this program, so as not to confuse the topics. Nor will we carry out any performance measurements, because the system on which the executions are run is based on a PCIe 2.0 bus which is really slow, impacting significantly on the final time results.

The key concept to **multi-GPU programming** is the use of the `cudaSetDevice(int d)` function which defines the GPU device that will be addressed until it is called again with a different device identifier.

The kernel to perform vector matrix multiplication on multiple GPUs is the same as the one we had in our CUDA Streams program, so let us follow the main program to understand the changes.

After we declare and initialize the vector and matrix on the host machine comes the first interesting part. An important thing to note is that we are assuming a system with two GPUs – that is why our for loop is using a limit of 2:

```
float *d_vec[2], *d_mat[2], *d_res[2];
for (int device = 0; device < 2; device++) {
    cudaSetDevice(device);
    cudaMalloc(&d_vec[device], rows * sizeof(float));
    cudaMalloc(&d_mat[device], chunkSize * cols * sizeof(float));
    cudaMalloc(&d_res[device], chunkSize * sizeof(float));

    cudaMemcpy(d_vec[device], h_vec, rows * sizeof(float),
        cudaMemcpyHostToDevice);
}
```

Here we have declared three arrays of pointers to handle the data that will be used on each device, and then our for loop allows us to perform the memory allocation and memory copy for each device. Here we are using cudaMemcpy , which is a synchronous function, but even if were using cudaMemcpyAsync with CUDA Streams, we have the restriction imposed by the PCI bus, so there is a limit to how much we can transfer at the same time even if the targets are different devices.

All our code will have for loops to allow for the changing and addressing of the two devices that are available. Our next code block copies half of the matrix to each GPU.

```
for (int device = 0; device < 2; device++) {
    cudaSetDevice(device);
    cudaMemcpy(d_mat[device], h_mat + device * chunkSize * cols,
        chunkSize * cols * sizeof(float), cudaMemcpyHostToDevice);
}
```

Again, we set the device accordingly and then transfer the data. Now it is time to execute our kernel, as follows:

```
int blocks = (chunkSize + BLOCK_SIZE - 1) / BLOCK_SIZE;
for (int device = 0; device < 2; device++) {
    cudaSetDevice(device);
    vectorMatrixMulKernel<<<blocks, BLOCK_SIZE>>>(d_vec[device],
        d_mat[device], d_res[device], chunkSize, cols);
}
```

We first define the size of our grid and reuse it for both GPUs. Besides setting the device that should be used, we also use the index of our for loop to address the memory we allocated on each GPU:

```
for (int device = 0; device < 2; device++) {
    cudaSetDevice(device);
    cudaMemcpy(h_res_gpu + device * chunkSize, d_res[device], chunkSize *
        sizeof(float), cudaMemcpyDeviceToHost);
    cudaFree(d_vec[device]);
    cudaFree(d_mat[device]);
    cudaFree(d_res[device]);
}
```

Finally, we copy the results from both devices to the correct position in the results array. As you can see, it is not much more difficult to use multiple GPUs than it is to use streams on a single GPU.

The real concern is that, to work on the same problem together, both devices will be competing for PCI bus availability, which can drastically penalize performance. A good idea is to use this resource in scenarios where we can have datasets loaded at the beginning and then perform different computations on different GPUs throughout the application lifecycle.

Summary

In this chapter we learnt how to use a new tool in our IDE to allow us to debug our code in a visual way. This is a very handy tool to be proficient in, for many will be the times when you must find the proverbial needle in the haystack. After that we returned to a topic first introduced in *Chapter 5*, but now we were able to explore many aspects of the use of CUDA streams and also the impact of data transfer size on performance. We learned about the relations between chunk size, transfer size and the number of data partitions.

By using our profiler from *Chapter 7* we were able to visualize the overlapping of memory transfers and computations. This not only shows that the new technique really works, but also enables us to leverage one more use of NVIDIA Nsight Compute which we learnt about previously.

We concluded the chapter by talking about the use of multiple GPUs, even though this is a more unusual setup.

In the next chapter we will learn how to expose our code to the Python programming language so that we can pack our GPU code into libraries, allowing more users to benefit from it.

Exercises

It is interesting to revisit the weighted moving average of *Chapter 6*, which was already improved by the exercises in *Chapter 7*. Now we invite you to use CUDA streams to improve that example even further, by breaking the data transfer and overlapping it with kernel execution.

9

Exposing Your Code to Python

Every library developer must choose how to make their code available to users, but when using C++, one option is simply to let users compile against the binary library. However, many users who need GPU acceleration have some piece of code that handles data in **Python**. If you are one of those users, this chapter is for you!

You will learn first about the alternative ways of exposing your code to Python, and then about concrete examples that will show you how to call the GPU code.

The chapter wraps up with a section on performance considerations for each of the alternatives.

The chapter's main topics, then, are the following:

- Using Ctypes
- Wrapping with your own code
- Performance considerations

Technical requirements

We will use the environment configured in *Chapter 3* with VS Code and our development container. If you have chosen to install the CUDA Toolkit on your machine, you can simply run the build commands on a terminal. We will also learn how to use VS Code to debug GPU code. The code is provided in the GitHub repository `https://github.com/PacktPublishing/GPU-Programming-with-CPP-and-CUDA/tree/main/ch9`.

Integrating with Python

Up until now we have been working with C++ to develop our programs and CUDA kernels, but it can be very useful to leverage all the functionality already available in Python and make everything work together. However, bridging the gap between C++ and Python can feel like introducing two people from completely different social circles — they speak different languages, have different customs, but when they get along, the results can be spectacular. Integrating a GPU-accelerated **C++ library** with Python can unlock performance benefits while keeping the ease of use and flexibility that Python developers enjoy. Let's start by exploring why this integration is valuable, the approaches available for making it happen, its potential pitfalls, and how memory management plays a crucial role in the process.

We already known that C++ unleashes raw power and control over hardware, making it the perfect choice for performance-intensive tasks – and for dealing with GPUs. However, Python is present in many modern scientific computing projects, as is machine learning. By making our GPU-accelerated C++ library accessible from Python, we provide high-speed computing capabilities to a broader audience, including data scientists, engineers, and researchers who may not be comfortable with C++ but who need high-performance solutions nonetheless.

A great benefit of exposing our libraries to Python is accessibility. As implied above, Python's ecosystem includes a vast array of libraries for data analysis, visualization, and machine learning. By integrating our C++ code with Python, users can call high-performance GPU computations from Python scripts, enabling a more dynamic workflow between writing algorithms, visualizing results, and conducting further analysis. Additionally, this integration makes it easier to develop prototypes in Python while offloading compute-heavy operations to C++.

We will explore two common approaches to exposing our code. The first alternative, **ctypes**, is a built-in module in Python that allows C functions to be called directly from shared libraries (`.so` or `.dll` files). This approach is relatively straightforward because it is a Python-only approach. However, it requires careful attention to function signatures and memory management, especially when dealing with pointers.

The second, more sophisticated, approach involves writing a wrapper (a.k.a. C program) manually using the **Python C API**. This method provides finer control over how the Python interpreter interacts with C++ functions, allowing for more Pythonic behavior in function calls and memory management. While it requires writing additional C++ code to handle Python objects, it provides the flexibility to define custom types, manage memory allocation efficiently, and handle Python exceptions more elegantly.

A major challenge when integrating the two programming languages is managing memory correctly. Python employs automatic memory management with garbage collection, whereas C++ requires explicit memory handling. This difference can lead to memory leaks or segmentation faults if not managed properly. However, we will be dealing here with memory allocated on Python's side and just manipulated on the C and CUDA side, making it much safer.

And since we mentioned our beloved CUDA, another challenge arises when dealing with GPU memory. As we know, GPU memory allocations work differently from CPU memory, and improper memory management can degrade performance. Although Python does not understand GPU memory, we do (luckily), and we can ensure that buffers are properly allocated and freed again when no longer needed. We will make use of our GPU memory management functions to make sure that everything is properly handled.

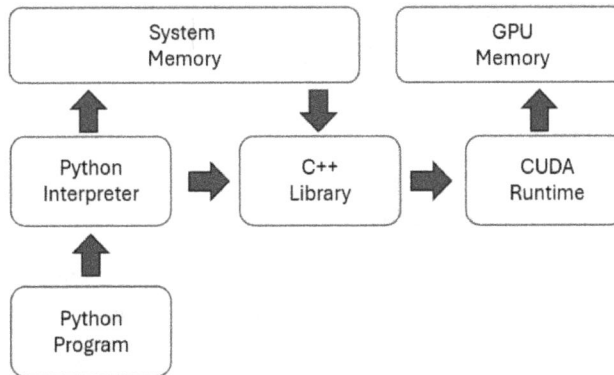

Figure 9.1: Python does not handle GPU memory directly

As shown in *Figure 9.1*, Python does not interact directly with GPU memory, instead relying on our library code to perform any memory handling correctly.

Another common issue is dealing with data types, because, as strange as it may seem (just kidding!), Python is what we call a **dynamically typed programming language**. This means that variables do not have a declared type, but the values they contain do. Due to this characteristic, Python objects like **NumPy arrays** need to be translated into a format that C++ functions can understand. This requires careful handling of data types and memory layouts. If not handled properly, performance gains resulting from the use of C++ may be negated by inefficient data copying. A well-designed wrapper should aim for zero-copy memory sharing when possible, by leveraging techniques such as NumPy's array interface or memory-mapped buffers.

With these considerations in mind, we will examine in the next section our first approach to loading a dynamic linked library that interacts with the GPU, and using a function declared in the library from a Python program.

Creating the C++ Library

We started this chapter talking about integrating a C++ library with Python, but up until now we've only created C++ programs that use the GPU – and all of them were executable programs, not libraries. So let's see how we can turn our code into a library! We will use as our example a very simple vector addition kernel that receives two input arrays, one output array, and their size to perform addition of the input arrays' elements and store the results on the output array. Note that we pass a single value for the size because the arrays must be of the same size.

A C++ library, in simple terms, is a collection of precompiled code that can be linked to multiple applications, saving time and leveraging code reuse. For our purpose of integrating with Python we'll need to create a shared library (dynamically loaded), and CMake provides everything we need to accomplish that.

Static versus shared libraries

Although a library is a collection of precompiled code, there are different ways to access library functionality. With a **static library** the code is copied into the final program, meaning that if we compile ten programs using the same static library, they all will have their own separate copy of the code in their final file. On the other hand, when using a **shared library** our program does not include the full library code. Instead, it depends on the runtime system to dynamically link the necessary functions from the library. One of the greatest advantages of using shared libraries is that, as long as the function name and parameters (i.e. the function signature) does not change, we may update the internal algorithms of the library without having to recompile the whole application.

One major advantage of libraries is to enable modular projects in which different aspects of the application are taken care of in different, functionally distinct, layers. We call this *separation of concerns*, and it is fundamental in a GPU project because it means we can isolate all the GPU-related code in a separate library and have different teams working at the business application level and at the internal application level.

To create our library our CMakeLists.txt file will change a little bit to include the following instructions:

```
add_library(vector_add SHARED src/vector_add.cu) set_target_
properties(vector_add PROPERTIES CUDA_SEPARABLE_COMPILATION ON) target_
include_directories(vector_add PUBLIC include)
```

Instead of the add_executable that we have been using, we now use add_library and adding SHARED specifies the type of library to create.

Then, by using set_target_properties we make sure that **nvcc**, the NVIDIA compiler, knows that this will be a library by specifying CUDA_SEPARABLE_COMPILATION ON.

Finally we must add the include directory that contains our header files (with definitions of our functions so that other executables know what is available in our library) so that CMake can track this.

The code for our library is slightly different from that on which we have been working, but it is a small change. First, the kernel does not change: it uses the structure that we had before:

```
__global__ void vectorAddKernel(int *a, int *b, int *c, int N){
    int idx = threadIdx.x + blockIdx.x * blockDim.x;
    if (idx < N) {
        c[idx] = a[idx] * b[idx];//a bug on purpose for debugging
    }
}
```

But we need to provide a way for the external world to call this kernel. Before we were using the kernel in our own programs, but now we are writing the kernel to provide a GPU-accelerated feature to someone else. What we can do is turn our main function into a proxy-like function, as follows:

```
void vectorAdd(int *a, int *b, int *c, int N) {
    int *d_a, *d_b, *d_c;
    cudaMalloc((void**)&d_a, N * sizeof(int));
    cudaMalloc((void**)&d_b, N * sizeof(int));
    cudaMalloc((void**)&d_c, N * sizeof(int));

    cudaMemcpy(d_a, a, N * sizeof(int), cudaMemcpyHostToDevice);
    cudaMemcpy(d_b, b, N * sizeof(int), cudaMemcpyHostToDevice);

    int threadsPerBlock = 256;
    int blocksPerGrid = (N + threadsPerBlock - 1) / threadsPerBlock;
    vectorAddKernel<<<blocksPerGrid, threadsPerBlock>>>(d_a, d_b, d_c, N);
```

```
    cudaMemcpy(c, d_c, N * sizeof(int), cudaMemcpyDeviceToHost);

    cudaFree(d_a);
    cudaFree(d_b);
    cudaFree(d_c);
}
```

To ensure that we export our function we need to include our header file, which is accomplished with `#include "../include/vector_add.h"` at the beginning of our C++ file. Note that we are not allocating any host memory as we did before; here we receive the host memory – even the array that receives the results – from the caller of the function. If we need to allocate memory inside our library, we must provide the user with memory management functions that allow for it to be deallocated.

One last resource we need to provide is something that we haven't been using much: a header file describing the functions supported by our library. This file is under the include folder of our project and is as follows:

```
#ifndef VEC_ADD_H
#define VEC_ADD_H
extern "C" {
    void vectorAdd(int *a, int *b, int *c, int N);
}
#endif
```

Now, with our library compiled we will see the file `libvector_add.so` in the build folder.

In the next section let's see how to use this new library together with a first Python program by declaring the necessary information about our function using Ctypes.

Using Ctypes

Having a library is useless if we have no way of using it in our program. Luckily there is a Python module called `ctypes` that allows interaction with shared libraries written in C or C++. It enables our Python programs to call library functions as if they were native Python functions. This mechanism provides an easy way to leverage high-performance C++ code while still benefiting from Python's flexibility and ease of use.

Using ctypes we can load shared libraries, declare function signatures, and invoke native functions easily. A great advantage is that it does not require any modification to the original C++ source code, making it an appealing option for lightweight integration.

Another interesting thing is that it is purely Python based, meaning that we can write code on the Python side to define what we want to use from the library without the need to compile anything. However, ctypes has its limitations: for example it requires manual mapping of function signatures and necessitates handling raw memory pointers.

Since Python is dynamically typed and C++ is statically typed, every function call must explicitly specify argument and return types, and this can cause some headaches. However, ctypes lessens the pain by providing data types like ctypes.c_int and ctypes.c_double, which correspond to their C counterparts.

A code example will help clarify what we are dealing with:

```python
import ctypes
lib = ctypes.CDLL("../../build/libvector_add.so")
lib.vectorAdd.argtypes = [
    ctypes.POINTER(ctypes.c_int),
    ctypes.POINTER(ctypes.c_int),
    ctypes.POINTER(ctypes.c_int),
    ctypes.c_int
]
```

Here we pass in the path to the shared library we are going to use, and the declaration of the data types we will be dealing with in our function. Although it may seem a little awkward to Python programmers who don't usually need to deal with data type declarations it is straightforward enough to read.

As for the function call, assuming that we've already imported numpy at the beginning of our Python program, we will have something like this:

```python
N = 1000000
a = np.array(range(N), dtype=np.int32)
b = np.array(range(N, 2*N), dtype=np.int32)
c = np.zeros(N, dtype=np.int32)

lib.vectorAdd(
    a.ctypes.data_as(ctypes.POINTER(ctypes.c_int)),
```

```
        b.ctypes.data_as(ctypes.POINTER(ctypes.c_int)),
        c.ctypes.data_as(ctypes.POINTER(ctypes.c_int)),
        N
    )
```

Here we use numpy to create the input arrays with random integers and the output array filled with zeros. Then, when performing the function call, we need to access the internal pointer for the data to pass into our library. And it's as simple as that! Although a little verbose, it is straightforward to follow what is going on.

We are specifying the data types for both declaration and function call, but the **dynamic type resolution** of Python has an impact on the performance of ctypes calls because it means that function calls are resolved at runtime. This introduces a small overhead, as Python determines the correct function signature and converts arguments dynamically. While the overhead may be negligible for occasional function calls, performance bottlenecks can appear in applications that require thousands or millions of calls per second.

It is clear that with ctypes we have a fast way to access our library from Python, especially because when dealing with GPU our code is (most of the time) all about kernels, and creating proxy functions to expose them makes a lot of sense.

There are other ways to access our code, however, and in the next section we will dive into the world of the Python C API to create a wrapper that acts as a **Python extension**.

Wrapping with your own code

A Python extension is a module written in C or C++ that can be loaded into Python like a regular module. It provides a bridge between Python's friendly scripting environment and lower-level languages. We can create an extension for anything that would require the use of a lower-level language, including when we want to interface with an existing C++ library and offer access to GPU functionality while still benefiting from Python's ease of use. A good example is PyTorch, which has a C++ backend and also CUDA support while offering a higher level API through Python.

Creating an extension requires the Python C API, which lets us define new types, expose C++ functions to Python, manage reference counts, and handle Python objects within C or C++ code. The general workflow consists of defining **wrapper functions** that translate between Python objects and native C++ structures, compiling them into a shared library and then loading them as Python modules. However, the compilation process is managed differently, and the shared object is created in such a way that the Python interpreter knows how to load that extension for us to import into our Python program.

Let's break down the steps involved in creating our extension.

An extension needs to include the definition of the functions that will be available to Python, an array that will reference all the functions, a module definition and an initialization function that Python calls when it loads the module.

Now, we will skip the function definition for a moment and go through this infrastructure first.

```
static PyMethodDef VectorAddMethods[] = {
    {"vectorAdd", pyVectorAdd, METH_VARARGS, "Perform vector addition
        using CUDA"},
    {NULL, NULL, 0, NULL}
};
static struct PyModuleDef vectoraddmodule = {
    PyModuleDef_HEAD_INIT,
    "vector_add_wrapper",
    NULL,
    -1,
    VectorAddMethods
};
```

Examining this closely, we first have the array of functions, with a single entry and the module definition that uses that array. What `PyMethodDef` expects is the name that will be exposed, the function implementation, a flag to define the arguments expected by the C function, and a description.

Our function will be called `vectorAdd` and will be performed by the `pyVectorAdd` function (which we will see a little later). We use `METH_VARARGS` to indicate that we will have a tuple of positional arguments, and finally we have a description of our function.

After that, we have a flag value set to `{NULL, NULL, 0, NULL}`.

Now we can define our module and provide the `VectorAddMethods` array.

We initialize the `vectoraddmodule` definition with a required macro, and then we give it a name. Here we are not providing any description, so we use `NULL` for now, but an important point is that by passing `-1` as an argument we inform the Python interpreter that our module does not need to allocate any space for an internal state. Finally, we pass in our array of functions.

There is one more thing in terms of infrastructure that we need to take care of before discussing the actual function: module initialization.

```
PyMODINIT_FUNC PyInit_vector_add_wrapper(void) {
    void *handle = dlopen("../../build/libvector_add.so",
                            RTLD_LAZY);
    if (!handle) {
        PyErr_SetString(PyExc_ImportError,
        "Could not load libvector_add.so");
        return NULL;
    }
    vectorAdd = (vectorAddFunc)dlsym(handle, "vectorAdd");
    if (!vectorAdd) {
        PyErr_SetString(PyExc_ImportError,
            "Could not find vectorAdd in libvector_add.so");
            return NULL;
        }
    return PyModule_Create(&vectoraddmodule);
}
```

Here we are using an approach to loading our library via dlopen which allows us to dynamically load each of the function pointers from the external library without having to provide the library at compile time. There is extra work to be done in referring to each function pointer name, but the interesting thing about this approach is that it allows a plugin-like architecture where we can switch between implementations of the library. The part related to the extension is the last line, where we call the PyModule_Create function and pass in our module's configuration that we defined previously.

Now it's time to see what our function looks like:

```
static PyObject* pyVectorAdd(PyObject* self,PyObject* args){
    PyObject *py_a, *py_b;
    int N;
    if (!PyArg_ParseTuple(args, "OOi", &py_a, &py_b, &N))
        return NULL;
    int *a = (int*)malloc(N * sizeof(int));
    int *b = (int*)malloc(N * sizeof(int));
    int *c = (int*)malloc(N * sizeof(int));
    for (int i = 0; i < N; i++) {
```

```
        a[i] = (int)PyLong_AsLong(PyList_GetItem(py_a, i));
        b[i] = (int)PyLong_AsLong(PyList_GetItem(py_b, i));
    }
    vectorAdd(a, b, c, N);
    PyObject* result = PyList_New(N);
    for (int i = 0; i < N; i++) {
        PyList_SetItem(result, i, PyLong_FromLong(c[i]));
    }
    free(a);
    free(b);
    free(c);
    return result;
}
```

The first thing to notice is that we are parsing a tuple of parameters with a pattern of "OOi". This means that we are receiving two Python objects (a.k.a the input arrays) and an integer that represents their sizes. We are not passing in the results array, so our Python version of the vectorAdd function is a little different from the library version. This is exactly because the objective of an extension is to provide more functionality to the programmer.

We could also have a set of data type and size validations, although we are skipping this for now for the sake of simplicity. But bear in mind that when bridging two different worlds like Python and C++ it is always reassuring to have code that safeguards us.

We then create the host memory as arrays to copy data from Python and store the results. With a for loop, we iterate over all the elements of each Python list and copy them to their C++ counterparts that we'll use in our function call.

Next we call the vectorAdd function loaded from the shared library during module initialization. This passes in the three arrays and their size; after completing the call we can copy the results from array c to a newly created Python list that will be returned. We then safely free the memory that was allocated and return the results.

One last piece to our puzzle is how to build this extension. We do that with a file called setup.py.

A change in the near future

As of this writing, setup.py is still the tool to build Python extensions, although for packaging and installing Python projects it has been deprecated in favour of modern tools like pyproject.toml.

Our setup.py file will be like the following:

```
from setuptools import setup, Extension
module = Extension(
    "vector_add_wrapper",
    sources=["vector_add_wrapper.c"],
)

setup(
    name="vector_add_wrapper",
    version="1.0",
    description="Python binding for CUDA vector addition",
    ext_modules=[module],
)
```

To build our extension we can use the following command:

```
python3 setup.py build_ext --inplace
```

Having built our extension in the current folder, if we execute our Python program from this folder, the interpreter will be able to find our library. If we need to install our extension to the system, we can use:

```
sudo python3 setup.py install
```

This command uses setup.py to first define which files should be built for this extension and then specifies the setup process with the module name that we will use to import in our programs.

Now, here is what the Python program that uses this extension looks like:

```
import vector_add_wrapper as vaw
import random
N = 10000000
```

```
a = [random.randint(0, N) for _ in range(N)]
b = [random.randint(N, 2*N) for _ in range(N)]
result = vaw.vectorAdd(a, b, N)
```

We see two differences from the previous version based on ctypes: first, the code looks a lot more like pure Python code, and this is because the extension is doing the heavy lifting for us backstage; second, we are using Python lists to input data that is being randomly created via the random module. In the previous version we used numpy arrays and passed in their internal pointers to actual data.

There are several issues to consider here. First, copying data may take a long time as the size of the arrays increases, but not only does it take longer (throwing away all the benefits of GPU execution) but also it *doubles* the amount of memory our data occupies in the system main memory, because as we are copying each element from the list to the array they now reside in two different memory locations. Finally, to access the list elements we have to make two function calls, one to get the value and the other to convert it to the correct data type. Later we will see that for smaller sized arrays this does not greatly impact overall performance, but with large arrays it can totally degrade performance.

For now, we know that if we could directly access the internal data from numpy as we did with ctypes then that could really improve our results. So in the next section we will update our extension to integrate with numpy and leverage that.

Passing numpy arrays to your library

In our first integration we passed in numpy arrays to our library using ctypes, and using numpy is essentially ubiquitous in scientific computing with Python. It provides efficient, contiguous memory storage, vectorized operations, and uses accelerated CPU-based libraries. By integrating the C API of numpy into our C extension, we will be able to use the data that has been created and preprocessed on the Python side to execute further calculations inside our GPU. This means we can put together the best of two worlds and but retain the Python feel. In many cases, the performance gains can be orders of magnitude higher than pure Python implementations, especially for operations involving large arrays.

We will change a little bit of our previous code to make the numpy API available. The first change is to import it in our vector_add_np_wrapper.c file with:

```
#include <numpy/arrayobject.h>
```

> numpy as np
>
> Python allows us to import a library and give it a different name by using 'as', and it is usual for applications using numpy to say 'import numpy as np' so that they can refer to the library as np instead of by its full name. We also use this approach here to differentiate our initial wrapper and the version that integrates with numpy, namely wrapper_np.

After the include, there is one more thing we need to do in terms of infrastructure: initialize the numpy module inside our module initialization function by adding a call to import_array(), like this:

```
PyMODINIT_FUNC PyInit_vector_add_np_wrapper(void) {
    void *handle = dlopen("../../build/libvector_add.so", RTLD_LAZY);
    if (!handle) {
        PyErr_SetString(PyExc_ImportError,
            "Could not load libvector_add.so");
        return NULL;
    }
    vectorAdd = (vectorAddFunc)dlsym(handle, "vectorAdd");
    if (!vectorAdd) {
        PyErr_SetString(PyExc_ImportError,
            "Could not find vectorAdd in libvectorAdd.so");
        return NULL;
    }
    import_array();
    return PyModule_Create(&vectoraddmodule);
}
```

With this we have everything in place to use the API. It is even possible to manipulate data within the C extension, but what we really need is to be able to use what comes from the Python program and pass it into our GPU library. So we need to update our pyVectorAdd function as follows:

```
static PyObject* pyVectorAdd(PyObject* self,PyObject* args){
    PyArrayObject *a, *b, *c;
    int N;
    if (!PyArg_ParseTuple(args, "OOOi", &a, &b, &c, &N))
        return NULL;
```

```
        int *a_ptr = (int*)PyArray_DATA(a);
        int *b_ptr = (int*)PyArray_DATA(b);
        int *c_ptr = (int*)PyArray_DATA(c);
        vec_add(a_ptr, b_ptr, c_ptr, N);
        Py_RETURN_NONE;
    }
```

Note that we are not now copying data from one data structure to another, but are using the internal pointer to the externally allocated array. And we do not need to copy results either, because they are being filled inside our GPU library, which is receiving the pointer to the array that numpy allocated.

Again, it is always a good idea to have safeguards in place to check types and these kinds of things, but for the sake of simplicity we are not adding those.

Our setup.py will also need to change to include our numpy include, so that when the extension gets built it will be able to link correctly to it. Below are the changes that need to be made to the file:

```
from setuptools import setup, Extension
import numpy
module = Extension(
    "vector_add_np_wrapper",
    include_dirs = [numpy.get_include()],
    sources=["vector_add_np_wrapper.c"],
)

setup(
    name="vector_add_np_wrapper",
    version="1.0",
    description="Python binding for CUDA vector addition",
    ext_modules=[module],
    include_dirs=[numpy.get_include()]
)
```

While basically the same as we have seen before, we have now imported numpy so that we can find the include directory and pass it into setup.

We build the extension using the same command as before:

```
python3 setup.py build_ext --inplace
```

The application changes a little bit, because now we will use numpy arrays as we did in our first example:

```
import vector_add_np_wrapper as vaw_np
import numpy as np

N = 10000000
a = np.random.randint(0, N, size=N, dtype=np.int32)
b = np.random.randint(N, 2*N, size=N, dtype=np.int32)
c = np.zeros(N, dtype=np.int32)
vaw_np.vectorAdd(a, b, c, N)
```

This is exactly what a Python programmer would expect from an extension: use numpy arrays to generate their data and pass it in for processing as if it were any other library.

With this small change we've got rid of the memory doubling problem we had before and have also increased performance – but we'll check the numbers in the next section.

Analyzing performance

We've now seen two ways to make our GPU code available to Python. It is clear that ctypes is very straightforward, despite that awkward way of defining the functions that will be used. Creating an extension, on the other hand, offers a very clear interface to the end user even though it is a little more laborious.

However, it is not only style that counts here; it is also clear that our extension implementation that did not use `numpy` arrays involved extensive data copying. The question is: how much does that affect the overall performance?

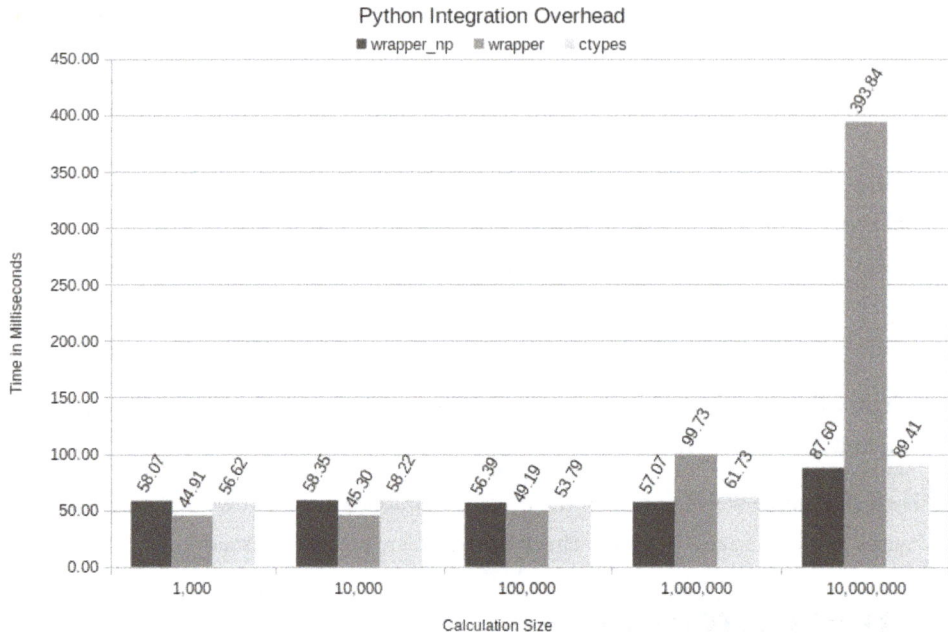

Figure 9.2: Execution time for each type of Python integration

🔍 **Quick tip**: Need to see a high-resolution version of this image? Open this book in the next-gen Packt Reader or view it in the PDF/ePub copy.

🔖 **The next-gen Packt Reader** and a **free PDF/ePub copy** of this book are included with your purchase. Scan the QR code OR visit packtpub.com/unlock, then use the search bar to find this book by name. Double-check the edition shown to make sure you get the right one.

As we mentioned before, we are calling the second version of our extension `wrapper_np` to denote that it uses numpy access. Note that with an array size of up to 100,000 the simple wrapper wins, while the other versions `wrapper_np` and `ctypes` are technically in a draw.

However, when we really increase the array size, to one million or ten million elements, we see that there is no way that data duplication can match using data pointers directly.

To be fair, in our comparisons we've measured only the execution time of the call to the extension, meaning that we did not count the time necessary to generate the random data. Also, we executed each program ten times and calculated the average time, and to make sure that the times were not affected by outliers we removed the lowest and highest values.

Another important factor is that our library was compiled using a debug profile in CMake, but even using a release profile would make no difference to performance, because the bottleneck is not within the GPU library but within the wrapper used.

Summary

In this chapter we learned how to access GPU kernels from Python, which is an important topic that opens up a whole new world for us to explore. We can mix the acceleration that GPU kernels can achieve with the ease of use of Python.

We looked at two distinct approaches to effecting the integration: by using `ctypes` and by creating a Python extension. The great advantage of the `ctypes` approach is that it is purely Python-based, and does not involve compiling anything extra. The second approach allows finer grained control, but we must compile the extension to make it available. Two variants of the Python extension approach were discussed, the first involving copying data and the second using `numpy` internal data pointers directly, which is much faster.

Regardless of the approach taken, we should expend some effort on reusing memory, or we lose the gains that the GPU can provide, as we saw in the performance analysis section.

In the next chapter we discuss where we go from here. Which libraries already exist, and how we can leverage them together with our own kernels? Stay tuned!

Unlock this book's exclusive benefits now

UNLOCK NOW

Scan this QR code or go to `packtpub.com/unlock`,
then search this book by name.

Note: Keep your purchase invoice ready before you start.

10

Exploring Existing GPU Models

Knowing how the GPU works is a fundamental part of employing it effectively in our projects. To help explore its hardware features and relate them to GPU programming concepts we've examined a variety of algorithms, and seen how our implementations of them can best exploit the GPU's architecture. In particular we've seen how learning to add vectors and multiply matrices helps us to understand CUDA threads, blocks and grids. We've also learnt about optimizations and how to handle memory transfers and memory access more efficiently.

In this chapter we investigate several topics that can have an important bearing on our time to market and the reliability of our projects. The first of these topics is libraries for working with GPUs. We'll first learn about existing libraries and then consider the conditions under which it is appropriate to write our own code. Then we discuss the idea that running sequential code on the GPU can sometimes eliminate or reduce performance-limiting data movements. In the last section we will explore the use of interpreted languages to help test the code on multiple levels.

Thus, to summarize, this final chapter will cover these topics:

- Using existing libraries and frameworks
- Writing your own code
- Moving sequential code to GPU
- Testing our code for greater quality

Technical requirements

We will use the environment configured during in Chapter 3 with VS Code and our development container. If you have chosen to install the CUDA Toolkit on your machine then you can simply run the build commands on a terminal. The code is provided on the GitHub repository, which can be accessed here: `https://github.com/PacktPublishing/GPU-Programming-with-CPP-and-CUDA/tree/main/ch10`.

Using existing libraries and frameworks

The code we have used in previous chapters helped us understand how to use the GPU, and you may wonder whether libraries already exist that offer the most optimized version of, let's say, matrix multiplication. And this is exactly the case: there are. Thankfully, we don't need to reinvent the wheel, because CUDA already provides a suite of mature, optimized libraries and frameworks designed to offer efficient implementations for common computing tasks, drastically reducing the development effort for our applications. The complete list of available libraries can be found at `https://developer.nvidia.com/gpu-accelerated-libraries`.

Those libraries target specific categories of problems, and although they are numerous, we will focus on two libraries that are similar to what we have worked on in previous chapters. This will enable us to compare our previous development efforts with the use of the libraries. The first library is **cuBLAS**, which is a CUDA implementation by NVIDIA of the Basic Linear Algebra Subprograms (BLAS) library. It includes code for matrix multiplication, vector operations, and other foundational numerical computations. Anyone who has used traditional BLAS libraries before will be able to transition to cuBLAS smoothly.

The second library we have is **Thrust**, a parallel algorithms library resembling the C++ **Standard Template Library** (STL). It offers a familiar syntax comfortable for developers who are just starting out in GPU programming, and provides a high-level interface to GPU computing with vectors, reductions, sorting, and more.

Using cuBLAS to multiply matrices

When using cuBLAS in our programs we need to keep in mind that it will not handle memory transfers for us: we need to provide the data that we want to process, by copying it to the GPU device memory. We do that with the `cudaMemcpy` command that we used previously.

The complete code for the example is in the `ch10/cuBLAS` folder of our GitHub repository, so let's focus on the specific details of using the library.

Our program will need to allocate the buffers on the device and copy data so that we can call the specific function to perform the matrix multiplication. Following is the code we need to create a cuBLAS context and perform these operations:

```
cublasHandle_t handle;
cublasCreate(&handle);
float alpha = 1.0f;
float beta = 0.0f;
cublasSgemm(handle,
            CUBLAS_OP_T, CUBLAS_OP_T,
            N, N, N,
            &alpha,
            d_A, N,
            d_B, N,
            &beta,
            d_C, N);
float* d_C_fixed;
cudaMalloc(&d_C_fixed, size);

cublasSgeam(handle,
            CUBLAS_OP_T, CUBLAS_OP_N,
            N, N,
            &alpha,
            d_C, N,
            &beta,
            nullptr, N,
            d_C_fixed, N);
```

We are using two cuBLAS functions due to the way that it handles data. Let's break down this code step by step. We create two variables `alpha` and `beta`, because the operation that will be performed is:

$$C = \alpha\, op(A)\, op(B) + \beta C$$

So, we use `alpha` as `1.0f` to multiply the `d_A` matrix, and we use `beta` as `0.0f` so that no operation is performed with the `d_C` matrix. Let's understand this point in more detail. From the equation, we notice that the *C* matrix could be used as an input as well if it already exists, and furthermore it could be multiplied by a scalar value, beta, before being added to the result of the *A*B* matrix multiplication. However, since we are just interested in the matrix-multiplication part, we are passing a `nullptr` as the original *C* matrix and `beta` with value `0.0f`. Now comes a big difference from our original matrix multiplication code: BLAS libraries usually work with matrices stored in column-major format, which means that instead of having all the elements of a row contiguously in memory, the functions expect to find all elements of a column. Due to this characteristic, we pass in the `CUBLAS_OP_T` operators to inform cuBLAS that it should consider the transposes of the matrices when executing the calculations. That way, cuBLAS will produce the correct value with our row-major matrices.

Column-major format

The original implementation of BLAS was in Fortran, which stores matrices in column-major format, meaning that all the columns are held contiguously in memory. This contrasts with C/C++ languages, which store matrices with rows contiguous in memory. The whole ecosystem of libraries that came from BLAS uses the column-major format and it is retained to this day. Many optimizations are possible to reduce performance penalties otherwise incurred when accessing rows.

However, the resulting `d_C` matrix is stored in column-major format, so before returning this to the host we need to find a way to transpose it to row-major format, as the original matrices were.

A very interesting alternative is to use the matrix addition function from cuBLAS but not provide a second matrix. That way, as we pass in the `CUBLAS_OP_T` it will only perform the transposition of the input matrix, generating a row-major version of the `d_C` matrix.

Finally, we must call `cublasDestroy(handle)` to clean up the GPU environment.

After these two operations we can copy the d_C_fixed matrix to the host and use it as needed. We obtain, for matrices of order 1024, the following execution times:

```
CPU matrix multiplication took: 1404.17 ms
Device data copy time: 0.886167 ms
Device data copy back time: 1.42023 ms
Device compute time: 3.29795 ms
cuBLAS overhead time: 8.79119 ms
Total GPU time: 14.4082 ms
```

As we can see, the total time to execute on the GPU, even allowing for data transfers, is 100 times faster than the single threaded CPU version (approximately 14 ms vs. approximately 1400 ms). We are considering as the overhead the time necessary to create the cuBLAS handle, and the compute time includes both the matrix multiplication and the matrix transposition.

Using Thrust to write GPU code

Now, let's see how to use the Thrust library to sort an array of integers and another array of double. This is an important example because it is exactly the code that is presented on the library website with a chart indicating the performance achieved. Our previous study on performance optimization has prepared us to read the information more clearly.

This time our code is simpler than that which we needed to initialize for cuBLAS because Thrust encapsulates many aspects of the GPU interaction for us. We can allocate a vector on the host and fill it with the data we want to sort. After that we can copy data to the device by simply using the following line of code:

```
thrust::device_vector<T> d_vec = h_vec;
```

Assuming that host_vec was previously declared and filled, this code will declare our device buffer and copy data to it. This is very convenient, although it offers less control than when we allocate and copy manually. After the copy completes, we can call the sort function which is very similar to the STL version:

```
thrust::sort(d_vec.begin(), d_vec.end());
```

Now the execution times are as follows:

```
  ==== Sorting float (33554432 elements) ====
CPU sort time:          2411.68 ms
GPU copy time:          12.9508 ms
GPU copy back time:     13.4571 ms
GPU sort time:          17.7616 ms
GPU total time:         44.1696 ms
```

Notice that the time to copy data was very high when compared to the time needed to sort the entire vector. Also, here we are considering the times necessary to copy data into the GPU memory and back to the host. Data transfer times are almost the same as the time needed to perform the sorting itself. However, the total time required to sort on the GPU, even when we consider the data transfer times, is still very much faster than the single threaded CPU version from the STL. Bear in mind that the comparison presented on Thrust's website (`https://developer.nvidia.com/thrust`), where we may find documentation and examples, does not consider a single-threaded version; instead the comparison is with the **Threading Building Blocks (TBB) library** from Intel and it does not take into account this huge amount of time necessary to transfer data. This is something that we always must pay attention to when reading the specifications of libraries that we are thinking of using.

In the next section we consider when it makes sense to write our own kernels, given that there are libraries already packed and ready to help us.

Writing your own code

Creating GPU-accelerated programs is different from sequential CPU code, but there is an interesting software engineering aspect that is constant in both worlds: we must consider when we should write our own code and when to use an existing library. In large, enterprise-level, projects we try to avoid reinventing the wheel as much as possible, for many reasons. One of them we already discussed on the previous section: a library tends to have a dedicated team that is specialized in the library's domain. This means that its *business* is the library, while most of the time our business is an application for a specific case that will make use of the library to achieve our results. Another reason is that when we decide to create code that competes with libraries we may take on responsibility for maintaining that code, and our ability to discharge that responsibility effectively can be affected by many factors. We may have less time to correct a specific bug than is needed, or the original author may leave our team, and these kinds of risk can directly translate into higher costs.

This does not mean that we should always chose to use libraries blindly. Although CUDA libraries are optimized and offer high performance, they are general-purpose implementations that may not immediately fit our specific problems. We have to analyze our problem to uncover the details relevant to determining the best solution. To give a specific example, let's say we need to compute the multiplication of matrices of complex numbers that are compounds of two 64-bit floating point values, one for the real part and the other for the imaginary part. This problem can be solved by cuBLAS, but due to its data representation the performance is much slower than if we were using 32-bit floating point values. Assuming we could use the single-precision version, that would affect the numeric precision of our entire solution, because the values would need to be defined as single precision when the matrices were first filled. This a very simple example, but it illustrates the kind of problem we have to think about.

We must also take into account the fact that many libraries are proprietary code from NVIDIA. This means that we cannot simply change the code: we have to conform with certain formats. An example from the previous section was that when using cuBLAS we had to transpose the result of the multiplication. It could be argued that that will be the case with most BLAS libraries, but it doesn't change the fact that it affects our data. And to explore the example of complex numbers from the last paragraph a little further, having to cast each single element from a double-precision floating-point matrix during access will affect the effectiveness of memory operations as well as waste a lot of memory space. And even then it would only work with a custom kernel, because cuBLAS uses different implementations for single- and double-precision floating-point numbers, as well as for single- and double-precision complex numbers – which are themselves based on the single- and double-precision floating-point numbers respectively.

One could argue that we could typecast the entire matrix, but that would make the cuBLAS function use only a part of each number, and the second half would be considered as a new number, resulting in the production of garbage results. This is because a double-precision floating-point number uses eight bytes, whereas a single-precision floating-point number uses four bytes; meaning that when we type-cast a `double` to a `float` half the number is discarded.

But if we consider that one double-precision number occupies the space of two single-precision numbers, the access to the second position of an array that was type-cast would be the second half of the initial number, instead of the first half of the second number. Let's use a diagram to help make sense of things:

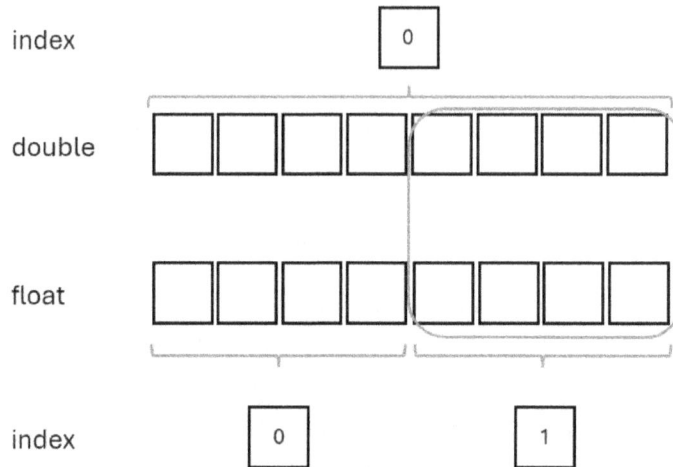

Figure 10.1: Memory layout for double and float numbers

As we can see in *Figure 10.1* what we would get at index 1 by seeing the position as a float would be the remaining bytes from position 0 if it was still a double.

To overcome this problem, we could type-cast each element, one by one, from the original matrix to a new one, but it would extend the overall execution time, which could in turn remove the benefit of using an optimized library at all!

But this does not mean there can be no guidelines on what to do in this type of situation. We can ask ourselves whether we are creating a new algorithm with its own new data structures, which demands more fine-grained control over memory accesses, *or* whether we are creating an application that needs accelerated versions of well-established numerical methods. This should be the first level of decision. Let's say we've figured out that we simply need existing numerical methods, so we decide to use the existing libraries. Then comes the second-level question: are we spending more time trying to accommodate our data into a format that fits the existing libraries than actually solving our problem? If the answer is yes, we should consider creating our own custom kernel, even knowing that it won't be the most hardware-optimized version of the code, because at the end of the day, although execution time matters, the total development time also has to be considered.

Fortunately, we have by now – since we have reached our last chapter – developed the techniques necessary not only for creating our own custom kernels, but have also learnt what it takes to profile and debug our code to help figure out what we can do to improve our bottlenecks.

However, no one said that we are forbidden to use a mixed approach. If our objective is to create a new program that can be decomposed in terms of existing numerical methods and new algorithms, we may try to use the best of both worlds. We can use streams to overlay memory transfers with calls to cuBLAS, provided we keep track of which parts of our data structures have already been copied.

It is a very good idea to separate calls to existing libraries and calls to custom code in different modules, so that we do not lose track of what is responsible for each computation stage.

In the next section we will discuss the execution of sequential code on the GPU, when possible, but again we must evaluate impacts on execution time.

Moving sequential code to the GPU

We learned that moving data to and from the GPU can be costly, and we learned that we can overlay those actions with computation to decrease the time taken to transfer data. However, there are times when we need to perform an intermediate sequential step between two GPU processing phases, and we then have to decide whether to move data out of GPU memory or whether we are going to move our sequential code into the GPU, even though it will not fully utilize the available resources.

Although it may seem a little counterintuitive at first, this is a very legitimate question to ask. It is not a matter of right or wrong, but rather of what will execute fastest and what the associated cost is – even if the cost is maintainability.

One important thing to keep in mind, based on the measurements we observed in *Chapter 8*, is that typically we can hide the computation time by correctly partitioning the data, in that the total execution time is given by the sum of the times needed to transfer the data to the GPU. This is because after completing the first data transfer we start a partial computation and a copy of partial results out of the GPU memory, and those two steps occur simultaneously with the copying of a new input chunk.

This means that the total time is dominated by the time required to transfer data in; the other parts are faster than each chunk transfer. In a naive approach we could argue that it would not make a difference if we could always overlay transfers and computation that way, because by the time we complete the full cycle the results will be on the host already to perform the sequential step. The caveat here is that transfer time is usually *larger* than compute time; that is why we use it to hide computation times. If we add the times necessary to process many steps over the same large matrix we would always be at the top boundary of our optimization. We also can use CUDA streams to overlap memory transfers to one kernel while we are executing another kernel.

On the other hand, if we used the overlaying strategy for the first memory transfer, but later we used a sequential kernel with data that was *already* in GPU memory, the total execution time would need to be larger than the time required to copy a new version of the matrix again – even if we used overlaying.

Of course that there is no simple way to know the total execution time upfront, but considering the difference in clock speed for CUDA cores and that they have less branch prediction power than the CPU we could try to estimate what the minimum amount of time required would be to compute a given sequential algorithm. Using this estimate we might decide to implement a prototype that would provide evidence of the execution time.

Another strategy we might use, if data dependencies allow, which is not always the case with GPUs, is that as soon as the partial results are calculated and transferred back to the host, we start our sequential code on those chunks of data. That way our sequential code will proceed in lock step with the availability of data. However, this code is much more complex to write and maintain than having a sequential version of the code on the GPU.

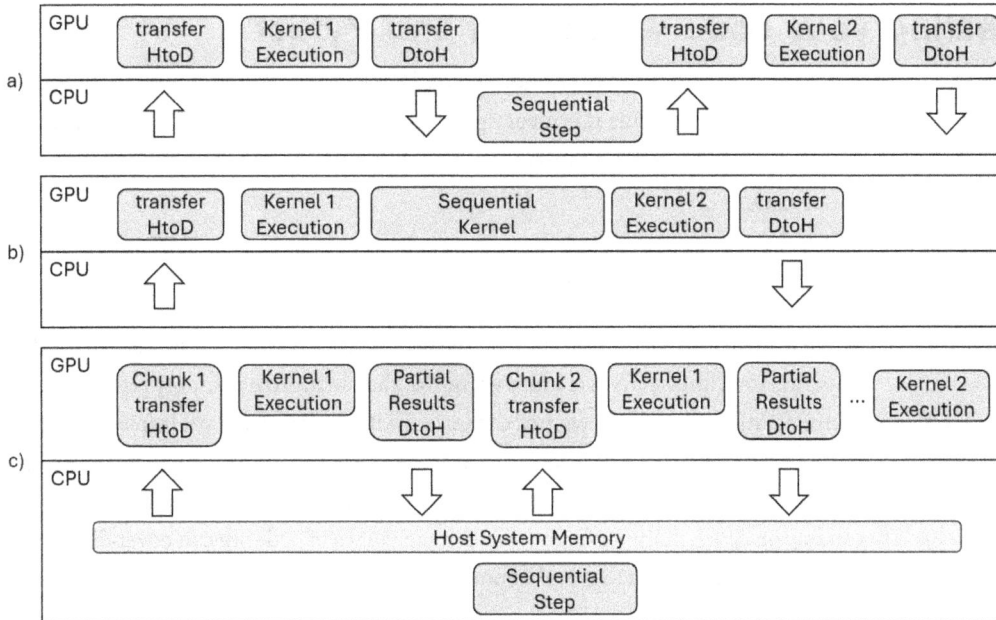

Figure 10.2: The strategies for interacting with sequential code

In *Figure 10.2* we have the three strategies represented visually for easier comprehension. In a) we can see clearly the impact that bringing data back to the host for a sequential step will have. If we are performing a vector-matrix multiplication the result will be a vector that is lighter on data transfer DtoH (Device to Host), whereas if we are performing a matrix multiplication then the final result will also be a matrix, which will demand more of the data transfer and hence the execution time will be increased.

In b) we see execution of the sequential part of the code on the GPU. This may take longer to execute than on the CPU for the individual step but may be faster overall.

Finally, c) demonstrates how we could overlap blocks in order to process pieces of data on the GPU and the CPU at the same time, making the whole computation move forwards faster. However, in this case many more data transfers are performed and that could affect the overall execution time.

In the next section we will discuss the benefits of using our CUDA-accelerated code with interpreted programming languages as one of the alternatives for testing. The other alternative is unit testing at the C++ level.

Testing your code with GTest and Pytest

Creating our code is the first part, but we cannot deliver it until we've made sure that everything is working properly. To guarantee this it is a very good idea to have automated, repeatable tests in place that will execute again and again to make sure that any new changes do not introduce regressions into our code.

> **TDD starts with the test code**
>
> When using test-driven development, we first create a test that calls our code, let's say a function, and then we create a version of the function that simply returns false or null. With that version, we run the test and it will fail. Then we implement the minimum amount of code necessary to make the test pass. We then iterate these steps, creating multiple tests, until we have fully functional and tested code that we can rely on. With many different tests for each piece of code we can cover different error scenarios, corner cases and boundaries, drastically increasing our code quality.

However, we don't need to create sample programs to run our code; instead we can use test frameworks like **GTest** from Google for testing C++ code, and if we want to test Python code we can use **Pytest**, which can be easily added to our Python installation.

Let's start with GTest, since most of our code has been in the realm of C++.

Using GTest with our code

We will be using our simple program that adds vectors as the example code for testing, but as in *Chapter 9*, our project will now have a bit more structure, with separate folders for an include file, the source code and the test code. This will enable our test code to know about our wrapper function, which is necessary because GTest does not know about GPU kernels. As a result we have to create a function for it to call, and this function will be responsible for handling GPU interactions.

We will focus here on the test code, since the kernel is simply adding the elements from the input arrays as we have already seen.

```
#include <gtest/gtest.h>
#include "../include/vector_add.h"
TEST(VectorAddTest, SimpleAddition) {
    int N = 5;
    float A[N] = {1, 2, 3, 4, 5};
```

```
    float B[N] = {10, 20, 30, 40, 50};
    float C[N] = {0};
    vectorAdd(A, B, C, N);
    for (int i = 0; i < N; i++) {
        EXPECT_FLOAT_EQ(C[i], A[i] + B[i]);
    }
}
```

Fully comprehensive documentation for GTest can be found here: `https://github.com/google/googletest`. Since our interest is in how to use it together with our GPU code we will not deep dive into its features, but instead will look at how the calls reach our GPU device.

In this code we use the `TEST` macro to define a test case. The first argument is the name of the test suite and the second argument is the name of the test case. The code provides simple values to use as inputs for our function call, and calls the `vectorAdd` function with them. Up until this point nothing really happened in terms of testing; what we need to do is validate the result of our function call with some other values that we know to be true.

In this case we know that we have to add the respective elements, and we are doing this inside a `for` loop, and we are adding in place. Note that if our kernel was doing anything much more complex than simple addition then we could have a situation where we needed, for example, to load results from an external text file and use pre-calculated values as the source of truth for our implementation.

There are many ways to assert that a value is correct, but here, since we are using floating-point numbers, we use the `EXPECT_FLOAT_EQ` macro.

This is the coding part, but we still need to build and execute the program, so let's see how to do that.

Our `CMakeLists.txt` file must include some other directives to allow test creation, as we can see in the listing:

```
cmake_minimum_required(VERSION 3.10)
project(VectorAddTest LANGUAGES CXX CUDA)
enable_testing()
find_package(GTest REQUIRED)
add_executable(vector_add_test test/test_vector_add.cu src/main.cu)
target_link_libraries(vector_add_test GTest::GTest GTest::Main cuda)
add_test(NAME VectorAddTest COMMAND vector_add_test)
```

```
add_library(vector_add SHARED src/main.cu)
set_target_properties(vector_add PROPERTIES CUDA_SEPARABLE_COMPILATION ON)
target_include_directories(vector_add PUBLIC include)
```

The first thing to notice is enable_testing() to initialize CTest, which is the testing infrastructure from CMake. CTest will be very useful if we want our project to be controlled by a CI/CD pipeline.

> **CI/CD pipeline advantage**
>
> A CI/CD (Continuous Integration/Continuous Deployment) pipeline is a set of automated processes that enables developers to build, test, and deploy code changes. It begins with continuous integration, where we merge our code changes into a repository, triggering automated builds and tests to catch bugs early. Continuous deployment (or delivery) then automates the release process with minimal manual intervention. This pipeline accelerates development cycles and is important for ensuring high code quality through consistent testing.

We use the find_package function to get the references to binaries and header files of our GTest library installation. An interesting thing to notice is that the test itself is a program. It is specialized in its content, but for the build system it is just another executable that has to be compiled and linked with the correct libraries.

After that we let CTest know that this test exists by calling the add_test function.

The other part that we already have in our CMakeLists.txt is the creation of a shared library that we'll be using in the next section when we talk about Pytest.

We can build our test and shared library by running make on the build folder as we did before.

Now there are two ways to execute our tests. The first is to directly call the test code by using:

```
./vector_add_test
```

This will yield the following output:

```
Running main() from /build/googletest-j5yxiC/googletest-1.10.0/googletest/
src/gtest_main.cc
[==========] Running 1 test from 1 test suite.
[----------] Global test environment set-up.
[----------] 1 test from VectorAddTest
[ RUN      ] VectorAddTest.SimpleAddition
[       OK ] VectorAddTest.SimpleAddition (88 ms)
[----------] 1 test from VectorAddTest (88 ms total)

[----------] Global test environment tear-down
[==========] 1 test from 1 test suite ran. (88 ms total)
[  PASSED  ] 1 test.
```

This approach is a good option when we want to execute a single test suite. The other alternative is to call CTest:

```
ctest
```

This will generate the output:

```
Test project /workspaces/GPU-Programming-with-C-and-CUDA/ch10/gtest/build
    Start 1: VectorAddTest
1/1 Test #1: VectorAddTest ...................   Passed    0.11 sec

100% tests passed, 0 tests failed out of 1

Total Test time (real) =   0.11 sec
```

This approach is a good option to use before committing code to the repository because it allows us to determine whether all tests are passing. The output is a little more concise, because this is what would run on a build server in our CI/CD environment. On a build server we want to run all available tests and mark the build as a success or failure depending on the results.

In the next section we will learn how to use Pytest to add another layer of tests for our code.

Using Pytest with our code

In the previous section we generated a shared library for our C++ code. As we know from *Chapter 9*, this is a fundamental step in exposing our function to Python, and for the sake of simplicity we will use the ctypes approach that we saw before.

First, we create a module that loads our shared library and uses ctypes to declare everything that will be used:

```
import ctypes
import numpy as np

lib = ctypes.CDLL('../3_gtest/build/libvector_add.so')
lib.vectorAdd.argtypes = [
    np.ctypeslib.ndpointer(dtype=np.float32, flags="C_CONTIGUOUS"),
    np.ctypeslib.ndpointer(dtype=np.float32, flags="C_CONTIGUOUS"),
    np.ctypeslib.ndpointer(dtype=np.float32, flags="C_CONTIGUOUS"),
    ctypes.c_int
]
def vectorAdd(a: np.ndarray, b: np.ndarray) -> np.ndarray:
    assert a.shape == b.shape
    n = a.size
    c = np.empty_like(a)
    lib.vectorAdd(a, b, c, n)
    return c
```

This code acts as a Python wrapper to our library code, which in turn is a wrapper to the GPU kernel, as we saw in the previous section.

Note that this code is only exposing the call to the library; it is not really our test. For that we need a separate file:

```
import numpy as np
from vector_add import vectorAdd
def testVectorAdd():
    a = np.array([1.0, 2.0, 3.0, 4.0], dtype=np.float32)
    b = np.array([5.0, 6.0, 7.0, 8.0], dtype=np.float32)
    expected = a + b
    result = vectorAdd(a, b)
    for i in range(len(expected)):
```

```
        assert abs(result[i] - expected[i]) < 1e-5,
            f"Mismatch at index {i}: got {result[i]},
            expected {expected[i]}"
    np.testing.assert_allclose(result, expected, rtol=1e-5)
```

Because our function starts with the prefix `test` Pytest knows that it should execute it. Here we are using numpy to create two arrays and calculating the expected result with `expected = a + b`. After that we call our Python function from the module we created before. Now we are presenting two ways to validate the result.

The first approach is similar to what we did in GTest: we use a `for` loop to iterate over all values and assert that they are within an expected tolerance. This could be considered the more common way to do it.

The alternative is to use numpy's `assert_allclose` function, which iterates over the values of two arrays and checks whether all values are within the specified tolerance. In essence, both alternatives are doing the same thing.

To execute our code we can use:

```
pytest -s test_vector_add.py
```

This prints the output:

```
==================== test session starts ==================== platform linux
-- Python 3.8.10, pytest-8.3.5, pluggy-1.5.0 rootdir: /workspaces/GPU-
Programming-with-C-and-CUDA/ch10/pytest collected 1 item
test_vector_add.py .
=================== 1 passed in 0.16s =======================
```

This is similar to what we did before to execute the C++ test individually, and it is important to know about this alternative because if we want to print something inside the test for debugging purposes this is the way to go.

The other alternative is:

```
pytest
```

This will execute all the tests found by Pytest, and the output is:

```
================== test session starts ==================== platform linux
-- Python 3.8.10, pytest-8.3.5, pluggy-1.5.0 rootdir: /workspaces/GPU-
Programming-with-C-and-CUDA/ch10/pytest collected 1 item
test_vector_add.py . [100%]
================== 1 passed in 0.17s ======================
```

This is very similar to what happens when we called CTest, and is what we would see in a CI/CD environment.

If there are any errors in our code then the corresponding asserts will fail, and we can then go through our debugging process to fix whatever is necessary. Let's suppose that instead of adding the values our kernel was multiplying them. In that case, a test that expects an addition will fail as in the following output listing:

```
================== test session starts  ==================================
= platform linux -- Python 3.8.10, pytest-8.3.5, pluggy-1.5.0 rootdir: /
workspaces/GPU-Programming-with-C-and-CUDA/ch10/4_pytest collected 1 item
test_vector_add.py F
================== FAILURES  ==========================================
_____ testVectorAdd_____
def testVectorAdd():
    a = np.array([1.0, 2.0, 3.0, 4.0], dtype=np.float32)
    b = np.array([5.0, 6.0, 7.0, 8.0], dtype=np.float32)
    expected = a + b

    result = vectorAdd(a, b)

    for i in range(len(expected)):

        assert abs(result[i] - expected[i]) < 1e-5, f"Mismatch at index {i}:
got {result[i]}, expected {expected[i]}"

E AssertionError: Mismatch at index 0: got 5.0, expected 6.0 E assert 1.0
< 1e-05 E + where 1.0 = abs((5.0 - 6.0))
test_vector_add.py:12: AssertionError
```

```
================== short test summary info ==============================
FAILED test_vector_add.py::testVectorAdd - AssertionError: Mismatch at
index 0: got 5.0, expected 6.0
================== 1 failed in 1.88s ====================
```

As we can see, if the code has errors, the test will capture the situation and we can pinpoint what is going on and proceed to correct it.

Summary

We have almost reached the end of the final chapter, and this is a good time to step back and reflect on everything that we have studied throughout the book.

We started by defining parallelism, and considered how it can be used to improve the performance of computational tasks. At first no code was needed, just some reflection on activities from our daily lives to make things clear and simple. Then we discussed the programming environment, and since GPU programming needs such a specialized toolkit, we presented the alternative of using Docker to keep everything tidy. This approach is doubly interesting because it can be used for other programming environments as well.

The next chapter brought us to the development of a simple program as our first milestone. We executed code that actually used the GPU! However, that first program was not really a true parallel program, so we then changed focus to look at programs that really exploit the power of GPU cores for bigger problems. In addition we learnt how to move data into and out of our GPU devices.

After that many new concepts needed to be explained, so we spent some time going through each facet of GPU programming to make sure that at every stage we had laid the foundations for what was coming next. We then moved on to the design of parallel algorithms and how to make the most of our GPU hardware. We discussed the challenges and characteristics of these approaches to programming problems.

Then it was time to examine performance optimization strategies, and also to look at the profiling tool that helps us find the hotspots that demand our attention when applying optimization techniques. We saw the use of shared memory in practice and its effects on overall execution time.

We learnt that another layer of performance improvement is possible when we overlap memory transfers and computation by using streams. And we leveraged the use of our profiler to validate the optimal data transfer size to use.

What good would our code be if we couldn't integrate it with other programs? That question motivated us to explore how we can pack code into libraries and how to call our GPU code from Python.

Finally, in this last chapter we've looked at the paths before us now that we know how to create GPU programs. We've seen that there are libraries that can boost our productivity like cuBLAS and Thrust, and we've discussed strategies for deciding when we should write our own custom CUDA kernels and when we should rely on existing libraries. We've seen that it may be useful to move even sequential code to the GPU if it ends up avoiding data transfers that could eat into the performance gains provided by the GPU.

The chapter rounded off with a glimpse of how we can test our code, both at the C++ level as well as on the Python level if our code is already exposed as a shared library.

And with that, we've reached the end of our journey together to the heart of performance programming using the GPU. Hopefully you now feel you have the knowledge needed to venture forth and exploit the power of the GPU in your own projects. Bon voyage!

Unlock this book's exclusive benefits now

UNLOCK NOW

Scan this QR code or go to `packtpub.com/unlock`, then search this book by name.

Note: Keep your purchase invoice ready before you start.

11

Unlock Your Book's Exclusive Benefits

Your copy of this book comes with the following exclusive benefits:

☁ Next-gen Packt Reader

✦ AI assistant (beta)

📄 DRM-free PDF/ePub downloads

Use the following guide to unlock them if you haven't already. The process takes just a few minutes and needs to be done only once.

How to unlock these benefits in three easy steps

Step 1

Have your purchase invoice for this book ready, as you'll need it in *Step 3*. If you received a physical invoice, scan it on your phone and have it ready as either a PDF, JPG, or PNG.

For more help on finding your invoice, visit `https://www.packtpub.com/unlock-benefits/help`.

> **Note:** Did you buy this book directly from Packt? You don't need an invoice. After completing Step 2, you can jump straight to your exclusive content.

Step 2

Scan this QR code or go to `packtpub.com/unlock`.

On the page that opens (which will look similar to *Figure 11.1* if you're on desktop), search for this book by name. Make sure you select the correct edition.

<packt>   Q Search...   Subscription 🛒 👤

Explore Products   Best Sellers   New Releases   Books   Videos   Audiobooks   Learning Hub   Newsletter Hub   Free Learning

Discover and unlock your book's exclusive benefits

Bought a Packt book? Your purchase may come with free bonus benefits designed to maximise your learning. Discover and unlock them here

Discover Benefits   Sign Up/In   Upload Invoice

Need Help?

✦ **1. Discover your book's exclusive benefits**   ⌃

    Q Search by title or ISBN

    CONTINUE TO STEP 2

👤 **2. Login or sign up for free**   ⌄

☁ **3. Upload your invoice and unlock**   ⌄

Figure 11.1 – Packt unlock landing page on desktop

Step 3

Once you've selected your book, sign in to your Packt account or create a new one for free. Once you're logged in, upload your invoice. It can be in PDF, PNG, or JPG format and must be no larger than 10 MB. Follow the rest of the instructions on the screen to complete the process.

Note: If you are still facing issues, reach out to `customercare@packt.com`.

Need help?

If you get stuck and need help, visit `https://www.packtpub.com/unlock-benefits/help` for a detailed FAQ on how to find your invoices and more. The following QR code will take you to the help page directly:

Note: If you are still facing issues, reach out to `customercare@packt.com`.

‹packt›

packtpub.com

Subscribe to our online digital library for full access to over 7,000 books and videos, as well as industry leading tools to help you plan your personal development and advance your career. For more information, please visit our website.

Why subscribe?

- Spend less time learning and more time coding with practical eBooks and Videos from over 4,000 industry professionals
- Improve your learning with Skill Plans built especially for you
- Get a free eBook or video every month
- Fully searchable for easy access to vital information
- Copy and paste, print, and bookmark content

At www.packt.com, you can also read a collection of free technical articles, sign up for a range of free newsletters, and receive exclusive discounts and offers on Packt books and eBooks.

Other Books You May Enjoy

If you enjoyed this book, you may be interested in these other books by Packt:

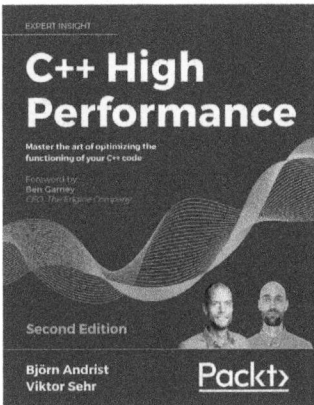

C++ High Performance - Second Edition

Björn Andrist, Viktor Sehr

ISBN: 978-1-83921-654-1

- Write specialized data structures for performance-critical code
- Use modern metaprogramming techniques to reduce runtime calculations
- Achieve efficient memory management using custom memory allocators
- Reduce boilerplate code using reflection techniques
- Reap the benefits of lock-free concurrent programming
- Gain insights into subtle optimizations used by standard library algorithms
- Compose algorithms using ranges library
- Develop the ability to apply metaprogramming aspects such as constexpr, constraints, and concepts
- Implement lazy generators and asynchronous tasks using C++20 coroutines

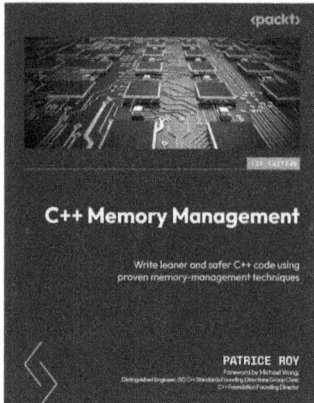

C++ Memory Management

Patrice Roy

ISBN: 978-1-80512-980-6

- Master the C++ object model to write more efficient and maintainable code
- Automate resource management to reduce manual errors and improve safety
- Customize memory allocation operators to optimize performance for specific applications
- Develop your own smart pointers to manage dynamic memory with greater control
- Adapt allocation behavior to meet the unique needs of different data types
- Create safe and fast containers to ensure optimal data handling in your programs
- Utilize standard allocators to streamline memory management in your containers

Packt is searching for authors like you

If you're interested in becoming an author for Packt, please visit authors.packtpub.com and apply today. We have worked with thousands of developers and tech professionals, just like you, to help them share their insight with the global tech community. You can make a general application, apply for a specific hot topic that we are recruiting an author for, or submit your own idea.

Share your thoughts

Now you've finished *GPU Programming with C++ and CUDA*, we'd love to hear your thoughts! Scan the QR code below to go straight to the Amazon review page for this book and share your feedback or leave a review on the site that you purchased it from.

https://packt.link/r/1805124544

Your review is important to us and the tech community and will help us make sure we're delivering excellent quality content.

Index

www.ingramcontent.com/pod-product-compliance
Lightning Source LLC
Chambersburg PA
CBHW081058220326
41598CB00038B/7146